TRUE GHOST STORIES

Vivienne Rae-Ellis is a Tasmanian writer and television presenter and interviewer now living in Bath, who has published both non-fiction and fiction in Australia and England. Her most recent book, *Black Robinson* (1988), was about the first man to be appointed Chief Protector of the Aborigines in New South Wales.

TRUE GHOST STORIES
of our own time

compiled and edited by
VIVIENNE RAE-ELLIS

faber and faber
LONDON · BOSTON

First published in 1990
by Faber and Faber Ltd
3 Queen Square London WC1N 3AU

Photoset by Parker Typesetting Service Leicester
Printed in England by
Clays Ltd, St Ives plc

All rights reserved

This collection © Vivienne Rae-Ellis, 1990
Introduction © Brian Inglis, 1990

A CIP record for this book is available
from the British Library

ISBN 0–571–14271–0
0–571–14273–7 (Pbk)

Contents

Foreword vii
Preface ix
Acknowledgements xiii
Introduction by Brian Inglis xv

PART ONE
Varieties of Ghost 1

Sensitives 4
Timewarps 15
Deeds of Violence and Violent Death 23
Monks 41
Apparitions of the Dead 45
Ghost Identification 54
Guardian Ghosts 63
Apparitions of the Living 75
Through Children's Eyes 78
Ghosts of Pets 83
Pets' Reactions 98

PART TWO
Ghosts Heard, Smelled, Felt and Perceived 103

Voices and Sounds 106
Ghostly Odours 117
Ghosts Felt 124
Presences 129
Possession 136
Blood 141

PART THREE
Hauntings 145

Historic Houses 148
Churches and Colleges 164
Theatres 172
Hospitals 173
Commercial Premises 177
Terraces, Flats, Council Houses 185
Pubs 193
Airfields 198
Towns 200
Rural Ghosts 206
Highway Encounters 212
Ghosts of the Oceans 225

PART FOUR
Poltergeists 233

Poltergeists 235
Disrupted Holidays 251
Violence 255

Note 258
Select Bibliography 259
Index 260

Foreword

To preserve people's privacy, all names other than those of contributors and their immediate families have been changed; where requested, contributors' names have also been changed. However, the full name, address and occupation of each contributor has been held on file, and subject to the contributor's permission being granted the original versions of the events described are available for inspection.

Are ghosts the product of our imagination, or are they real?

My research indicates that while most people refuse to accept that ghosts exist, a personal experience of some paranormal event may cause even the most contemptuous sceptic to admit that he or she will in future at least keep an open mind on the matter.

If one reaction annoys me more than the credulity of someone willing to believe anything he hears on the topic of ghosts, it is that of the dogmatic sceptic who refuses point blank to consider the possibility of their existence. They are often scientists – I don't have to look beyond those closest to me for a prime example – who dismiss anything remotely connected with the supernatural.

A wiser individual will approach this mysterious subject without prejudice, remembering Samuel Johnson's view on the existence of ghosts: 'All argument is against it, but all belief is for it.'

I urge you to cast aside any preconceptions you may have, read the following pages with an open mind, and draw your own conclusions.

Vivienne Rae-Ellis, Bath, October 1989

Preface

When I began researching material for this book, my picture of ghosts and their surroundings was the traditional one: a grove of dark forbidding laurels crowding the door of some ancient pile, mist swirling around the battlements, and inside the ubiquitous figure of a Grey Lady or a Laughing Cavalier gliding along dusty corridors before disappearing through a solid brick wall. An experience I had at one of Essex's most striking early houses was soon to confirm that impression.

Late one night in 1984 the telephone rang in my flat in Canberra, Australia. A friend from Essex was on the line.

'I've found the perfect place for you to stay when you're next in England,' she said. 'It's a stately home called Layer Marney Tower.'

The Tower is an eight-storey gatehouse erected when Henry VIII was a boy by another Henry, the first Lord Marney, who died in 1523, leaving the building just as it appears today. The owners, Major Gerald Charrington and his wife Susan, welcomed me on a hot, sultry evening in May, and showed me over the wing I was to lease for the next three years.

After unpacking – my few possessions vanished into huge antique chests and hanging cupboards in a large room dominated by a canopied four-poster bed – a ferocious storm broke directly over the Tower.

Keyed up by the excitement of my first night alone in this ancient building and apprehensive of the violence of the storm, eventually I fell asleep – only to be woken by a strange twitching of the bed-covers. When I slipped off to sleep again, the same thing happened: the blue bedspread was pulled down towards the foot of the bed, disturbing me. I turned on the reading lamp, but no one was in the room.

Switching off the light I settled back against the pillows, frightened by the intensity of thunder and lightning, and listened to the rain lashing branches against the mullioned windows. But every time I went into an uneasy doze the bedspread was moved by an unseen hand, waking me up. I left the light on finally, and slept fitfully through the rest of the night.

It was some weeks before I discovered that if the bedroom door was left unlocked, allowing unimpeded access from the bedroom to the long corridor stretching the length of the east wing, I would be left to sleep in peace. If I locked the door, I was always disturbed by a 'presence' which, though not in any way threatening, was definitely there – invisible and inexplicable.

That particular section of the east wing had been burnt down many years ago, as I learnt later, and rebuilt in 1910. The ghostly presence appeared to want to move freely between the Tudor and Edwardian sections of the building. But no one was able to suggest why, and the identity of the spirit remains a mystery.

Layer Marney Tower is a building of great charm, enhanced by a peaceful atmosphere that is evident to many sensitive visitors. My ghostly experience there was exciting rather than frightening. I wish I could say the same of the following incident.

A few years ago I was staying in a small hotel overlooking a beach swept by the tides of the English Channel, on the south-west coast of England. Occupying a room on the second floor with a balcony facing the sea, I was engaged in writing the final chapter of a book.

The weather was warm and sunny. The hotel was only partly occupied in the early weeks of May by regular guests, mostly retired schoolteachers and clergymen and their wives. Each evening after dinner we gathered in a small room at the rear of the dining-room to watch the late news on television, after which most of us retired.

On one particular night after I had been there about ten days, I said goodnight and for some reason, instead of using the main staircase, I made my way up to the second floor by the narrow back staircase formerly used by servants when the hotel had been a family home. Handbag in one hand and my other hand on the stair-rail, I approached the last flight.

About three steps from the landing outside the bathroom on my floor, I was suddenly 'threatened' from the rear by what I thought was a man holding a long knife. He seemed about to plunge it into my neck. I spun round. There was no one there. But my sense of fear and evil was so strong that the hair on the back of my neck literally stood on end. I knew I had to escape.

Dashing up the remaining stairs, I tore along the corridor to my room and, fumbling the key into the lock, I threw open the door and rushed in, slamming and bolting the door behind me. Still the fear persisted. The feeling of evil was indescribable. I knew without any doubt that I was in imminent danger from an invisible hand.

I remained in the hotel for forty-eight hours, sleeping uneasily with all the lights on each night, and using the main stairway to reach another bathroom on the first floor – nothing would have induced me to return to the bathroom landing on the second floor – before I bowed to fear and checked out. I was too ashamed of my unaccountable terror to mention the incident to anyone.

Much later I learnt that a woman had been murdered on that floor towards the end of the nineteenth century, a story the owners had suppressed, and I gathered that I was by no means the only person to have experienced that sense of evil and threat to life on the second floor of an otherwise innocuous hotel.

My unpleasant experience changed my attitude towards the supernatural, and led indirectly to the compilation of this book. Now, having corresponded with hundreds of people in all parts of Britain who have offered new, contemporary evidence of ghostly sightings, I realize that my earlier conception of ghosts was misleading, to say the least.

In this new material there are many examples of 'traditional ghosts'. But a surprising number of experiences are contemporary ones, told by people about houses, cars, fishing boats and favourite pets: there are fascinating accounts of ghosts of animals as well as of human beings only recently dead.

The stories come from people in all walks of life, the majority of them having had no interest in the supernatural before their experience took place. Many of them admit that they have been reluctant to talk to friends or relatives about them for fear of ridicule. Other correspondents say that they have drawn comfort from the knowledge that they are not alone, and that similar disturbing incidents have been reported by other men and women, who are willing to share their experiences publicly.

No attempt has been made to prove the validity of these stories. I have relied on the fundamental honesty of people who, invited through the national press to offer accounts of personal experiences for publication, have done so at the cost of considerable time and effort. They include businessmen, housewives, artists, nurses, farmers, academics and labourers.

I am deeply indebted to my contributors, and to the editors of journals and newspapers who published my appeal. The response from readers in the Midlands and northern areas of England was remarkably high, an intriguing point which might warrant further investigation.

The majority of the stories appear in the words of the contributors, and they have only been edited when it has proved necessary to make clarifications, avoid repetitions or shorten the text. As Brian Inglis pointed out, the same ghost may manifest itself in various ways, and may not be easily categorized. To avoid having a string of tales with no connecting themes, his advice has been followed, and the accounts have been divided into four sections: first, reports of the common types of sightings; second, descriptions of occasions on which a ghost has been heard, smelled, felt, or experienced in any other way; third, hauntings – where the ghost appears to be associated with some particular place; and fourth, poltergeists.

Acknowledgements

I am delighted to have Brian Inglis's support in the publication of this book, and thank him most warmly for his assistance. Barry Watts, a fellow Australian author, gave me valuable practical advice in the early stages of the project.

Introduction
by Brian Inglis

Most of us have been asked, or have asked the question, 'Do you believe in ghosts?' On the face of it, it is a strange question, in view of the fact that ghosts have been reported from every part of the world, in every era, often by people whose word we would accept unquestioningly on any other matter. Why the doubt? Why do many people feel embarrassed at having to claim 'seeing is believing'?

Perhaps the question is best put in another form: 'Do you accept that people have experienced encounters with what appear to be ghosts?' Even the most die-hard of rationalists would surely not reply, No! The distinction is important, because it leaves open the tendentious issue whether there are ghosts 'out there', occupying space, or whether they are hallucinations, like Macbeth's dagger. The rationalist's tendency has been to assume that if ghosts are hallucinations they are not merely explained, but effectively explained away; we need not bother our heads about them. But this is to ignore the mass of evidence that hallucination experiences (if for argument's sake we accept this proposition) are so often meaningful. They have a story to tell, or to find out about. It is as if ghosts are challenging us, warning us that there are forces at work we do not understand – which many of us refuse even to acknowledge – and which ought to be seriously investigated.

Vivienne Rae-Ellis's collection is significant for a number of reasons. It shows that people are experiencing ghosts today of much the same varieties as they have been experienced throughout history, and as they have been reported in similar collections during the past century. And it also shows that although there are people who are particularly sensitive to atmosphere, so that they may literally conjure up ghosts, for many of us seeing a ghost may be a once-in-a-lifetime experience, coming out of the blue when we are awake and in our right minds, not primed to expect anything 'spooky'.

The mind's eye picture of a ghost for most of us is a transparent wraith, floating around battlements or through doors. But this type, though occasionally reported, is a relative rarity. More commonly apparitions, as the name implies, seem to be real people. The term ghost also has the disadvantage that the wraith is generally regarded as being the earthbound spirit of somebody who has died, usually a violent death (or of the murderer who has done the deed, and is condemned to haunt the place where it was committed). Hauntings of this kind are indeed quite frequently reported, with circumstantial stories to account for them. But apparitions are often of the living, or of nobody in particular. We are stuck with 'ghost', as it remains the stock colloquial term, but this collection provides a useful corrective to the 'wraith' conception, and also to the hardly less common assumption that ghosts are usually *seen*: sightings may be most commonly reported, but ghosts are heard, felt, and smelled, as well as establishing their presence by physical activity of the kind that has come to be known as poltergeist outbreaks.

Poltergeists, too, have been reported all over the world, in every age, and they present an intractable problem. The hallucination theory cannot accommodate them: the sounds of, say, smashing crockery may turn out to be hallucination of hearing, but not the sight of the smashed crockery on the kitchen floor. They are also an unwelcome reminder that such visitations can be mischievous, malicious, and even dangerous. Yet this is rare. As a number of the contributors have found, ghosts can be friendly. They can even provide useful warnings. In other cases they may appear to be neutral, nothing to be frightened of – perhaps even, as in Noël Coward's 'Stately Homes of England', something to be proud of. And there are often indications that the alarm they can generate appears to represent a desire – say, to try to have some wrong put to rights: it is as if the guilt has in some way poisoned the atmosphere, which needs to be purged.

This is speculation. But speculation, surely, is precisely what these accounts should be encouraging. It is ridiculous that ghosts should still be widely regarded, and feared, as 'supernatural'; anything which is actually experienced, as Alfred Russel Wallace pointed out, must be natural, even if as yet unexplained.

To deride and dismiss such experiences as products of superstition is simply crass. Instead they point to the existence of forces influencing our lives which need to be investigated the better to exploit them when they are potentially useful, or to provide protection from them when they are sinister.

Brian Inglis, February 1990

Part One

VARIETIES
OF
GHOST

Ghosts are complicated beings appearing in all shapes and forms, bearing little relationship to the familiar image of the transparent wraith, although that, too, is encountered. The great majority of apparitions seem to be real people until they fade away and vanish, when the startled witness is forced to question, perhaps for the first time, the complex phenomenon he or she has experienced. Such phenomena are experienced by people in all walks of life, often for no apparent reason, and when least expected. One of the most puzzling aspects of this collection of stories is that all the apparitions seen have been described as being clothed in some manner – no one has reported seeing a naked ghost.

Sensitives

For many people an encounter with a ghost happens only once in a lifetime. A few are 'sensitives' who have several experiences.

Jill Fletcher, an attractive young insurance broker from Essex, is a sensitive. Her story is fascinating, and contains a timely warning of the inadvisability of becoming too closely involved with the powers she describes. The following is a transcript of a tape she recorded at my request in 1988.

'I lived with my parents in a terraced house just outside the East End of London. When I was about ten my grandmother came to live with us, as her husband had died and she was no longer capable of looking after herself due to ill-health. I was not particularly kind to my grandmother but she always seemed very fond of me.

'Every night at 4 a.m. she would get up, stomp across the landing to visit the bathroom and pull the chain, a routine which always woke me up as my room was next door.

'When I was fourteen my grandmother died, and after that strange things began to happen. One night I was woken (as I used to be when she was alive) by the sound of the toilet flushing at 4 a.m., and this started to occur often. I would hear my grandmother's door open, her heavy footsteps cross the landing and the toilet flushing.'

But Jill Fletcher was not alone in hearing strange noises in the house.

'My mother and I would also often hear the sound of someone washing up in the kitchen and always when we went to investigate there was no one there, and no sign of any water or dishes in the sink.

'I had a plastic elephant among my soft toys which, when my grandmother was alive, she particularly liked. She had found a little chequered scarf to tie round its neck. I kept the elephant on a cupboard three feet in depth sitting wedged in with other soft toys. On countless occasions this elephant would be found in the middle of my bedroom floor – so much so that I had only to leave the room for a few moments and it would be found there on my return.

'Other things began to happen also. After my grandmother died my father converted her bedroom into a small office for himself, in which the freezer was kept. While she was alive my grandmother, for safety reasons, was fanatical about pulling all the plugs out of sockets overnight. On many occasions my father would find all the plugs pulled out of their sockets including, of course, the freezer. My father would be furious and blame my mother and myself, but we never ever touched them and could not explain how it happened.

'One particular summer my parents went away on holiday when I was about sixteen or seventeen, and I was left alone in the house. During this time I began to feel my grandmother's presence more strongly . . . My bedroom door was opened in the night even though I had left it firmly closed. One particular evening I was sitting in the conservatory watching television with our corgi dog, Sandy, sitting at my feet. The heavy, very stiff door between the conservatory and kitchen flew open. I assumed it must have been a gust of wind and closed it, sitting down again in my chair.

'Sandy suddenly got up from my feet and walked away and, on turning round, I saw my grandmother. She was sitting in her favourite chair, wearing the blue plastic pinafore she wore every day, dangling her hand over the side of her chair stroking the dog – just as she always used to do. A few moments later she had disappeared.

'I saw her again, in exactly the same manner, later that week and this time I said hello to her, but she only smiled at me before vanishing. I also saw her when I went upstairs and on glancing towards her room saw her sitting in a chair in the corner. During the last few days of my parents' absence I went to stay with friends, as I felt so disturbed by all of this.

'Some months later I started to see a new boyfriend who told me he was psychic so I invited him home for coffee, making no mention at all about my grandmother and the strange happenings in the house. He went up to the bathroom and when he came down he was as white as a sheet and said there was something up there, a presence he didn't like at all, and he decided to go home there and then. He never spoke to me again. I don't know what my grandmother had said to him, but she obviously didn't like him.

'After this I decided to visit the British Spiritualists' Association and I attended several readings. Among other things a gentleman there described my grandmother in great detail and said she was extremely worried about me and her presence would not leave me until she was satisfied that I was going to lead a happy and fulfilled life with a good man to look after me. He also mentioned that my mother would have an operation on her fingers, although at that time there was no sign of any such problem.

'About eight weeks later my mother started to complain of pain in her thumbs. On seeing a specialist she was told the bone needed to be replaced in her hands. Subsequently she did have an operation on her fingers.

'I eventually left home and went to live with John, who ultimately became my husband. My grandmother's presence still continued in the house and only gradually disappeared when I eventually married John.

'We moved to a semi-detached house in Romford previously owned by an elderly lady who had lived there with her husband, who had died a few months earlier. This house had a long kitchen with a door leading out of the lounge and a door opposite leading from the kitchen into the garden. For about two years I used to feel a cold shiver when I was in the kitchen and sensed the presence of someone walking from the lounge through the kitchen into the garden. I stopped feeling disturbed about this eventually, and it was then I began to see an elderly gentleman walking from the lounge out through the door into the garden. He was dressed in a shabby grey suit and knitted waistcoat. He had thinning grey hair, quite a kindly face and wore small round tortoiseshell spectacles.

'Several years later we moved again, this time to a village, and struck up a friendship with Mike and Sandra [*names changed*] who lived near by. Sandra's mother was involved in spiritualism and said I definitely had a gift in this area and I should be used as a channel. She asked me if I would like to join her "circle" and I agreed. At this time I was happy and well-adjusted, with no problems in my life.

'The "circle" met and about eight to ten of us would sit in

darkness and ask for healing for certain people who needed help. When I joined the circle I knew no one who needed such help but subsequently I seemed to be a magnet for everyone's problems, so much so that my own marriage began to suffer. My husband's job started to go badly, as did my own. I would hear voices in many different languages and went into a trance many times.

'On one occasion I found myself experiencing the sensations of a witch being burnt at the stake – a most horrifying experience. I felt that I was losing control of my own life, which seemed to be taken over by unknown forces. I then decided that I must leave the "circle", and subsequently things started to improve. My husband's job situation got better and I was promoted. My mother stopped suffering pain in her hands and everyone round me stopped bringing their problems to me, with the result that my life is now very happy once again.

'I firmly believe that there is something on the other side; very strong forces indeed, and I am a receptacle for them. I still often hear voices and sense presences.

'Finally, I will just tell you about an incident that happened at school when I was about fourteen. There was a group of us, about eight to ten girls, who used to practise using Ouija boards, and on one occasion we had gone up to the physics laboratory before school to have a seance. The windows were fastened with strong metal catches, all firmly slid into their bolts. We started on our session and glasses were moving backwards and forwards when we decided to ask the spirit to show himself.

'Suddenly every single window in the lab flew open and three glass experiments were smashed into thousands of pieces. We all fled screaming from the room, and were punished by the school for causing so much damage.'

Mrs Olive S. Sone, retired, now lives in Kent. She has enjoyed the acquaintance of a number of ghosts in the past, seeing her first manifestation when she was only a child.

Sitting on a swing in the garden of a lodge-keeper in 1924, she was suddenly aware of a pretty little girl standing by her. The child was 'dressed in a pink and white dress and a poke bonnet and pantaloons, holding a rag doll. Her smile was like sunshine,' recalls Mrs Sone. Then, some years later, she and her friend Helen went for a walk one lovely day along a road where there was once a prison, by that time in ruins.

'Nearby stood a big house and all of a sudden we saw six big black cars come down the long drive towards the double gates. In the cars were six brides, each with a man at her side. As the cars got to the gates they all disappeared. We were so scared we ran like the devil. Even though we are seventy years old now, we still talk about this incident.'

Mrs Sone's sensitivity to the supernatural continued. When she moved into a house on 28 July 1941, she discovered she was sharing her accommodation with not one ghost, but two: one indoors, and one outdoors, both of whom remained with her for a number of years.

The outdoors ghost wore the uniform of a soldier of the Coldstream Guards in the First World War, and Mrs Sone saw him each night in her garden, feeling around as if he were searching for something he had lost.

'One day I decided to go and see what he was looking for. I found what it was and I still have it. It is his collar brooch, I took it indoors and cleaned it, then I sent it to Pall Mall.'

According to Mrs Sone the army authorities were very interested in her story, and identified the badge, which they returned to her. Oddly enough, after finding the collar badge, Mrs Sone never again saw the ghost of the soldier in uniform.

The indoors ghost became a very familiar figure to her, and she looked upon him as a friend. The first strangeness she noticed about the interior of the house was a strong scent of pipe tobacco.

'No one in my family smoked a pipe. This went on for about three years, then one day my dog came up to me, and her fur was standing on end.

'I was making the beds at the time and all of a sudden I felt the sheets being pulled. I looked up and saw the most handsome man standing there as though in the shadows. He was very much like a cavalier, dressed in green velvet. I used to talk to him. He never spoke to me, but I think he understood what I was saying. He used to follow me all over the house. He chuckled a lot, and he seemed to be my guardian angel. He used to play about when I made the beds. My dog's fur stood up on end when she knew he was around, but I told her not to worry.

'My children used to say how cold it was. I said, "Don't worry! Yorky is around!" (That was the name I gave him.) My eldest son's wife always felt cold [when Yorky was there], and my second husband felt it also. The only thing was, Yorky did not like my late husband. I miss my Yorky. He really was my friend. He was with me until I moved to my present address. This house has none of those feelings. I miss him even now.'

Mrs Juliet MacLauchlan and her husband have lived abroad for the last twenty-five years, and are currently in Belgium. But in 1980 they decided to buy a house in Kent, although Mr MacLauchlan intended to continue to work abroad. Juliet MacLauchlan describes the search for a suitable house in the following transcript of a tape-recording made in 1988. Profoundly affected by the events she describes, she says it has been difficult to talk about them.

'We had a shortlist of five houses to look at and the Old Rectory at St Mary in the Marsh was second on the list. From the outside it looked very unprepossessing, unkempt and untidy. But as soon as I entered the hall I knew immediately that this was the house I wanted. There was a warm, welcoming atmosphere which I felt very strongly.

'We bought the house and in the spring of 1981 we arrived to clean and redecorate it. As we entered we immediately encountered a lovely welcoming feeling spoilt only by a strange, strong smell emanating from the drawing room. We found a loose floorboard, put down some rat poison, and the smell disappeared.

'On another occasion I returned alone to the house and on entering the front door and walking into the hall I was assailed by the feeling that there was someone in the house, but I felt no fear. I spent ten happy days working in the house and I felt very approved of. Then in mid-June my husband, myself and our two daughters all moved into the house with all our goods and chattels and the smell was back, stronger and more persistent than ever, although it disappeared after a couple of days, and we settled down to living in the house.

'My husband then returned to Germany, my elder daughter to study in Sweden and my younger daughter stayed with me. Again I had the feeling that there was a ghostly presence in the house – although I have always been a very logical person, rather sceptical about such things.

'In September my husband returned and we started to gut the kitchen area. The kitchen door was old and heavy and I decided it ought to be removed since it was in the way of improvements I wished to make. On that particular evening my husband and I took our supper into the dining-room, leaving the kitchen door open. On returning to the kitchen just before midnight we found the door very firmly shut. It would have needed a very heavy push to close it, particularly as there was a bump in the floor which would have hindered its progress. I commented that my ghost had closed it just to show my husband how inconvenient it was. He laughed, but removed the door for me before returning abroad.

'Life continued and my husband then moved from Germany to Belgium and I continued to live happily in the rectory, never feeling lonely, but convinced that I was somehow wanted . . .

'During 1982 there was a very warm period which necessitated watering the garden close to the house and the same characteristic smell reappeared throughout the whole of the ground floor, although previously it had been obvious only in the drawing room.'

Mrs MacLauchlan wondered if the cause might have been seepage from the garden, penetrating the house. She became very worried about it but, once again, it suddenly disappeared.

'In mid-June my husband returned feeling unwell and one evening after a dinner party he collapsed. The house felt in turmoil. The local doctor came, gave my husband an injection and left. I stayed in the bedroom with him. There seemed to be someone else in the room with me, guiding me. Later my husband had another attack, but I remained totally calm and in control, which is not normally my nature as I am partly French and of a volatile disposition. I was, however, sustained by the presence of someone in that room, sometimes sitting in a chair, sometimes moving about, and I knew with absolute certainty that my husband was going to be all right.'

Later Mrs MacLauchlan asked the former rector of the parish, who had also lived in the house, if he had any reason to believe it might be haunted.

'He replied that during the winter of 1962–3 he and his wife moved into the rectory, which had been empty for some time. From time to time they would hear a piano playing in the house and were conscious of a person standing on the landing looking through the window towards the church. They also experienced an awful smell in the house which persisted for a while, before vanishing.

'Then, as they were clearing the house of rubbish left by previous occupants, they came across some sheets of beautifully handwritten music. They continued to hear the piano playing, but no one else heard it. Finally they could bear the situation no longer and decided to burn the boxes containing the sheet music – whereupon the piano was never heard again.'

On making inquiries the rector learnt that a previous tenant, a bachelor clergyman, had employed as housekeeper a woman distantly related to him, who played the piano. She lived in the house until she died. Juliet MacLauchlan resumes her story:

'On one occasion my elder daughter was in the rectory alone, as we had gone to a dinner party. The following morning she asked me why I had returned to the house shortly after we had left for our party. She said she had heard my skirt rustling as I crossed the hall and climbed the stairs. I assured her that I had most certainly not returned at that time, and in any case the skirt I had been wearing would not have rustled in that way.

'One weekend a friend, Amanda Walton Price [*name changed*] whom I met during the period we had been living in the house, was staying with us and I told her of the ghostly presence in the rectory. She then related an experience she had had in a house when she had encountered a Roman centurion who seemed in fact to be a rather unpleasant individual. She asked if she might walk round the rectory and on returning half an hour later she told me she was certainly conscious of a lady in the study, and of something older too. At a later meeting she told me of a visit to a fortune teller who had mentioned Amanda's encounter with a ghost of a lady in a rectory and the smell, which the fortune teller said was caused by that lady having injured her leg, the wound being dressed with unguents to heal it. Amanda assured me that she had mentioned nothing to anyone about the rectory and its occupants.

'Another friend who used to call and see me at the rectory had two whippets. They used to run around the house happily, except that Mousey would never enter the study without great coercion.

'About five times I smelled cigarette smoke very strongly in the drawing room. No one in the house smoked and it certainly was in the room and had not come from outside – I could not understand it.

'When my husband recovered from his illness and returned to Belgium, I decided to join him and we decided to sell the rectory. I felt my ghost was in accord with this decision, but she certainly did not like some of the people who came to view the house, and I was conscious of her utter disapproval. In fact she didn't seem very happy with the people who eventually bought the house, and they stayed for only some eighteen months.

'The Marsh is a very fruitful source of ghostly tales – of headless horsemen and the army officers who, prior to embarkation for Dunkirk, had lived in Poplar Hall, Appledore. Their apparitions appeared during a service of communion to lay their spirits to rest.

'As I said earlier, I find this story very difficult to tell, as I was so deeply affected by it, and I miss my gentle guiding presence. There are certainly no ghosts in my house in Belgium.'

Mrs Joan Read, a retired local historian from London who has contributed a number of psychic experiences to this book, recalls a particularly disturbing incident when she visited a house in Greenwich, whose occupant wanted to learn more about the history of her home.

'I made the appointment for 10 a.m. and, as it had turned out to be a lovely, hot summer's morning, I strolled across Blackheath and through Greenwich Park to Park Vista for my appointment.

'The kitchen, a new unit, had been built as an addition to the front of the house. It overlooked the front gate. The lady of the house saw me at the gate and had the door open and the kettle on almost immediately. Two large dogs bounded out to meet me, tails wagging, looking for a welcome.

'We sat down in the kitchen and the lady began her story. Her husband had been very ill and was still in hospital. She had been worried and weeping for several nights when, on what she knew was a critical time for him, a little stout man, wearing what looked like a leather apron over his shirt, appeared in the room with her. He touched her on the arm and told her not to worry as her husband would survive the night. She thought she had dreamt it, but when she rang the hospital, she was told that her husband *had* survived the night!

'Nevertheless, her husband was still a very sick man. She worried a lot about him. Then, she noticed, the little man seemed to be about the house frequently. Sometimes she saw him and often she had the feeling he was close by as she felt a reassuring grip on her arm.

'"Do the dogs notice him?" I asked, as animals are said to have a fear of the supernatural.

'"Yes, the hair rises on their backs and they always leave the room. In fact, he doesn't appear everywhere in the house. This kitchen for instance, he has never been felt out here. He seems to stay on one side of the house, upstairs and downstairs. Would you like to wander round the house on your own, while I clear the kitchen?"

'I moved with the dogs to the dining-room behind the kitchen, then upstairs, looking at the old staircase, peeping into the bedrooms, then descending the stairs again, turning at the bottom to enter the sitting room. Here, the dogs went back to the kitchen, growling!

'It was cool in the house, but I felt a little too warm, so I went out into the garden. I knew the house was an old one, and in the garden I could see a lot of the flat Tudor bricks set in the wall of the house. This must be the side of the house that was old.

'The sun was rising higher and it was getting hotter. There was little shade in the garden so I re-entered the house.

'"It's getting very hot!" I called.

'"Sit by the fireplace, it's usually cool there."

'A large wooden armchair stood beside what could only be an open log fireplace. I was fascinated by the Tudor brickwork ... I passed my hands over it then, still admiring it, I sat down in the chair.

'As I sat, I cooled down. Then I began to feel cold, very cold! I clutched the arms of the chair – then felt it slowly rise! My feet left the floor and then the chair slowly descended. My mind was in a whirl. I quickly went out to the kitchen and explained what had happened.

'"He doesn't like you very much," replied the owner of the house.

'"Well," I answered, "I did come with an open mind."

'"You may think so. He definitely doesn't like you; he thinks you are asking too many questions, even in your mind. Oddly enough, he didn't take to my husband when he came home for a short time. My husband never saw him or felt him, yet I know that there were times when I could either see him or feel him in the house. You are sure that the chair rose?"

'"Yes, very sure!"

'"Well, there you are. He's proving he's here!"

'"Do you think he belongs to the house? What kind of age are his clothes? The apron was probably part of his trade but what other clues do you get?"

'"His apron is so long and he is only about five foot tall, so he seems to be all apron; but I suppose he gives the impression of being an Elizabethan workman."

'"An ostler?"

'She agreed that he might well be an ostler.

'Before my visit I had had a good look at maps covering the Park Vista area. The old Palace of Placentia had stood near to the river, a walled area around it. Along one of the roads leading to it had stood a small house with a yard around it. I had a strong impression that the little man looked after travellers' horses. I had no proof; it was just a very strong impression, strengthened when I studied the fireplace.

'I did not stay long after that – and I have never returned.'

Timewarps

Some people have quite remarkable experiences which appear to involve their being transported back in time to witness an incident which took place many years earlier, and often feature a number of apparitions, including those of people, animals and even objects. These have become known as timewarp experiences.

A friend told me about the bizarre experience of Susan, her highly respected employee. A woman of mature age, neat, precise and rather shy, Susan is reluctant to discuss the event with strangers, and wishes to remain anonymous. She did agree to talk to me, however, and the following story is taken from a recording of our conversation in Bath on 10 May 1988.

In about 1968 Susan and her late husband were driving along a tarmac road near Marksford on the outskirts of Bath. It was very familiar territory to the couple, who often walked their dogs in that area, near their home. Susan was sitting in the passenger seat next to her husband who was driving. There was no one else in the car.

The journey was uneventful until all at once, with absolutely no warning, Susan found herself flung backwards in time.

'Suddenly the road was a track and there were a lot of people around a stage coach which had overturned. There were armed men, boxes strewn about the ground and deafening noise. But no one appeared to be hurt. I don't know what century it would have been – probably about a hundred years ago I should think.'

The coach, painted black and trimmed with red, appeared to have overturned recently, spilling boxes and baggage all over the rutted track. The four horses were hysterical with fear, but still in harness, struggling to keep on their feet as the armed men who appeared to be highwaymen rushed around shouting orders to passengers and coachmen. The confusion was indescribable.

Susan was unsure of her own role in this scene: 'I don't know what part I was playing in this, whether I was boy, man, girl or woman, but I was right in the middle of it, and totally unafraid.'

This aspect of the experience seems to be the one which surprised her most of all. She emphasizes how utterly unafraid she was of the armed men (whom she described as being dressed in dark coloured clothing, perhaps red). The confidence she felt in the midst of the confusion was quite foreign to her normal nature. In retrospect she believes she may have been a member of the highwaymen's gang.

Beyond that she could not say whether she was young or old, male or female, or what kind of clothes she wore. She had the impression that the people involved in the scene were young rather than old. She could not see any individual's facial features, or estimate the number of people involved in the chaos. But she was convinced that she had arrived on the scene at the precise moment the coach had overturned.

Projected without warning into the centre of this noisy disaster in time past, Susan was acutely aware, throughout the experience, of her other being, her current life in the twentieth century. She was aware of being two people at once, she said, but in two different time scales.

She described her reaction as one of impatience and almost anger, certainly of deep regret, at being dragged back into the present when her husband stopped the car at a crossroads and spoke sharply to gain her attention. He demanded to know what was wrong – he had spoken to her several times and she had not replied. When he glanced at her as he waited for the traffic to pass, he was disturbed by her appearance.

'You look so strange,' he said.

A straightforward, matter-of-fact man who had never experienced anything remotely resembling what his wife then described, he accepted her explanation because, he said later, his wife was so clearly not with him on the half-mile stretch of road between the time of her last remark and the moment at which they reached the crossroads.

Susan could not remember anything about the car journey along that section of the road, nor could she remember stopping at the junction. It was only when her husband spoke her name for the third time that she was drawn back from the scene of the stage coach to re-enter the twentieth century.

Susan subsequently walked her dogs along that particular section of road on many occasions, hoping that she might be allowed back to the scene to repeat the experience she had found so enjoyable. But nothing of the kind ever happened to her again.

About a year later, however, early one morning as her husband prepared to leave for work, she had a premonition: she knew he would be involved in an accident that day.

About to warn him, she thought better of it, realizing that he might worry unduly and perhaps *cause* an accident. She was terribly ill at ease all morning and was tempted to confide in a friend she was entertaining to coffee but decided against it as she was frightened of being ridiculed.

Her friend left the house and at one o'clock Susan had a sandwich while she listened to the news on the radio. A few minutes later she felt totally calm and relaxed: the nightmare, as she called it, was suddenly over – she didn't know why.

When her husband returned home at his usual time, he was carrying items normally left in the car.

'You've had an accident!' exclaimed Susan.

'How do you know?' he demanded.

Susan described her premonition and her husband then admitted that he had been driving around a wide bend when he had skidded on ice, badly damaging the undercarriage of the car. He was unhurt. The time of the accident was exactly 1.02 p.m., when Susan had been listening to the news on the radio.

Susan has never had any other psychic experiences, before or since these two. She appeared to me to be completely reliable, a woman not given to romantic invention, who had been thoroughly shaken, not only by her extraordinary journey through time, but also by her enjoyment of it.

Dr Harris [name changed] *is a retired general medical practitioner who now lives in Devon. When he was twenty-two he was living at a students' hostel in Perivale Avenue, Ealing, while studying at University College Hospital in London.*

'I arrived at Ealing Common Station from London one evening at about six o'clock. It was dark; the lamps were lit. As a change I decided to walk back to the hostel through Montpelier Avenue. I usually went by a slightly quicker road parallel to it.

'Some way along I passed a policeman standing on a corner, also a small brown dog. A few hundred yards further, on the right side of the road where I was walking, I came to a fairly large white house, lit up, with a large gate and a path through the garden to the front door.

'Just before I got to the gate a black coach came out with, I think, two dark brown horses, although there might have been four. They stopped just outside the gate and I noticed that you could see the horses' breath, but there was not a [sound of their breathing] or anything else to be heard.

'Then I noticed a number, say four, of dark people-shapes come out of the house, who were pushing someone else into the back of the coach, who didn't seem to want to go.

'I thought this was all very odd, and went back to the policeman, who accompanied me back up the road, but I could not then find any trace of the white house, or garden or gate, or any sign of the coach! I understand that there used to be some large houses in this part of Ealing in Regency times.'

John Allison is a retired teacher, now living in the West Midlands. The son of a clergyman, he was brought up deep in the Lincolnshire countryside in a huge, rambling old house built during the Napoleonic Wars for a Miss Coverdale. The house was far too big for an impecunious country parson and his family, according to Mr Allison. Nevertheless, his father accepted a post in the neighbourhood, taking up residence in the house shortly after the end of the First World War. It was not long before the Allison family realized that it was not alone in the building. The first intimation of another presence came at the end of a long corridor upstairs.

'My mother was in the bathroom while my brother and a friend, both aged six, were playing in the corridor by the door which divided the corridor from the back stairs and several unused rooms. As my mother came out of the bathroom she found the two boys looking at each other with puzzled expressions.

'"Where has she gone?" they asked.

'"Where has who gone?" queried my mother.

'"An old lady stood and smiled at us," she was told. "She was dressed ever so funny. We thought she went through that door, but now we can't find her."'

No one of that description lived in the house at the time, and the children's experience was dismissed as a figment of their imagination. However, shortly afterwards, a visitor arrived to stay the night. He was shown to the guest room which had a large window with a view on to the roof of the columned porch and beyond it to a long gravel drive winding down to a large white gate.

'I can still remember the click of that gate when it shut,' remembers John Allison, who continues: 'It was dark when the visitor awoke. He was aware of the sound of carriage wheels on the drive and concluded that this was what had woken him. He heard the carriage stop by the front door below him; then he heard the front door being opened and shut. He glanced at his watch; by the bright moonlight which filtered into the room he saw that it was 2 a.m. He wondered idly who the night visitor might be, but then heard again the sound of the opening front door, followed by the grating of wheels on the drive, a pause, the creak of the gate, the click as it shut, and the sound of wheels fading away into the distance.

'In the morning my father inquired conventionally whether his guest had slept well, and was regaled with details of the night sounds. Privately my father concluded that his guest had been the victim of a nightmare. No one had called during the night, and the front door was found locked and bolted as usual.

'A few weeks later another guest was shown to the same room, an old friend of the family. To my father's surprise, he too told of the sound of wheels in the night, [his account agreeing with that of the first guest] down to the smallest detail.

'My father came to the conclusion that some important event in the life of Miss Coverdale was being re-enacted, though what it was was anybody's guess. Anyway, it was sufficient to persuade my father to carry out the prescribed rites for the laying of spirits, and the room was purified.

'Later, the room was in daily use. Indeed, I slept in it myself on several occasions, but there were no more night disturbances. If the spirit of Miss Coverdale still hovered over the house, unseen and unheard, it must have been a friendly one, for I remember it as a happy place.'

(John Allison adds in a postscript that although the bedroom next to the one described also overlooked the drive and was in constant use, no one occupying it ever experienced anything remotely unusual there.)

Mrs S. M. Woodyatt from Devon describes friends who ran a hotel overlooking Dumpton Hill near Honiton in Devon during the Second World War. She talks of them as down-to-earth, practical people who, on one occasion, were shocked by the state of one of their guests.

An American colonel had booked into the hotel for a rest. It was November and one foggy morning before breakfast he decided to climb Dumpton Hill. He set off in high spirits but returned some time later looking as white as a sheet and asking for a stiff drink. Responding to the proprietors' anxiety at his appearance, he told them what had happened. They, in turn, described the incident to Mrs Woodyatt.

The summit of the hill was crowned by half a dozen trees, shrouded in mist that particular morning. As the colonel neared the top he claimed a whole regiment of men suddenly burst out of the trees, all wearing chain armour with crosses on their breasts. They swept towards him, on and on, charging out of the trees on top of Dumpton Hill. He freely admitted to being absolutely terrified, and his hosts bore witness to the evidence of shock in his manner and appearance on his return to the hotel, as we have seen. But no one was able to offer him any explanation for the incident.

When I was out to supper on 4 December 1988, my Bath hosts' daughter was intrigued by comments on research for this book. 'I believe in ghosts,' she said. 'I've seen one!' And this is the story Erica Lynall (now in her early twenties) told me.

'Ten years ago, when I was eleven years old, I was living in a converted coach house of the type common to large Georgian houses, in Bathampton Lane, Bath. I had a very small room at the front on the top floor (there are only two levels, and it is a very small building). My bed was right next to a window.

'One night for some reason I woke up. I had a strange feeling or urge to look out of the window, so I sat up on my bed and opened the curtains. I saw the figure of a coachman dressed in what I would call a typical Georgian coachman's outfit: three-cornered hat, a large overcoat and riding boots. He was hovering in a sitting position as if he were upon a coach with the reins in his hands, although there was no coach and no horses.

'I did not feel frightened. My reaction was more a sense of curiosity, and I distinctly remember telling myself to keep calm lest he sensed any fear. I had no doubt in my mind that he was a ghost. It could not have been anything else. He did not look at me – he was looking slightly to the right of where I was, just as if he were thinking or waiting for something. His face was almost in profile from where I sat, but it was not very distinct.

'I was not sure what I was looking at exactly, and I remember shutting the curtains and opening them again, expecting the ghost to be gone. But he was still there.

'I could see next-door's wall, so it cannot have been a misty night. The next day I went to look outside, and there was nothing there that I could possibly have mistaken for a human form, no overhanging trees, for example.'

Her parents confirmed Erica's story, remembering quite clearly her description of the ghost which she told them about immediately after the event.

The following account is the only example of its kind that I received in the course of my research. Mrs Rosemary McCarthy of Somerset moved to the country, settled in, and decided to take a walk around her new home.

'I live in a pretty village near Wells. The village is old and has a most attractive church. One day soon after I arrived I was walking past the church when I noticed a most beautiful grey stone cottage at the back of the churchyard. I asked who lived there, but was told there was no cottage there, and nobody else had ever seen one.

'It seems probable that there were cottages there in the past, as was the custom. I was not frightened, but I know absolutely what I saw. It seemed such a happy, peaceful cottage that I'm quite sure whoever lived there had a happy, peaceful life.'

Rosemary McCarthy emphasizes the point that it was broad daylight when she saw the cottage.

Deeds of Violence and Violent Death

The most frequently seen ghosts in folklore and fiction are those of men and women whose lives have been cut short by violence, by murder, suicide, execution or accident. The following stories about real events appear to support the approach of many writers of fiction: ghosts of identifiable individuals whose lives came to an abrupt end are frequently encountered.

For more than sixteen years, Mr Gordon Headon (now a Head General Porter) of South Yorkshire had worked in the Crown Hotel, mostly on night duty. In that time he had heard many stories about ghosts being seen in the hotel, but he had paid little attention to them, dismissing them as of no interest.

However, in 1978 a small fire broke out in the staff block. It was quickly contained and put out, with little damage to show for it. But it seems to have started a chain of events. Mr Headon tells of his meeting with a ghost.

'It would have been roughly 6.15 a.m. Daylight was just breaking, and having completed my duties for that night, I sat down on the foyer settee to enjoy a freshly brewed cup of tea. The doors of the hotel were still locked, as we had few residents in that night, and breakfast didn't start until 8 a.m.

'The hotel has two doors leading into the foyer, the main door on to the High Street and a side door leading to the Colonnade which is on the right hand side of the foyer.

'A young woman, I judged her age to be about the mid-twenties, walked from this side door through the foyer, and rounded the corner to enter our lounge bar. Walking directly towards the bar itself, she walked right through it, and as quickly as she appeared, vanished.

'I shook my head in total disbelief, and went to try the door she had appeared from, to satisfy myself I still had the door locked. It was.

'Two days later I had more or less convinced myself that I must have been overtired, and had seen nothing at all, when I was strongly reminded that whatever I had seen had indeed walked through a solid locked door and a closed and locked bar.'

A regular guest of the hotel, well-known to Gordon Headon, occupied bedroom 15 situated in the oldest part of the hotel. The guest had booked the room for two nights on this occasion, but on the morning after his first night he went down to reception, suitcases in hand, and asked for his bill, saying he would not be staying a second night.

'Thinking perhaps we had upset him in some way, I inquired the reason for his early departure. At first he was reluctant to tell me his story, perhaps assuming I would think him a bit crazy. However, I persuaded him to tell me what had happened. It seems that he was awakened at around 4 a.m. by a feeling that he was not alone. He opened his eyes and saw a young woman standing at the far end of the bed with her back towards the window. In a darkened room he should not have been able to see her clearly, but he did, a fact which did not dawn upon him until later . . . He was very puzzled to know how she had entered the room, as his door was locked.

'"What are you doing here?" he demanded. But getting no answer, he reached for the bedside light and switched it on. The girl remained at the foot of the bed, looking down at him. He jumped out of bed, walked towards her and, thinking she might be sleep-walking, he put his hand on her shoulder to try to get her to respond to his question. His hand passed right through her, and he could still see it.

'He swore to me that the girl looked as solid as we do. When he realized I wasn't laughing at him, he asked what I thought about it. I replied that I thought I had seen the same girl.'

The two men discussed the figure they had seen and realized that their descriptions matched exactly. They had both judged her to be about twenty-five years old. She wore a white blouse with full sleeves at the wrist, buttoned high at the neck. Her skirt was long and black, while her hair was piled on her head in a bun. She wore flat black shoes and black stockings.

'Both of us were convinced we had seen a ghost, and I was

determined to discover who she was. I searched for anything I could find, both at our local library and in a Doncaster branch, but I found nothing.'

One day Mr Headon told a friend who happened to be a police constable about the ghost. The policeman thought for a moment and then described a murder which had taken place at the Crown Hotel shortly after the end of the Second World War.

Apparently the chef at the time had been having an affair with a young waitress. They had quarrelled, and the chef had strangled the girl. But in a fit of remorse he hanged himself from the rafters of the old staff block in which they had both lived. Later, that particular part of the hotel had been converted into guest rooms.

Excited by this information, Mr Headon returned to the public library to renew his search for evidence of the story, and eventually he found it. He came across evidence that a murder had indeed taken place at the hotel as recalled by the police officer. And there was another remarkable detail: when the unfortunate girl's body was discovered, she was wearing the same clothes as those he and the guest had described as being worn by the ghost!

Four years later, in 1982, the general manager of the hotel arranged to have the story investigated by two mediums. They were told nothing of the circumstances, nor of the whereabouts of the hotel they were being taken to. Mr Headon, who was asked to participate, was disconcerted to find himself confronted by no less than sixteen people in one of the hotel's meeting rooms.

Claiming she could see and communicate with the ghost of the girl, who she said was standing next to Mr Headon as she spoke, one of the mediums then confirmed the details given earlier: she told everyone that the spirit was a girl of twenty-four, who was dressed exactly as Mr Headon and the guest in room 15 had recounted.

Unable to see any sign of the ghost himself, Mr Headon said that he was very suspicious of the medium until she revealed personal information about himself and his assistant that she said had been conveyed to her by the spirit.

According to the medium, the girl had met a tragic end. She had frequently followed Mr Headon around the hotel and failed to communicate with him. Mr Headon wrote:

'It wasn't until we had the fire, which the medium described as a major disturbance, that the girl had been able to show herself.'

The medium said that the girl had not fully realized what had happened to her: she did not know that she was dead.

'She would explain things to the spirit, which she did, seemingly speaking to herself once again . . .

'She ended by turning to me, saying that the girl now understood that she was no longer in our dimension, and that she would no longer try to communicate with me, but asked: as she felt lonely, would I mind if she walked with me sometimes, as she didn't mean any harm. As I was in no position to argue with someone I could no longer see, I agreed.

'From that day to this I haven't seen her again, or even felt her presence.'

Gordon Headon's attitude to this psychic experience is comparable to that of many contributors to this book: having previously dismissed accounts of supernatural events as being of no consequence, he had reversed his opinion completely after his own personal sighting, and had not been able to rest until he discovered some explanation for that unnerving experience.

Mrs Joan Church of Wiltshire is the daughter of a woman who was the seventh child of a seventh child. Traditionally, individuals with this background are considered to enjoy special powers. Joan Church certainly appears to have inherited from her Scottish mother a sensitivity to the supernatural. On the occasion recounted below, she must also have inherited nerves of steel.

In 1954 Joan Church and her husband and their three children returned from Malaysia after spending three and a half years in Kuala Lumpur. Mr Church's parents had recently moved into a new flat in Maidenhead which was being redecorated. Unable to accommodate the visitors, Mr Church senior arranged for the family to stay at a nearby residential club where they returned each night to sleep after spending the day with their relatives.

Joan Church had not visited Maidenhead before. The club appeared to offer a high standard of accommodation, with pleasantly furnished rooms; but for some reason she was very conscious of a cold and peculiar atmosphere in the rooms allotted to her family. The children's room was connected to their parents' by an arched opening without a door. Joan Church describes what happened on the first night.

'I got up to make sure the children were warm, having come from a hot climate, especially the baby, who was only six months old.

'When I returned to bed I was annoyed and astonished to find a very old lady asleep where I had been myself. I assumed that my husband had forgotten to lock the door, and that she had wandered in by mistake. She looked twisted and haggard.

'I did not want to touch her, so I said loudly that she must get up and leave as she was in the wrong bed. I shook my husband and told him what had happened.

'All this time I was looking at her and thinking how strange she looked. My husband woke up and I pointed to her and said, "Look. You must have left the door open."

'As he moved and turned to look at her, she slowly vanished. My husband said I must have dreamed it, but I knew very well I had not. When I got back into bed it felt horribly cold and unpleasant, and I felt utterly revolted.

'The next night we were all very tired and I suggested to my husband that he should go over to the flat and say goodnight to his parents, and I would stay with the children.

'About fifteen minutes later, having gone downstairs and stopped to have a drink at the bar, he came back looking very upset, and refused to leave us, saying he would not go to his parents that night.

'It was only after we left the club a few days later that he told me what had happened. At the bar the manager had begun to tell him about the murder some years ago of an old lady who owned the house. The murder had been committed by a casual workman who had hidden the body in the room we had occupied and later in a trunk in the hall. My husband was so upset at the implications of this, and what I had seen, that he refused to leave me alone there until we left. My father-in-law did not know about the murder, and was horrified to learn about our experience there.'

VARIETIES OF GHOST

Mr Simon Reynolds is a London art dealer. This story dates from the 1950s, when he attended Ampleforth College.

'The late Father Sebastian Lambert of the Order of St Benedict was the down-to-earth housemaster of St Cuthbert's House, Ampleforth College. He had been housemaster for as many years as anyone could remember, and was known as a respected disciplinarian ... Normally a man of few words, just sometimes he could be persuaded to gather his flock of restless boys about him, usually in front of his office fire on a dark winter's evening, to relate tales from his own distant past.

'A true story, from one of those evenings in the 1950s, has left a clear and deep impression upon me.

'Father Sebastian was travelling one winter weekend somewhere in the heart of Wales. He was due to connect trains at a small provincial station but because of stormy weather his train arrived too late for the connection. To his aggravation he found himself stranded in a hamlet that did not even boast a hotel. Racking his brains he recalled that one of his old boys lived near by in, if he remembered rightly, a substantial house.

'Father Sebastian telephoned and was much relieved to find his past pupil at home. The problem, however, was that a house-party was in full swing and the house was full to capacity. Father Sebastian pleaded that he did not mind where he could lay his weary head provided it was dry and warm. "All right," said his host, "You are more than welcome, but the only room we have is one that we have not used in years; the servants however can air it and kindle you a good fire, and I will send a car down to collect you from the station."

'It was still early evening when Father Sebastian arrived at the stately old house, in good time to change for what proved to be a substantial dinner party.

'The room to which he was shown was indeed sparsely furnished but had evidently, at one time, been a guest room of some importance. There was a large double four-poster bed entirely surrounded by rich and heavy velvet curtains; opposite the bed a second door led into a smaller bedroom, apparently unoccupied and unfurnished. The door to this room was closed and between it and the bed, overlooking the park and opposite the cheerfully burning fire, was a large window.

'After dressing for dinner Father Sebastian descended to the drawing room to join the other guests. The dinner was convivial but being tired he soon withdrew to his room. To his surprise he found the fire almost dead, with the cold evening air gusting between a wide-open door to the adjacent room and a fully opened window. Cursing the negligent servants he closed and securely locked both door and window. Nevertheless the lingering cold of the room drove him quickly to his bed, where he drew the bed curtains closely around him. Exhaustion overtook him and within minutes he fell into a deep sleep.

'Sometime in the early hours of the morning he woke with a start. He could see absolutely nothing within the confines of his bed curtains, but he clearly heard a door creaking open. To his great alarm it was not the passage door to his room – it was the door opposite his bed, the door to the adjacent room which he had personally locked the previous night. He lay frozen to his bed as slow footsteps crossed the room, approaching the bed relentlessly, but with apparent stealth.

'Next came the gentle rustling of the curtains at his feet. Father Sebastian sat bolt upright. Transfixed with fear, he peered into the gloom. As the curtains divided, the white light of a full moon flooding from the window clearly illuminated the head of a man gazing fixedly at the petrified priest. Father Sebastian's description of the face he saw was stilted; even years later he was obviously unwilling to recall the moment in all its horror.

'"Evil! The face I saw was the very personification of evil! The eyes carried a message of hate that I have never before or since seen in mortal eyes," Father Sebastian related. "All I then remember was the weight of a hand on the foot of the bed!"

'When some hours later he reopened his eyes, it was already daylight. His memory of his night's ordeal was vivid. However, he could only surmise that he had fainted as the apparition made its way from the foot of the bed. Throwing open the bed curtains he saw the door to the ante-room was wide open: so was the window.

'Father Sebastian dressed and made his way down to breakfast. His host welcomed him but, noticing how pale he looked, he inquired as to how his guest had slept. "Sadly, not too well!" retorted the priest. Pressed by further anxious inquiries he related his experience the previous night.

'"That," replied his host, "is why I was reluctant to offer you that room. Once it was our chief guest room, but it has been unused for years. Shortly after my great-grandfather built the house he invited a large house-party to spend the weekend." Among the guests were a young newly married couple and an older gentleman, a neighbour and friend of the bride's family. These acquaintances had not been advised that they were joint house-guests but due to the limited accommodation available they had been placed in adjoining rooms, Father Sebastian's for the bridal couple and the empty ante-room for the bachelor guest.

'The first evening of the house-party passed uneventfully but the morning sun rose on a horrific scene of unaccountable death. The bachelor was found by the gardener lying dead beneath the open windows of the principal guest room. The gardener raised the alarm and a search was undertaken. The bridal couple had not stirred so their host entered their room. All was silence, the fire dead in the hearth, the window wide open, the door to the ante-room creaking ajar on its hinges. Pulling back the curtains of the bed, the host found both bride and bridegroom lying dead, strangled, their bodies spreadeagled over the tangled bedclothes.

'Subsequent police inquiries apparently ascertained that the deceased bachelor had long entertained an unwelcome infatuation for the dead girl. Knowing his fierce and jealous disposition, the girl's parents had forbidden him the house and had purposely refrained from telling him about their daughter's marriage to the young man of her choice. Evidently the shock of discovery, coupled by the close proximity of the bridal pair, had turned the mind of the lonely, rejected suitor. He had entered their room while they slept, killed them with the utmost ferocity and subsequently thrown himself from the bedroom window.

'Father Sebastian was the innocent victim of the restless spirit of the murderer, eternally condemned to re-enact his crime.'

Mrs Shelah Newman of Sheffield was about ten years old one sweltering hot summer when her parents were invited to look over an empty house in the neighbourhood.

The house was notorious as the scene of a particularly brutal murder committed by a previous owner, after which it had remained empty for three or four years. No one wanted to live there; passers-by shuddered and spoke in whispers as they hurried past; even birds avoided the place. But human nature being what it is, when Shelah's aunt and uncle obtained the keys to look over the property, her parents immediately agreed to accompany them. As it was during the school holidays, little Shelah was taken along too.

The back of the house, built up on stilts on the edge of a bank, protruded into a dark and silent wood. As they went in, the only sound was the creaking of the heavy front door. When it came open, every one of them was aware of the sudden drop in temperature in the air around them. Shelah Newman takes up the story.

'I don't think any member of the party felt over-enthusiastic, but we were determined to proceed. Apart from the noise made by the door, the silence was positively uncanny – thick dust muffled our footfalls, yet there was a tendency to keep on looking behind us, and the entire party was shivering and complaining of the chill.

'By the top of the steps leading to the cellar kitchen I found myself unable to move: the chill had moved towards my throat. I found I was unable to breathe, with a clammy pressure I couldn't account for on my neck.

'I can remember having to be taken outside. My mother scolded and blamed me for causing a scene. But I don't think anyone was really sorry – there were pointed looks and mutterings among the adults for the rest of that day.'

When she was much older Shelah Newman discovered details of the murder committed in the house and realized the significance of her experience: the owner had brutally attacked and strangled his wife on exactly the same spot where she had, on that summer's day, experienced the sensations described.

There was a curious reaction to this visit to the haunted house: afterwards everyone, adults and children alike, came out in a rash. 'All the party came out in what could have been flea bites within a day or two of the visit.'

Over the following twelve months uneasiness increased in the area of the house. The former stillness and air of brooding menace was disrupted by inexplicable noises, and lights were reported as being seen dimly through the windows. Eventually the place was demolished, but according to Mrs Newman even the site where it stood was studiously avoided after dark.

Mrs Mary Outhwaite of Devon is a library assistant who has had a number of psychic experiences. The following account is a transcript of a tape recording made by Mrs Outhwaite in 1988.

In her mid-twenties Mary Outhwaite was working as a Girl Friday in an ancient building in Surrey called the Wire Mill where, she was told, nails for St Paul's Cathedral were made. It was there, on 9 January (her birthday, so she has reason to remember the date), that she saw her first ghost.

'The building was then run as a sort of Country Club with a large lake at the back and a bar which was mainly patronized by the locals – mostly a farming community. On this particular evening, about midnight, the bar had emptied, apart from the proprietor's niece Penelope [*name changed*], a girl of about fourteen or fifteen years old, who had fallen asleep stretched out on a sofa in front of a brightly burning fire.

'Although the room was warm I suddenly felt a distinct drop in temperature and, on looking over into the corner where the Christmas tree had been, I saw a strange, shimmering, gauzy apparition hovering about a foot off the floor.

'I was not afraid and stared at it. It had no face or recognizable limbs, just this gauzy shape. It gradually disappeared by just fading away. As it did so the temperature in the room increased and Penelope woke up.

'Several months later the basement was going to be turned into a ballroom so the rotting old floor had to be dug up. Two skeletons were discovered, manacled by their wrists.'

The skeletal remains were removed before Mary Outhwaite had a chance to see them, but she wondered if they were connected to the wraith-like figure she had seen on the night of her birthday.

Mary Outhwaite is one of many contributors who comment on the absence of facial features in ghostly presences they have observed.

Victor G. Neville-Statham is a retired civil servant now living in Lincolnshire. He admits that psychic phenomena have always fascinated him and appears to have been receptive from an early age. He believes that some people are more sensitive than others, but thinks that such awareness needs to be cultivated. 'If you are really keen on learning to play an instrument,' he says, 'you'll learn. If not, you won't.' Fear of ridicule and modern life probably blunt our sensitivity, he adds, believing that everyone is, or can be, psychic. As a young man he investigated that famous haunted building, Borley Rectory in Suffolk, with some of his colleagues (see p. 164). The following incident took place during the Second World War, when he was living in London with his parents.

'In 1942 I had been discharged unfit from the army, and was working locally. We moved from where we were living – a flat – to a house in order that my young sister might have a room of her own. The house was vacant and my mother had permission to view it. There were two latchkeys (Yales), one of which my mother gave to me when we arranged to meet at the house to go over it together.

'I arrived at the house on my pedal cycle, wheeled my bike up to the front door and opened it. I decided to put my bike in the hall for safety.

'Looking down the hall I could see a clear-glass panelled door. Standing in the room beyond was a woman, her back to me. She was looking out of the window in front of her. This window was crisscrossed with paper strips, as were many in wartime, and the woman moved as though she were peering through the strips to the garden beyond.

'It wasn't my mother, who was tall and dark. This lady had fair hair, short and wavy, and wore a flower-patterned frock. I turned to close the front door and saw my mother entering the gateway.

'I told her that someone was in the room beyond, probably looking over the house. She reminded me there were only two keys, both in our possession, so how had she got in?

'We went into this room at the end of the hall and found no one there. The door to the garden was locked and bolted, and there was no key.

'After we had moved in a neighbour told me that the previous tenant, a lady, had committed suicide by drinking Lysol (a corrosive disinfectant). We had been in residence about a month when the noises started. There was a cupboard under the stairs and it would sound as though someone was shovelling coal there and throwing it up against the underside of the staircase. Then there were heavy footsteps along the hall, ending with a loud bang as though someone had thrown something heavy against the front door. These noises would occur after everyone had retired to bed, and gradually died away over the years.

'My mother and father both died there, and a white poodle I had is buried in the garden of the house. After I moved on retirement (it was a rented property), it was sold to an Asian family. I am told that so far, in three years, four separate Asian families have lived there, but will not stay because, as they put it, "It is a house of spirits". A figure is seen standing by an upstairs window, apparently looking out, and what appears to be a "white ball of fluff" comes down the stairs towards the front door.

'My father in his lifetime had a habit of standing looking out of an upstairs window (on to the street) and my poodle, which I was obliged to leave at home when I was at work, would come running downstairs to greet me on my return home each day.'

James (Jim) Ross lives in Tyne and Wear and is usually employed in the building trade. However, at the time of this experience he was temporarily working as an itinerant brush-salesman, travelling from door to door.

At the end of the village of High Spen he found himself one day in May in a pleasant country lane with the scent of spring in the air, and birds trilling in the hedgerows.

'The road led through Barlow to Winlaton which overlooks and joins the town of Blaydon, known to all Geordies, where the legendary Blaydon races were once run and won. Winlaton was, until the sixties, famous for chain-making.'

Enjoying the brief respite from the gruelling task of selling brushes, Jim Ross dawdled along the lane with his heavy suitcase in hand, occasionally glancing back to check on any overtaking traffic.

At one point, he writes, 'I turned and saw a figure of a man walking behind me. He had not been there a minute before. What made me stop in my tracks was his dress. He could have stepped straight off a Quaker Oats packet! He wore what appeared to be a shovel hat, black frock coat, breeches that buttoned at the knee, white silken hose, and silver-buckled shoes . . . "Quaint!" I thought. "My mates will never believe this in the pub tonight!"

'Next time I turned around he had disappeared! I looked over the hedge thinking he may have dived into the field. No one there. I walked back down the road to see if there was a gate or gap in the hedge. None. It was a tightly knit hawthorn hedge. Well. There was a mystery!'

Three years later Jim Ross joined a local history class and when researching another subject he came across a reference to Selby's Stile at the Winlaton end of Barlow Lane adjoining Cromwell Road, where there is now a bus depot.

He then discovered that the Selby who had had a stile named after him was one of the judges connected with the sentencing to death of Charles I. Fleeing from pursuers intent on revenge when Charles II came to the throne, Selby hid himself in remote Tyneside.

His flight failed to prevent his discovery and death, however, and he was found hanging in the woods by local people who, unable to identify him and being suspicious of a stranger, cut down the corpse, drove a wooden stake through his heart and buried him at the crossroads. Jim Ross had finally identified the man in the lane.

'As the history book said, his ghost is believed to haunt the area to this day, so that explained my ghost.'

Jim Ross adds a postscript: 'One thing I learned was that ghosts are not wispy vague things, but are solid to look upon, and are gone the next moment.' Many contributors make the same comment.

Deirdre Bishop [name changed] *is retired and lives in Hertfordshire. During the Second World War she served in the Women's Royal Naval Service (WRNS or Wrens as they were known) and was for some time stationed in North Hill House on the Andover Road on the edge of Winchester. The building was not particularly old.*

'On a few occasions some of the Wrens had reported being awakened in the night in great fear with the feeling of a presence peering down at them in a hazy light. There was a rumour too that a soldier, dressed in some uniform of indeterminate date, had been seen in the grounds. All this was, of course, dismissed by the male section of the community as mass hysteria in women when herded together.

'I shared a cabin with one other Wren in the attic of the house. This room lay at the end of a passage. One night I had a head cold and could not sleep, but sat propped up (I certainly was not woken from a dream). The night was hot and our door lay open to get some air. I say this to stress the point that there was no breeze to blow curtains or doors, or rock window-stays in any way – all was still.

'About 2 a.m. I heard footsteps slowly and heavily mount the stairs and progress towards our room. (Nowadays one would fear a rapist – but no such idea entered my mind in the war years! At any rate instinct told me this was not human.) There was no bedroom lamp by my side, only one near the door, and nothing would have got me there.

'The footsteps stopped by the door and then for a few seconds came the sound of (not clanking chains!) but rusty, revolving squeaking machinery. Then silence. Nothing entered the room – yet nothing went away! I lay there petrified until dawn. My cabin-mate, on hearing of all this later, remonstrated with me for not calling her. But I had been unable to open my mouth.

'On the opposite side of the road to North Hill House was a very ugly public house, and in all the years I had been stationed in Winchester I had never entered it until the week I was due to be demobbed, when I decided to go in one lunchtime for a beer. There over the fireplace was an etching of North Hill House, and underneath, its history. It had been built on a hanging site of the Middle Ages!

'Did I hear some poor chap heavily mount the steps to the gallows, the trap door rustily open, and then – silence?'

When Graham Elsworth was eight he was living with his family in the Kingstone district of Barnsley in a house in an old terrace that was being demolished.

It was January 1955 and the little boy was engrossed in playing with empty walnut-shell halves left over from Christmas which he had made into tiny boats. Floating his flotilla in a large puddle of rainwater among the ruins of the demolition site, he was overlooked to the left by the gaunt remains of a large, privately owned house which had been in a derelict condition for many years. The owners of the property had, some time before, been served with a demolition order, and had engaged a local man to tackle the dangerous job of felling the remains, which he attempted to do alone, without any assistance.

'On the first day of this man's employment, while attempting to dislodge a roof beam at the highest part of the ruined house, he slipped, lost his footing and fell to his death on the rubble below.'

After the death of the workman nothing had been done to complete the task, and the skeleton of the building rose high against the cold grey sky, dwarfing the boy.

Suddenly, without any warning, he heard a loud noise at the top of the derelict building and turning towards it saw in the darkening sky the figure of a man.

'My throat went dry. I wanted to scream, but no sound came from my mouth. My legs turned to jelly and my body started to tremble. I pointed to the man who appeared to be looking directly down at me from his perch high above. He smiled and then suddenly drifted out from the building, falling only yards from where I stood transfixed. I screamed, a terrified wail, which no one would have heard for we were almost the last family waiting to be rehoused.

'I turned and ran for home, my walnut shell boats left rocking on the rainwater pond ... Long before I got there my legs folded beneath me. I tried to stand but simply could not, my terror was so great. I may have crawled something like fifty yards on my knees, gibbering inarticulately. I knocked on the front door. My mother was appalled to see the state I was in.'

When Graham had calmed down sufficiently to describe what he had seen, his father went to investigate. He found nothing but the tiny boats floating in the puddle as the boy described them. There was no body, nothing tangible to account for his son's obvious distress.

'To this day I remain convinced it was a ghost I saw,' adds Mr Elsworth, formerly a bus driver and manager of a television rental shop. 'Rational explanation cannot explain away what I saw, and I do not feel I was fantasizing or hallucinating in any way. At any rate, I never did play in the same area again.'

What follows is another contribution from Mrs Joan Read (see p. 12), who worked as a local historian at Manor House Archive Department at Lee in south London. The names mentioned are historically correct and she requests that they be left unaltered.

'An elderly little man, wearing a large flat cap which made him look even smaller, approached me while I was on duty in the library.

'"Do you know of anyone who has suffered a sudden death along the Bromley Road?" he asked.

'"Recently?" I inquired, my mind racing to remember about any sudden deaths in that area.

'"About sixty or seventy years ago, I think."

'"Why do you think it's round about that date?" (I needed a few more clues before I could start searching for this strange request.)

'"It was the dress that she was wearing. The young woman, she was seen passing through the traffic in Bromley Road."

'I was intrigued, but still puzzled. This was 1967 and the period that he was inquiring about was the 1890s!

'He went on to explain. "Every year, about Bank Holiday, a young woman, in what looks like a white blouse with leg-of-mutton sleeves, and a long dark skirt, has been seen by residents living in the new flats on the corner of Bellingham Road, which overlooks the main Bromley Road traffic. One lady called her husband to verify it as she thought that she was imagining it but her husband, too, saw the girl pass through the car. It was late afternoon, they continued to watch, but she appeared no more. They told their neighbours who, in turn, watched and the girl appeared again! They have asked me to find out more about the girl."

'"Which Bank Holiday?"

'"August. She appears to have been seen several times at this time over the past few years."'

Joan Read succeeded in locating a reference on a family tombstone which appeared relevant: 'In loving Memory of ... Alice Emma Grant, the only and dearly loved daughter of George and Emma Grant of Catford who was killed instantaneously by a cycling accident in the Southend Road on 2 September 1898 aged 18 years.' [Southend Road, now Southend Lane, leads into Bromley Road.]

'Opening the large book of bound newspapers for that year, we soon spotted the headline in the *Lewisham Journal*: "Catford Lady Cyclist Crushed to Death".

> Alice Grant, Brownhill Road, Catford, was not an expert rider but she hired a bike from Weatherleys, Rushey Green, and went out with her friend Miss Jessie Pynegar, who also went to Lewisham Grammar School with her. They rode to Bromley and on their return they passed a green-grocer's cart standing in the kerb and a brewer's dray was approaching from Catford. Her friend called to her to be careful – although there was about 14ft between the two vehicles. Miss Grant immediately lost control of her bike, the front wheel hit one of the horse's legs, causing it to plunge, throwing her under the heavy, fully-laden dray, the heavy wheels passing over her body, crushing her to death. It was late on Friday afternoon and a local doctor was near by, but she had died instantly.

'"That's just what I wanted to know," said the little man, and left.

'He came back a couple of weeks later to confirm precisely where the accident happened. I could not resist asking him why he wanted the information. "I'm a professional ghost-layer," he said, and left.

'He was in my thoughts as I wondered how he could deal with Alice Grant. Would he walk up and down Bromley Road with bell, book and candle? Would she really be laid to rest?

'I was lucky. I saw him a few months later on top of a bus. I couldn't resist asking him about it, although in those days librarians were never expected to ask the reason why – just to answer the query.

'He smiled at me for the first time. "Yes my dear, she is now at rest, I hope."'

Monks

The absence of naked ghosts in this collection of stories has been noted. In this section the importance of the clothing worn by apparitions is stressed: it is frequently our only clue to the identity of ghosts, or to the period when they lived – and that is almost always in the past. Many sightings of this kind take the form of cowled monks.

Mrs Gwerfyl Chappell lives in Lancashire but at the time of this incident she was a child of seven living in the little village of Corwen, ten miles from Llangollen in North Wales.

'I'd gone to morning chapel with my grandfather, and, facing the pulpit, we were waiting for the preacher to appear through the vestry door on the left of the pulpit.

'The door opened and a cowled figure appeared dressed in a long *cream* habit with the cowl up. It hid his face when he turned to go up the pulpit steps, and as there was a seat at the back, when he disappeared from my view I thought he was sitting down.

'I wasn't frightened, I just thought it was a new kind of preacher. Eventually the usual preacher arrived, and when I asked my grandfather when the other man was going to speak, he'd seen no one!

'It was only a few years ago, in 1972 to be exact, that I found out there used to be monks at Corwen, and they were established near the old church there, the rear of the church being almost directly opposite the Wesleyan Chapel. I still don't know which brotherhood he belonged to.'

A number of contributors have described events which were witnessed by other people in their company, although most sightings seem to occur when people are alone. Harold V. Rutherford, a retired bank manager in Wales, recalls one such event which took place when he and his wife and two little girls lived in an ancient house called Paradise Grange, situated in the Cattle Market at King's Lynn. The house stood on the site of land once owned and occupied by Black Friars.

'Our bedroom was lit by a street lamp some yards away so that it was illuminated most of the night . . . Both our children were ill with measles at the time, and I woke up to see a dark figure walking across the room from the window and out through the bedroom door. It appeared to be dressed in the dark outfit of a monk, with a cowl.

'My wife called to me from the other side of the room. "Did you see that?"

'I said "What?"

'She replied "That figure which walked across the room."

'As she did not seem alarmed, I confirmed that I had seen it.

'A night or two later she got up to see if the girls were all right as Mary was very poorly. To her horror she saw the ghost bending over Mary. But it was very noticeable that the child seemed to improve quickly from then on. This made us inclined to think the apparition was the ghost of a Black Friar, perhaps a physician.

'To us it seemed a very benign character, and although we saw it once or twice again, we were never alarmed. We were asked several times if we had seen the ghost by people who knew the house.

'The great pity is that the town council in their wisdom demolished the lovely old house to make room for parking lorries. I swear this is a true description of an event which we are very proud to have experienced.'

In 1974 Joan Church's husband had gone abroad to work, leaving Mrs Church (see p. 26) at home to provide a base for the children, who were all away at university. With time on her hands she took a job selling antiques in a manor house in Wiltshire. When the owners of the business went away, they left her in charge of the house.

'One night I was startled to hear footsteps coming down the corridor, when there was no one in the place but myself and my dog.

'The dog fled under the bed, howling. Standing in the doorway, looking at me with mild interest, was a monk in a brown habit, with a cowl hanging down his back and a piece of thin rope around his waist. He was broad and stocky in build, with a large head.'

Joan Church said nothing about the figure of the monk to the family on their return to the house, but one day she overheard the owner refer to the 'monk's room'. When she asked him what he meant, he told her where the room was, and added that the house had, many years ago, been a home for monks. When Mrs Church described the figure she had seen, the owner laughed. 'You're not the only one by a long way!' he replied.

A little while later the cleaning woman at the manor house told her that the family always found it difficult to get help in the house. According to her, two girls who had been left alone there one night had experienced something which sent them running into the night, screaming at the top of their voices, and they refused to return.

Francis W. Skeat is a Fellow of the British Society of Master Glass Painters who now lives in Hertfordshire. As a child he lived with his family in Romeland Cottage in St Albans, a building which overlooks the Abbey churchyard and is said to have been built on the site of the Abbey charnel house, where monks were buried during the plague. Mr Skeat quotes the following account of a ghost that is said to haunt Romeland Cottage. It came from a former resident of the house, Dr Toms.

In 1904 Dr Toms's parents had a maid sleeping in the house. One night she went upstairs to bed and went to sleep.

'She was woken by a man dressed as a monk talking in a foreign language and who was very excited. He wore a medal round his neck.

'Next morning my father tried to talk the maid out of this experience but the following night it happened again.

'My father realized it was something unusual and consulted Canon Glossop, who talked to the maid. Her description of the medal tallied with those worn by pilgrims or monks at the Abbey.

'A clergyman living on Holywell Hill opposite Diocesan House called with Canon Glossop the third morning and exorcized the spirit, and it was never seen again.'

John Richard Hodges is an author and teacher living in Shropshire. As a child he lived in a large farmhouse near the Roman city of Wroxeter. The pride of the house was a magnificent carved oak staircase sweeping up four flights to the attic, which was believed to have come from a monastery, possibly from the summer house built for the abbots of nearby Haughmond Abbey.

John shared a bedroom with his brother, who was away at school most of the year and did not share his psychic experiences. But at the age of fourteen John was moved to his own room in the attic, a dark, unlived-in area which always frightened the children when they were young. He was in this bedroom when he had the following experience.

'I woke one night, suddenly wide awake as if something had touched me . . . I saw a figure leaning over, looking at me. I could not make out a face at all, just the outline of a dark cowl. I grabbed for the light cord which was by the bed and of course when the light came on he had gone. The family laughed in disbelief at my tale next day.'

A few years later, however, John was relieved to find someone who was more inclined to believe his story of the ghost. In conversation with an aunt who had once lived in the farmhouse and who loved it dearly, he discovered that she, too, had seen the same cowled figure in the house.

Apparitions of the Dead

A cowled monk is usually recognized as a ghost, possibly because so few are seen outside monasteries these days. But apparitions take many forms, sometimes appearing as ordinary men and women dressed in contemporary clothing, but in unexpected places. These ghostly forms can shock or disturb people who see them in houses or rooms where they assume they are alone. The presence of a ghost often follows or precedes a death, and occasionally warns of danger ahead. Because these apparitions come into view dressed like ordinary people, the onlooker is usually unaware that he has seen a ghost until the figure suddenly disappears. They are rarely heard to speak, but appear capable of making sounds: footsteps are frequently heard before a ghost materializes.

Here is another of Mrs Joan Church's experiences.

'We were staying at a small hotel virtually on the beach in Devon. The children were all away at boarding school and we were alone. My husband went down to buy some cigarettes late at night and I was sitting up in bed with the table lamp on, when a small boy of about six came in at the door and walked over to the wash-basin on the other side of the room.

'I saw how thin his legs were and did not move in case I frightened him. I was just about to say quietly, "I'm afraid, my child, that you are in the wrong room!" when, as I watched, he was somehow no longer there.

'The next day I asked a member of the staff if there was a small boy staying there. She gave me a strange look and said 'No. Not any longer, madam." She said she did not want to discuss it. I asked another member of the staff, and she said she thought that a child had been drowned there, but she did not know when, or anything else about it.'

After describing three ghostly experiences Joan Church ends her account by insisting that she is 'a very down-to-earth person'. But taking into account the fact that her mother displayed impressive powers of precognition, perhaps it is not surprising that she, too, should be 'sensitive'. Mrs Church is refreshingly honest about her attitude to these events, reflecting the feelings of many writers whose stories appear in the book.

'I am not sure what I saw in any of these cases,' she says, but concludes her letter with the comment that the experiences 'seem to defy explanation'.

Mrs D. Heale [name changed] *of York is unlikely to forget something that happened to her a long time ago, before she got married. She was living in the country with her mother at the time, and one bright moonlit night she went to see a film, returning on the bus at about ten o'clock. Entering the bungalow she intended to go into the sitting room but, forgetting what she was doing, she opened the kitchen door next to it instead.*

'It was as light as day with the moon shining in the window and there was a man sitting in the rocking chair. He had very dark eyes and a black moustache, a tweed cap with ear-flaps folded up and tied on top with a shoestring, a tweed suit, belted, and knickerbockers.

'He turned and looked at me and I fled. I thought he must be tall as his knees seemed to stick up. My mother (never afraid) went to look, but saw nothing. She said it must be the rocking chair (a very old chair) and put it out in the shed.

'A few years later we had a new kitchen built on at the back. I was washing up one Sunday afternoon on a hot summer's day when I heard footsteps coming down the hallway. I was drying a plate at the time.

'I turned from the sink and there was this same man standing in the doorway. The thought rushed through my mind: "I *thought* you were tall!" – his hat almost touched the top of the door.

'I wasn't scared. I put the plate on the table and was just going to say, "What do you want?" and he was gone.'

That bungalow has since been demolished. A garage now stands on the site in the village of Burton Agnes near Driffield, North Humberside.

Giles de la Mare is a director of Faber and Faber and the grandson of Walter de la Mare, whose descendants appear to have inherited the poet's well-known interest in, and sensitivity to, the paranormal. Giles de la Mare describes his daughter's experience.

'In late August 1981, my daughter Calina was invited by a friend called Sarah from her school in Hampstead to spend a few days at her family home near Leominster in Herefordshire – Croft Castle. She had never been there before, and was nearly ten at the time. William Croft, the early eighteenth-century composer, was an ancestor of Sarah's, and the house, which was partly medieval, had been owned by her family for centuries. Since Sarah was already in Herefordshire, my wife and I drove Calina there, spending the night in a wing of the castle, which was administered by the National Trust. Next morning, before the two of us left for London, we all climbed up to a prehistoric camp on a nearby hill, from where we could see across steeply rolling country to the foothills of Wales.

'When she returned to London, Calina told us all about her stay, in particular about an experience she had had in the rose garden. She and Sarah had been picking roses for Sarah's grandmother who lived in a flat in the main castle, as she still does today. After a while, they began to get a bit bored and Calina said she wanted to explore the part of the rose garden up the slope from where they were. Sarah didn't want to go, so Calina went off by herself.

'As she came towards a low hedge, she noticed that there must be a way out of the garden through a tall hedge on the left, at right angles to the low hedge and beyond it. She had seen a gardener with tweed cap and jacket and a grey beard pushing a wheelbarrow behind the low hedge and into the thick tall hedge. She rushed down the hill to ask Sarah to show her the way. Sarah was perplexed because there was no gate in the tall hedge – indeed, there was no way out of that part of the garden except in the opposite direction, to the right. Calina explained that there must be a gate since she had seen a gardener going through the hedge. He had had a grey beard. Sarah said that they didn't have a gardener with a grey beard, and anyway it was impossible. By this point, both girls had become quite frightened. Even more so when Calina's detailed description of the gardener made it clear to Sarah that she had seen Ernie Price, the castle's gardener, just as he had been before his death two months previously. Her description fitted exactly.'

A ghost resembling a real person can cause confusion and distress to the living, as demonstrated in the following story provided by Mrs Joan Read.

While she was working one hectic Saturday afternoon in the Manor House Archive Department at Lee an agitated young man came in who seemed to be trying to gain her attention.

'I walked into the next room, where it was quieter. He followed. I looked up expectantly and he leaned quite close, whispering "Can you help me? . . . I'm getting desperate! I don't know what to do. My wife says that she will leave me – I hope you can help – you are my last hope!"

'I smiled encouragingly. He went on: "A while ago my friend called. I opened the front door to him and asked him in. His eyes had gone past me and he was looking at the staircase. 'Not while you've got company,' he said.

'"Company?' I replied. 'I'm the only one in the house! My wife has gone out shopping.' He didn't believe me and said that he could see that a young lady was standing on the stairs waiting for me. I turned round, but I couldn't see anyone. He thought I was playing games, so I shut the door on him. I was livid! I'm sure he thought I had another woman there!"

'"Why have you come to see me?" I asked.

'"Things have got worse. He's called several times and still insists I have another woman in the house as he has seen her each time. It's got beyond a joke!"

'"Has your wife seen her?"

'"Yes. She came in the other evening as I was coming down the stairs, and from the look on her face I knew that she was going to accuse me of having an affair with another woman. We had a row.

She wanted to know who the woman was that had just gone past me, up the stairs and into the bedroom! I told her that there was no one, that I hadn't got a woman friend. She didn't believe me!"

'"You obviously haven't seen the woman. Did your wife or your friend describe her?"

'"They say she is young, younger than my wife and in her early twenties. My friend says she has a lovely smile and a good figure."

'"Where do you live?" I asked.

'"In the old coach house that belonged to Dacre House. We've made a nice home there, with various conversions."

'"Dacre House was a very old house," I told him. "It had a tragic history. Lord and Lady Dacre lived there and on Baron Dacre's death in July 1794 he was buried at St Margaret's Churchyard, Lee. Lady Dacre is said to have visited his tombstone every day, attended by one of her maids, until a highwayman robbed her of her gold watch and chain."

'"Who lived in the coach house?" asked the young man.

'"George Pickering, the coachman. There were three women servants: Ann Maunday, Ann Chapman and Sarah Sherman, the maid. But they lived in the house."

'"When did Lady Dacre die?"

'"In September 1808 at the age of fifty-three. There followed a number of relatively short tenancies before the old house was demolished."

'"I suppose my phantom lady could be one of those three servants," said the young man. "She might have had secret meetings with the coachman."

'"It could have happened that way," I replied. "It could have been Sarah the maid, whose life was wrapped up in caring for her mistress and the house. But it might have been someone who visited the house, or the coach house – someone we know nothing about. I just don't know."

'"Well, thanks anyway," said the young man. "I know a bit more about the old coach house now. I'll tell my wife about it and let you know – especially if I have more trouble with my phantom lady!"'

The young man never returned, and Joan Read heard no more of the phantom lady in the coach house.

VARIETIES OF GHOST

Mrs Shelah Newman (see p. 30) was formerly employed in a steel-works laboratory and now lives in South Yorkshire. Some years ago she used to walk to the bus stop with an elderly gentleman who lived in her area. He became ill, and Mrs Newman did not see him and heard nothing of him until one bright sunny morning a few months later.

'As I walked down the long path from the back of the house, I glanced to the left and there, walking slowly up past the hedge round the front garden, I saw the gentleman in question.

'He appeared to be dressed as usual, wearing his trilby hat. He was visible as far as the waist [the lower half of his body being concealed by the hedge]. He turned and looked straight at me, and I was forcibly struck by how pale and drawn he appeared to be. Not until later did I realize I could not hear the sound of his footsteps, although he appeared to be walking in his usual manner, apart form being slower.

'I happened to glance away, and when I looked back there was no one there. There was nowhere he could have disappeared to, and he had not collapsed on the pavement. I was unable to account for this as it seemed so odd – he was so solid and very real, despite his unexpected appearance.

'Not until evening did I discover that he had died about half an hour before I had seen him that morning.'

Sarah Winthrop [name changed] lives in a remote village in Lincolnshire. Her grandmother had three sons-in-law at the time of this incident, which took place during the First World War.

In her bedroom one night she quite plainly saw her son-in-law William, who suddenly appeared in front of her and said: 'Hello Mum! I've just come to say hello and tell you to look after yourselves. And Mum, look after Hilda and the boy for me. I shan't be coming back into your world any more!'

And he faded from sight. Sarah's grandmother said nothing to her daughter Hilda at the time. But a few days later Hilda received the telegram all wartime wives feared: her husband William was missing, believed killed. He never returned home.

Sarah Winthrop's grandmother, in turn, made her own death-bed appearance. Later in life she had moved to live in America, latterly in Asheville, North Carolina, and in 1936 she visited Sarah's family in England.

Towards the end of her holiday she became ill with some kind of a chill, but being passed as fit to travel by her doctor in England, she decided to return home. Sea travel was the usual means of transport then and Sarah accompanied her mother, Elsie, and her grandmother to Liverpool to wave the old lady goodbye. As the ship pulled away from the dock Sarah's mother wept uncontrollably, saying she knew she would never see her mother again.

Some weeks later Elsie told Sarah that in the night she had felt a hand softly touching her shoulder, as though someone wanted to wake her. When she woke, a figure dressed in white stood by her bed and said 'Elsie!' before fading from sight. Elsie was convinced that the apparition (as she always called it) signified that her mother had died.

'And she had,' recalled Sarah Winthrop. 'We got a letter from Asheville telling us that, a few hours after the ship sailed, Grandmother was taken ill, spending the whole journey in the ship's hospital.'

After she had been taken as a stretcher-case on the four-day rail journey to Asheville, her American doctors diagnosed cancer, and she died three weeks later at the age of 72.

'And the time she died,' Sarah discovered, 'was the exact hour (taking account of time differences between UK and USA) when the apparition appeared beside mother's bed.'

Edward A. Stott is a retired engineer. Now living in Cheshire, he served with the RAF in North Africa during the Second World War.

'On 27 July 1942 twelve Hurricane fighters of 33 Squadron RAF took off on the dawn patrol over El Alamein. This "A" flight included myself and a new pilot, Sgt Leicester [identified as Red Four].

'We met no enemy fighters but half-way back to base it was noted that Red Four was lagging behind the formation. "Red Leader to Red Four: catch up! Catch up! You are too far behind!"

'This command was shortly repeated. "Red Leader to Red Four: catch up formation and hold your position!"

'Red Four continued to drop further and further behind. Suddenly two enemy fighters were seen above and behind us. They dived on Red Four. He was shot down in flames.

'We returned to base and landed, then went to the mess tent for our delayed breakfast. Here we met "B" flight who had by now finished their breakfast. We discussed our flight and the sad loss of the young Sgt Leicester. They looked surprised, and said we must be mistaken.

'"Why should we be mistaken?" we asked.

'"Because Sgt Leicester had breakfast with us half an hour ago!"'

The 'B' flight pilots' claim that Sgt Leicester had indeed breakfasted with them was confirmed by several officers who were present. They were completely mystified by the denial of Edward Stott and his colleagues who insisted that it was impossible for the young pilot to have been in the mess that morning, because they, in turn, had seen Leicester's plane disappear in flames. 'B' flight finally accepted the loss of the new pilot. But all the officers who were witnesses to the incident were deeply puzzled by it.

Mrs Winifred Taylor lives in Hertfordshire, but she was brought up in London. As a baby she lived with her family in Islington where, in 1913, she contracted measles at a time when her sister was seriously ill with pneumonia. The children's mother had the responsibility for nursing both children.

'My mother was worn out and one of the aunties suggested she go for a walk to clear her weariness and get some air ... She was walking along Liverpool Road, Islington, when coming towards her she saw a funeral procession. In those days the horses wore black plumes. She saw every detail and knew it was the funeral of her daughter, Frieda, my sister. As she gazed at it, the funeral procession vanished.'

Frieda died, as her mother's vision indicated. Mrs Taylor comments: 'She spoke of this right through my growing up years. I know she spoke the truth as she was a committed Christian.'

A retired schoolteacher, Doris Olwen Lancaster now lives in Warwickshire. As a teenager she received a warning from her father, who had died six months earlier, which she chose to ignore.

'One Sunday morning, about six months after my father had died, my brother and I planned to go to a field about six miles from my home (then in South Wales) to pick mushrooms. My brother had gone to get his motorbike ready for us to leave and I was having a cup of tea in the kitchen, when my father appeared in the doorway to the hall and, pointing his finger at me, said "Don't go!" and vanished.

'Well, we did go, but the trip was non-productive – the farmer had put a bull in the field. On the way home it started to rain and we skidded. My brother suffered shock, but I was injured and was off school for three weeks.'

As Doris Lancaster freely admits, she paid a high price for not heeding her late father's warning. Although now nearly eighty, she still remembers the incident vividly.

Ghost Identification

Some ghosts may be instantly identified by relatives or friends of their former selves, who have no difficulty in recognizing characteristic features. Others may only be identified after a sighting from sketches, portraits or photographs; while yet others may appear featureless and totally unrecognizable, the face a blur, or simply a blank space.

Mrs Joan Church's aunt by marriage, Marina [name changed], died a few years ago. Mrs Church describes her as a woman of great integrity and accepts without question the story she told her as a truthful account of an incident she and her two children witnessed.

During the Second World War Marina was staying in Wales where her husband, a colonel in the army, was stationed.

'They had taken a small cottage [whose owner lived in the next village] and Marina, with her two small sons, was in the cottage one evening in the winter when a little woman dressed in Welsh traditional clothes came in the door and went up the stairs. My aunt was rather annoyed, as it seemed so rude.

'She waited and waited for the woman to come down again, prepared to say "Now that we have rented the cottage, I should prefer you not to come visiting here."

'But, to her dismay, the little Welsh woman failed to reappear. After some time Marina went upstairs to investigate: no one was there. Puzzled and somewhat alarmed, she searched for another exit from the top floor of the cottage, but found no way in which the intruder could have disappeared. She came to the conclusion that there must have been a hidden door on the top floor which she had failed to find, and decided to say nothing more about it, concluding that the woman had called to collect something and was probably rather eccentric.

'After a few weeks had passed, the same thing happened again.

Marina and her two children saw the woman come in and walk upstairs. When Marina's husband returned at the weekend they went to see the owner of the house and asked her to explain the visits [and indicate the location of the exit]. The woman looked at them and said, "There *is* no way out upstairs!"

'They described the appearance of their visitor and the owner exclaimed, "That's my mother!" My aunt, still very confused, said, "Well, you must ask her to stop coming to the cottage now that you've let it to us!"

'The woman, looking sadly at them, replied, "I can't do that. She died last Christmas!"'

Mrs Adrianne Browne of West Yorkshire writes:

'We lived at St Cuthbert's Vicarage, Billingham, Co. Cleveland, during the 1970s. An elderly retired teacher who lived in a nearby cottage often talked about the clergy and their wives who had been there. She mentioned particularly a Canon Tennyson [*name changed*] and his wife, who had been there many years.

'One night I awoke and sat up in bed as the figure of an elderly lady walked into the room. She had a slight limp and was dressed in blue. Her iron grey hair was scraped up into a bun at the top of her head. There was nothing alarming about her and from what my friend had told me I felt sure that she must be Mrs Tennyson. After standing at the foot of the bed for what seemed to be several minutes she disappeared.

'The next day I visited my friend to tell her of this encounter. She wasn't at all surprised but calmly informed me that the apparition I described was not Mrs Tennyson but Mrs Carey [*name changed*], the wife of an earlier vicar.'

The following story is from Mrs Ida Walker, a retired special machinist who lives in the Midlands. A few years ago she and her husband were told by the authorities that their accommodation was due for modernization. They were required to leave their house while the work was being done, and were expected to return within sixteen to eighteen weeks, on completion of the

VARIETIES OF GHOST

work. But the authorities were over-optimistic in their calculation of the date of completion by the builders.

'We duly moved out. Then as we moved, we were both made redundant. So to try and help ourselves we took on an allotment.

'The house we moved into looked quite nice, but it was only small – we had two large dogs, a Labrador (a marvellous house dog) and a lovely golden Labrador bitch. But as the house had a good yard and our visit was supposed to be a short one, we said OK.

'After we moved in the cooker blew up. We blamed the removal men. The Labrador dog could walk through the so-called bolted door. The heating never, in the two years we were there, worked properly, and on one day alone we had about ten workmen in to see to the faults.

'One lovely spring day my husband said he was off to dig the allotment. I was to follow with the dinner and the dogs after I had pegged out two blankets. Well, hubby went off. And I was pegging out the blankets. I turned to speak to the dog lying in the doorway.

'Suddenly, over him, I saw the figure of a man at the foot of the stairs. He was grey-haired and fresh-complexioned. I said, "How did you get there?" wondering how he had got by Silva the dog.

'Then he just vanished. It was towards midday, and the sun was shining. I described him to the lady next door. She said, "Oh, that's Mr Smith. He lived there in the 1940s. He was a lovely man!"

She told Mrs Walker that her neighbour had suffered from poor health, but he had kindly looked after her children while she worked.

Mrs Walker continues: 'I was not frightened when I saw the ghost of Mr Smith, and it didn't worry me. But I was never happy while I was in that house, and was very glad when I came back to live at No. 78.'

Mrs Dorothy Mary Pittkin (known as Peggy) has lived in her home in Worcestershire for twenty-seven years. The house was built in the period 1810–13, replacing an older building occupying a position between two villages above the River Avon. A working mill stood on the site from the time of the Domesday Survey until 1909, when it was burnt down and never replaced. The Pittkins' house, which was the mill house, was built in Regency style with the light, airy interior characteristic of that period.

Mr and Mrs Pittkin bought the house on their return from New Zealand in 1961. Subsequently the house was divided into two, providing separate homes for the Pittkins and their daughter and her husband.

Peggy Pittkin had lived in the house for twenty-four years before she saw the ghost which has come to be known as the Child. Profoundly impressed by the event, she wrote an account of it that day. This is how she recounted what she saw on 28 May 1985, at 8.30 a.m.

'Joanna, my granddaughter, was standing half-way down the steps from the back door as my nephew and niece were about to leave to return to South Africa.

'I was standing by their car when Joanna came through the door with a girl behind her, and they both halted. The other girl was ten to thirteen years old. I couldn't tell her exact height as she stood on the step above Joanna. My thought was that she was a friend who was going with Joanna to her brother Paul's school sports near Hereford.

'The child was dressed in a fawn coat, with a dark brown velvet collar. The flared coat was worn over an off-white dress with a round neck and no collar. I remember thinking the dress looked grubby. Her hair was fair, flowing to the shoulders, caught back with a band off her face, and the hair was slightly wavy. Her eyebrows were darker than her hair, and her eyes were dark and her complexion pale, with a pretty face.'

Mrs Pittkin thought nothing more about the girl at the time because she intended to ask Janet, her daughter, who she was.

'The relations left, I returned to my side of the house and Janet came in to me a few minutes later asking if Joanna was with me. Here I did a curious thing. I was about to answer "They are upstairs in the bedroom" when I checked my words, altering them to "She is upstairs"; this was instantaneous, with no further thought.

'Joanna appeared [she was alone] and I knew I had seen the ghost. All I saw was a very ordinary girl in everyday circumstances, and utterly of this world. The clothes I should date between 1880 and

1910 when there was little change in style. Who is she? Why does she appear, not always in the same clothes?

'There is no doubt in my mind that I saw her; 8.30 a.m. was hardly the "witching hour", and I shall always remember what she looked like and how I thought it was Joanna's friend, a child of similar age. The circumstances were so normal, for I was involved mentally and physically with saying goodbye to part of my family.'

Peggy Pittkin has researched the history of house and mill and has collected many early photographs relating to the properties. In one photograph of a group of people taken at the turn of the century she recognized a young woman of about twenty years of age 'who is the image of the child I saw'.

Two other sightings of the Child have been recorded.

'A friend was staying here, and looking out of her bedroom window she saw a child skipping along the drive, though only her head was visible as we now have a hornbeam hedge here. This lady thought it was one of the family, until she realized no girl of that age was on the property.'

The second sighting occurred in 1978–9.

'I am convinced my husband saw the Child, thinking it was his granddaughter Joanna, for he was so angry when I said Joanna was at school. He remarked on the pretty pink dress she was wearing. His sight was failing by this time, therefore he would not have recognized her features.'

Mrs Pittkin's explanation for the appearance of this little ghost is that she was very happy as a child in her home on the banks of the Avon. That period may have been followed by a tragic or at least an unhappy adulthood, and for that reason her spirit may return to the place where she spent the halcyon days of her youth.

Geoffrey Houghton-Brown of London is an antiques dealer, painter and author.

'In June 1941 I bought at auction No. 25 The Circus, Bath. When I first saw this house it was empty and I knew nothing of the previous owners. I moved in some of my furniture on 21 July and slept in the back drawing room that night. I had not had time to hang any curtains, though there were shutters partly closed.

'I awoke suddenly and early next morning. The sun was shining in and I saw, standing beside my bed, looking at me, a rather tall elderly lady with white hair parted in the middle and dressed in the fashion of the period in black. She had long pendant diamond ear-rings. She was leaning on an ebony walking stick. She smiled at me in a kind but rather amused way and then vanished. It all happened in a flash but the impression left on my mind was so strong that I can still clearly visualize her.

'I thought nothing much about it until some weeks later I went into an antique shop and bought a piece of furniture. I asked the lady of the shop to send it to 25 The Circus.

'"Oh," she said, "that was Lady Adelaide Brocklehurst's [*name changed*] house, was it not?"

'"Yes," I said. "I think it was."

'"Such a nice lady. So sad that she broke her leg!"

'Immediately I remembered my ghost lady.

'"Did she walk with a stick?" I asked.

'"Yes, she did after her accident."

'"Was she tall and thin, with white hair?"

'"Yes, she was."

'"Did she wear long pendant diamond ear-rings?"

'"I don't remember. But quite probably she did."

'After that I felt sure that it was Lady Adelaide Brocklehurst whom I had seen.'

Mrs Janet E. Stringfellow is a shop assistant who lives in the north of England. She and her husband and daughter are a close family who once lived in a terraced house in Longsight in Manchester. While they were there, Mrs Stringfellow had this experience.

'One night my husband went out with a few of his friends for a drink. I had put my daughter to bed; she was only four at the time. I did a few jobs around the house, which wasn't very grand, but I kept it clean and looking quite nice. We were a happy family (and still are), with lovely neighbours.

'I went into the front room to watch TV. There wasn't much on, and my husband hadn't arrived home, so I went to bed. I got into bed and switched the light off, and got comfy on my right side.

'Suddenly I felt a tap on my left shoulder. I turned, thinking it was my daughter wanting the toilet. There was nobody there! I turned once again to get comfy, and there at the bottom of the bed was a grey figure! I just froze. She was wearing a long gown, and the sleeves covered her hands as if the garment was too big for her. She had long flowing hair down her back.

'I just lay there, I couldn't move! I tried turning around to look at the clock, but I could not move at all! Time seemed to stand still, as if the whole world had stopped. I tried to speak but nothing happened, she just stood there watching me. In the next instant, she was gone!

'I relaxed and went to sleep. The next morning I told my husband. He said that I was silly, and that I was dreaming. I answered "How could I be dreaming when I was wide awake?" He said that he didn't understand it.

'A few days later I went to see my mother-in-law. The terraced house had at one time belonged to her father and mother. I asked her how old her mother was when she passed away, and she told me that she was in her late forties. I then asked if her mother had long hair. She said she had, and that she brushed it a lot, so it was very straight down her back. I then asked her if she was of slim build, and her answer was yes. Looking a bit puzzled, she asked me why I wanted to know these things about her mother. I told her what had happened. She was surprised at what she heard, saying that I had described her mother! The thing is, I never knew her mother, nor had I ever met her. I just can't explain it, can you?'

Mrs Charlotte Bathurst of Gloucestershire is an artist who has had a number of psychic experiences. She says, 'The strange thing about ghosts is that they never appear when you expect them!' She agrees with other contributors that sightings of a supernatural kind are often so fleeting 'you have to think rather long and hard as to whether you have seen them or not'. In this, Mrs Bathurst's earliest encounter with a ghost, her artistic skills proved very useful.

'My first ghost was seen in my mother-in-law's house near Bath where I woke to find a man with an Edwardian suit, middle parting, leaning over me. I drew [a picture of] him in the morning, and my mother-in-law said "Oh, that's Uncle George! He always wore that suit when he stayed here, and had a middle parting. I expect he wanted to have a good look at the new daughter-in-law!"'

Mrs Norah Moss lives in Somerset. She told me this story over the telephone.

When Norah was a young girl she had a close friend (let's call her Claudia Best) with whom she stayed for the night from time to time in an old house which had been built by Claudia's great-grandfather.

Staying there on one occasion, Norah was dressing for school in the morning, and couldn't find her black stockings. She searched for them everywhere, including in a room which was sometimes let, as part of a small flat. When she went into it she saw a woman looking out of the window. Apologizing for disturbing her, Norah withdrew, assuming her hostess had let the flat without mentioning it to her young guest. The woman at the window smiled kindly as she left the room, but said nothing to her.

When she found her stockings Norah went downstairs and said to Mrs Best that she was sorry to have disturbed the family's lodger in the flat.

'Oh no, dear! We haven't let the flat!' replied her hostess. And when the girl described the figure at the window she exclaimed: 'Oh, that must be Grandma! I wonder what she's come to tell us! She always appears when something is going to happen in the family!'

It transpired that members of the Best family, including the grandmother and her husband, had died in the epidemic of influenza that swept the country after the end of the First World War, and the not infrequent appearance of the grandmother's figure at the end of Mrs Best's bed had always, up till then, heralded a death in the family.

Norah described in detail the appearance and dress of the woman she had spoken to, realizing only at that point that she was describing the costume of an earlier period. Intrigued, Mrs Best then took her guest into her own bedroom, which the girl had never been in before, and showed her a photograph of the grandmother in question: it was, without doubt, the image of the woman Norah had seen standing at the window.

The old house has now been demolished, and neo-Georgian dwellings occupy the site.

Mrs Louise Mary Sayer of Wiltshire describes elsewhere (p. 150) her schoolgirl experience in a haunted Scottish castle. Perhaps a sensitivity to the supernatural runs in her family, because her mother also had an odd experience when she and her sister, Janet, then in their twenties, joined the first Cook's tour of Versailles in the early 1900s. Mrs Sayer says that her mother, Louise Rattray, was an extremely balanced and sensible woman.

Louise Rattray told her daughter how Cook's tourists were led into the palace to be shown around the first large room open to the public. After half an hour or so, she noticed an unusually dressed woman walking through the room.

Mrs Sayer remembers her mother's reaction: 'She decided to follow her ... and leaving the others, did so. When she reached the next room surprisingly there was no one in it, and no door leading out of it.'

Disconcerted by the woman's disappearance, Louise returned to her party, and when the guide finally led his group into that room she asked if there was a hidden exit from it, explaining that she had seen someone walk into the room and disappear. When the guide asked how the woman was dressed, Louise described in detail the pale gold gown with long sleeves worn with a beautiful diamond necklace.

'The guide smiled and then asked my mother to follow him into a large gallery which she had not entered before. He pointed to a portrait of the lady she had seen, wearing exactly the same dress and necklace. The guide told my mother that the portrait was that of Marie-Antoinette. Her ghost had been seen quite frequently in the palace, he said, adding rather sadly that he personally had never been fortunate enough to see her.'

Guardian Ghosts

Friendly ghosts inhabit some houses, and although we all appear to be apprehensive at the thought of seeing one, numerous cases have been reported where the resident apparition has appeared to be offering assistance. That aspect of the sighting may not have been obvious at the time. In other cases the benign spirit of the ghostly inhabitant may be apparent in a harmonious atmosphere pervading a house. I believe my own home in The Circus in Bath owes its warm, welcoming air to the well-known hospitality of its first occupant, the celebrated painter Thomas Gainsborough.

As a child, John Richard Hodges lived near Wroxeter in a large farmhouse with a magnificent carved oak staircase (see p. 44). The young John spent most of his time at the farm and in the house, often alone, as his mother and father were frequently away.

'I used to enjoy reading and rarely listened to the radio or television. The house was quiet: just the sounds of the old grandfather clock in the oak hall. On occasions I would hear footsteps quite clearly on the staircase and often went to look to see who was there. [There was never anybody to be seen.] On occasions the lights would be turned on when I had turned them off, and vice versa. Whatever or whoever it was, was an amiable character as the house had the most marvellous atmosphere you can imagine ... one of peace and happiness, so I was never afraid of the footfalls or other activities.'

In 1987 Patricia Newey's husband had to work in Bath for several weeks and the couple took a short lease on a maisonette at 31 Daniel Street, close to the Holburne Museum, where they occupied the first and top floors.

There was, Patricia Newey says, a secure lock on the door at the foot of the staircase at ground-floor level. The bedrooms and bathroom were at the top of the building; the smaller first-floor room at the rear of the house had been converted to a kitchen/dining room, and the original double doors led into a most attractive drawing room overlooking the street. The house was furnished with plenty of modern electric light fittings in each living room and on the staircase.

'One October evening I came down the stairs from our bedroom and there, on the first-floor landing, was a man standing with his hand just touching the handle of the rear room on the first floor. I could see him quite clearly in the electric light above his head, which reflected on his bald pate. He was about five foot six or seven in height and I should think in his early sixties. He was in shirt sleeves and wing collar and had a gold watch chain on his waistcoat. He was stout, slightly florid and wore gold-rimmed "library" spectacles. In fact he looked like some of the portrayals of Mr Pickwick, and I should think he was Victorian. He carried a casually folded broadsheet newspaper in the other hand.

'I should stress that I was not in the least frightened. Indeed, I was not even particularly surprised by him. I opened my mouth to speak to him but at that moment my husband called out that it was time for the *Nine O'clock News*, and the man was just not there. I didn't say anything at the time because quite honestly I thought I had flipped, as they say.'

Sarah Winthrop (see p. 50) moved with her companion to Lincolnshire in 1969. 'I live now in a remote village where the villagers are still in the Middle Ages. If I told them my ghost stories I would immediately be considered ready to be put away. I'm already thought to be queer – simply because I am from the city.'

One morning Sarah washed some clothes, hung them out in the garden to dry, fetched them in some time later and put them away to air. Then she went into her bedroom and sat with her back to the window to take off her shoes and put on her slippers.

'I felt strongly that someone was in the room, or looking in from the outside – what kind of neighbours had we, that looked into rooms through the window?

'I turned to see who it was and now, looking back, I wonder how I took it so calmly. But standing at the corner of my flat, ordinary window was a young cavalier. He was standing at his window (similar to the ones seen in Hampton Court Palace) and he was turned towards me, his right hand on his window ledge, his left on his hip, holding the wide-brimmed hat they wore, with the curling feathers in it.

'I could not identify colours very well because although I was sitting in my room at about 11 a.m., he was standing at his window in moonlight, so that he had a bluish light over him. He seemed to be fair haired, about nineteen to twenty years of age, slender, and about my own height of 5'5" . . .

'All I felt at the time was indignation at his intrusion into my bedroom. I never questioned who he was – I mean ghost or whatever. "How dare you come into my bedroom! This *is* my bedroom you know! Leave this instant and do not ever come back!" I said. Now I wish I had not. I would have liked to try talking to him. But he smiled apologetically, bowed, and as he straightened up, slowly faded, leaving me staring at where he had been and regretting my haste to send him away.'

The late Mr Arthur Lightfoot lived in an estate in a large city in the Midlands. When the prefabricated buildings of the original estate, which had been built in open country, were demolished to make way for flats, the Lightfoot family were the first occupiers of one of the new maisonettes above ground level, and they remained there for twenty years.

Mr Lightfoot's job required him to work over weekends, with Mondays and Tuesdays off. On those days he was alone in the flat as his wife was at work and his children were at school. Shortly before his death recently he wrote:

'One day I heard a key being inserted in the door downstairs, then heavy boots on uncarpeted stairs. (We had stair carpet fitted.) Then a shadowy figure passed by the glass partition that made a hallway between the living room and bedrooms.

'On opening the door, thinking it was my wife, I found nothing! I told my wife of this when she came home and all she said was I must have dreamt it.'

But there was more to come.

'I was relating it to my wife when my elder daughter interrupted to say the same thing had happened to her. She described it in the same way – the same things in the same order. Later my wife experienced the "visit".'

In a second letter Mr Lightfoot stressed the fact that over the period they lived in the maisonette *all* members of the family, including each of their four children, became familiar with the ghostly visitor.

'Within the family we called it our Friendly Neighbourhood Ghost. It didn't harm us, and we were not scared of it.'

Encountering the 'spiritual manifestation' of relatives from time to time is not unusual for Mrs Charlotte Bathurst (see p. 60). In this instance it was the nanny's turn.

'We had a house in the Isle of Man, inherited from a much loved aunt. She always changed into a long black dress for dinner, even when alone.'

After her aunt's death, the Bathursts were occupying the house with their children and their Irish nanny.

'We asked her if she minded our going out one wild night. She said no, she found the old lady with the long black dress great company – she had seen her every night!'

Mrs Bathurst adds that the children's nanny had not known her aunt, nor did she have any idea that it was the old lady's habit to wear a long black gown at dinner every night.

Mrs Margaret Offen lives in Tyneside. She wrote a moving account of her own experience.

'This is a true story of a very real ghost. But I must start this tale many years before the incident occurred – in fact, when this ghost was very much alive.

'It all started when I met my future husband – a widower of two years with two very small children. His wife had died tragically, leaving him with a little girl of five years and a small boy of two years, and her father of eighty years, who had lived with them since their marriage some ten years previously.

'Before we married, I had visited the house many times as we often took the children on outings or I just looked after them while their father attended business meetings.

'I always had great compassion for the frail old man who not only had to cope with his daughter's death, but also with the high spirits of these two healthy youngsters.

'I did notice that he had a special affection for the little boy . . . He cared for him through the day and kept saying what a lovely nature the child had.

'Two years later, he gradually grew much frailer. One cold winter's day he died, quite peacefully, in the small bedroom he had always occupied.

'We married in the following autumn, and the little boy, now six years old, occupied the bedroom his grandfather had always used.

'Many years later, we had all been out late to a church social and on returning home we prepared for bed.

'The boy, now a big lad of sixteen or thereabouts, went to bed first. I glanced at the clock before I checked that all the lights were out: it was exactly 12.20 a.m. I opened the door of the small bedroom to turn out the light – and beside the window was the figure of a white-haired old man. There was the familiar waistcoat and shirt-sleeves. He was leaning against the window sill and looking lovingly at the sleeping boy. It only seemed to be for a second, but it was all very real and not in the least frightening.

'I told my husband about the incident next morning as we got ready for church. I thought he would laugh incredulously, but he did not do anything, except ask what date it was. It was 19 February, ten years exactly since the old man had passed away.

'He had made the journey back to see that everything was still all right, and when he saw his beloved grandson was happy he went away contented – and so far he has never come back.'

May Stevens [name changed] lives in Lancashire. During the Second World War she married. One night she was alone in bed, as her husband was engaged on Home Guard duty.

'I wakened to hear footsteps – very light, but quite firm and clear – which came up to the bedroom door. Then I heard three knocks which sounded as if they were made with the knuckles of a person's hand.

'Needless to say I couldn't do anything, I was too scared. (I was young at the time.) Anyhow, from that night for approximately three months, I was wakened every night by my head being stroked firmly for about ten minutes on the right-hand side.

'I asked my husband to put his hand on my head [during the stroking] but he felt nothing, although the stroking was there when he moved his hand away.'

During this period May Stevens was working in an ammunition factory, and about three months after the peculiar regular nightly visitation began, she went to work as usual.

'I had lunch and a joke with my friends, sat down and set on my machine. Well, it caught my hair (right-hand side) and could have scalped me. But luckily I managed to turn the machine off in time with my foot, though I did lose a large clump of my hair.

'Needless to say, after my accident the stroking stopped!'

William George [name changed] *of Bath has loved only one woman throughout his life, his wife. After a happy and carefree holiday in Majorca the couple returned home to tragedy: Mrs George collapsed and later died. Her husband was devastated.*

'One night I drove around anywhere, crying bitterly, and after a while I knew I could not go on without her. I don't know where I was but ahead of me in the lights of the car I could see a high wall. I put my foot down hard, intending to smash the car into the wall and kill myself.

'I was quite cool and determined. [He had previously been engaged in the removal of unexploded bombs.] My eyes were glued on that wall when suddenly a brightish big car flashed across my path. I braked like mad and just missed it and my car hit the wall with a soft bump.

'I looked left to see the other car, but there was none, just the high return of the wall I had stopped against.'

Greatly puzzled by the appearance of the phantom car, William George found that all thoughts of suicide had vanished immediately, and they never returned. Then one night he had a kind of vision.

'I was undressing in the bedroom, which was always lit by a street light. I looked at the wall, and my wife and a grey old man appeared. She was crying while the old man was comforting her tenderly, as though coaxing her back.

'Shortly after that incident I visited my wife's people. As I was leaving I saw a photo on the sideboard. It was the man in my vision. "Who is this man?" I asked. Her aunt replied, "Oh, that's your wife's grandfather, my father!"'

After that experience, William George became convinced that life continues after death.

Mrs Pascale Schtraks, a young woman who lives in London, is a member of a family that originally came from Algeria. The story she tells is of an incident that took place twenty-five years ago. It was told to her by her grandmother, a witness.

'When my great-granddad died, all his children (including my grandmother) were in his flat, sitting in the big kitchen. Suddenly they heard noises coming from their father's bedroom. Somebody appeared to be up there, moving furniture and walking about.'

The family assumed a thief had got into the flat by the window but no one dared move to investigate. Suddenly there was a crash from upstairs, followed by absolute silence. The family rushed into the bedroom to find no sign of anyone. Everything appeared to be in order except for a picture frame lying upside down on the floor. No one could work out how or why this object had jumped from its place on the wall, especially as the picture hook was still firmly in place, and the cord on the frame was intact.

Inspection revealed that a certificate lying on its face behind the glass was a citation in recognition of the dead man's assistance to the Jewish community. A second document was then found secreted behind the first.

'At this moment the family saw that it was the place their father chose to hide his will! Not one of them knew of its existence previously.'

Mrs. Peggy Lambert of Yorkshire describes an event in the life of her mother's uncle. The true tale about her great-uncle's sick child has been handed down by word of mouth in the family. Mrs Lambert retells it here in the form of a short story.

'Inside the cottage the only sound was the spluttering of the oil lamp and harsh laboured breathing which came from the small child wrapped in blankets on the improvised bed in the corner near the fire. "Keep the child at the same temperature," counselled the doctor. "I will call again tomorrow." The parents obeyed, knowing little of medical matters, but understanding that pneumonia was a serious illness.

'For most of the day the mother sat by the bedside, wiping perspiration from the tiny face, moving only to prepare a hasty meal for her husband when he came in, anxious about the child and exhausted from his work on the land. He joined his wife in her vigil ... staying by the child's bed for some hours.

'Suddenly the man got to his feet. "Must have some air," he muttered. He pulled back the door curtain and lifting the door sneck, stepped out on to the back porch.

'The smallholding was built in a hollow high on the moors. It was poor land but with hard work he managed to scratch a living. The trouble was, they were so isolated. Not many people climbed up there and in winter they were often cut off for several weeks.

'As he stood there, trees in the nearby copse quivered, a slight breeze edging around them, and an owl hooted. An autumn ground mist hung over the pond in the mid-distance and the farmer ... looked towards the pond, thinking he saw a movement in the mist. Yes! There it was again! Suddenly he could feel the short hairs on the back of his neck prickling. Frozen with fear, he could scarcely breathe or even blink.

'There, gliding round the pond through the mist on the far side, was his mother. Yet how could that be? She had been dead several years, but he was certain it was her. Around her shoulders was the little shawl she always wore, her skirts tucked up as they were habitually when she was working on the land. As she drew nearer, her son could see her face, every feature of it familiar. And then he noticed that in her arms she was carrying a small bundle, bending over it protectively.

'Slowly she passed from his sight, drifting away until she and the mist were as one. The man gasped, and turning swiftly groped for the door. Stumbling into the room he saw his wife bending over the child's tiny bed.

'"She's gone, Tom!" she sobbed. "She's gone!"

'Clumsily he held the stricken woman, stroking her hair. "I know lass," he whispered. "I know!" and leading her to the chair he sat her down and then told her what had happened outside the cottage, encouraging his wife to draw comfort from the knowledge that their dead child was, at least, in the good hands of her loving grandmother.'

Mrs Beryl M. Elliott lives in London. At a very tender age she saw a ghost:

'It first happened at a comfortable modern house at Harpenden. I remember best the night nursery, which was down three or four steps at the end of a long passage, all carpeted in blue with a lot of shining white paint. I was not quite four years old at the time, but I remember that my cot stood along the wall on the opposite side of the room to the door. My brother was three years older than I and our parents thought it time we had a nursery-governess, so we said goodbye to Hettie, the nurse we had known all our lives, and Miss Petley arrived to take her place. We took to her at once for she was young, being only twenty-two. She shared my night nursery with me, and photographs she had brought with her hung on the wall beside my cot. I remember one was of two little boys with whom she had been before coming to us and of whom I was never tired of hearing stories.

'After lunch each day I had to take off my dress and rest in my cot. I think I was getting too old to sleep in the afternoons and, having nothing to do, I amused myself by turning the photographs to the wall. Knowing that this would be frowned upon and also it being approved if I slept, I did not make a sound, or answer the knock which every day I heard on the door, thinking it was Miss Petley coming to see if I was asleep.

'At last, one day, I said "Come in!" The door flew open and across the room, with a purposeful stride and making straight for my cot, came a tall, gaunt woman with searching and most piercing dark eyes. She wore on her head what I thought was a bathing cap, the kind which people used to wear years ago, with elastic round the edge similar to some of the bath caps worn today. Doubtless it was a mobcap, but I did not know of such things then. She came right up to my cot and leaned over it, fixing me with those dark eyes. I opened my mouth and screamed. I did not see her go. Whether she just vanished, or went the way she came, I do not know. All I know is that I was terrified.

'My cries brought all the household running. First to arrive was my mother, closely followed by Miss Petley, with cook following. The more I tried to tell them I was awake, the more I was told it was a bad dream, a nasty nightmare they said. No wonder, for who could believe a child who repeatedly said that she had been visited by a lady in a bathing cap? Perhaps the incident would have been forgotten altogether and never thought of again if it had not been for what happened some time later.

'During the next three years we moved about considerably, my father then being in the army. When he was posted overseas my mother took "rooms" for the Easter holidays in a fisherman's cottage at Seaton in Devon, as she had friends there with children of our age. I was then six and three-quarter years of age. It was a cosy little cottage in a row all joined together. It was the end house but one, in a cul-de-sac. An iron railing ran the length of the cottages and each cottage had a little iron gate and a garden path leading to the front door, which opened on to the only flight of stairs which ran steeply up from a tiny linoleumed hall. Opposite the cottages across the sandy, gravelly road was a high green hedge.

'Welsh was the name of the fisherman. We saw little of him but enjoyed the fresh fish he brought home. Mrs Welsh was a kindly soul who loved children and looked after us well. After lunch she would take her lace pillow and sit in the sun just inside the front door, which was practically at the foot of the stairs, to make lace. I still had to have a short rest after lunch each day, but now it was different. I rested on my mother's bed, which was a double one, in the sunny front bedroom. I would sit cross-legged on the bed, cutting out pictures from magazines for a scrap-book I was making, or spend the time colouring pictures with my crayons.

'On this particular day I was having my rest as usual. My mother, with my brother, had gone for half an hour or so to see her friends, and Mrs Welsh, ensconced at the foot of the stairs making her lace, had been asked to keep an eye on me.

'The bedroom door was ajar, I was cutting out my pictures and singing happily when I heard a knock on the door. I looked up and said "Come in!" and just as had happened before, the door was flung open and in came the same tall, gaunt lady in the mobcap. Those same intense black eyes gazing at me, she came right up to the bed where I was sitting, and bent her head right over me and close to mine.

'Again as before I screamed, again I did not see her go. Mrs Welsh came rushing up the stairs but could not pacify me and I was still yelling "The lady in the bathing cap! The lady in the bathing cap!" when my mother came home, and even then it took her some time to quieten my hysterical sobs.

'Poor Mrs Welsh, how difficult for her, for there was no explanation, and all she could say to my mother was that no one, absolutely no one, had been to the house, and that she had been sitting there all the time, and how my singing had suddenly stopped, followed so soon by terrified screaming.

'I have never seen my lady in the bathing cap again, and wonder if I ever shall. For years I felt frightened to call "Come in!" when hearing a knock on the door. I wonder why she visited me like she did – Harpenden and Seaton are some 180 miles apart. I was a very normal child, quite robust and athletic.

'Many years later, when I was about twenty-two years of age (and more for the fun of it than anything else for I am not unduly superstitious) I visited a fortune teller who did not even know my name. She was amazingly good and now, looking back over the years, I realize even more how good she was. One thing she told me that mystified me at the time was this: "There is someone who has passed on, who takes an intense interest in you. It is as though she has her hands on your shoulders, pushing you forward through your life. Can you think of anyone?" I could not, and told her so. Again she said "Think about this, for there *is* someone!"

'Could it be The Lady in the Bathing Cap?'

Apparitions of the Living

This category of ghost is one of the most intriguing of all. Is it possible for someone to be in two places at once? It appears from the following accounts that the apparition of a living person can often be so lifelike that it may be assumed to be the actual person concerned, although later evidence as to their whereabouts at the time of the sighting may show the assumption to have been wrong. Incidents of this kind are not uncommon.

Henry Franklin is now retired and lives in Cornwall.

'I had a friend, sadly now dead, called David Lloyd Davies [*real name*] who was a great field sports enthusiast. Some time prior to the 1939–45 war he was staying with the Earl and Countess of C— at their castle in West Wales near Tenby.

'The Hawkerstone Otter Hounds were hunting that country and David was duly hunting with them. They had had some good runs in the morning and after the lunch break the master asked David to cross the river and round up some missing hounds. On his way over he slipped and got caught in the branches of a sunken tree and was lucky to extricate himself as he was completely submerged.

'When he got back to the castle the butler met him and told him that a telegram had come from David's mother which said "Are you all right?" The butler said that he had taken the liberty of replying that David was indeed all right.

'When David next saw his mother she told him that she had been resting upstairs on the afternoon in question when David appeared to her, all dripping wet, and said "I have come from the depths!" Hence her concern and her telegram.'

David Lloyd Davies achieved fame among his friends as the only 'living ghost' they had ever met.

VARIETIES OF GHOST

Giles de la Mare (see p. 47) drew my attention to the following passage in the transcript of an interview which was broadcast on BBC Radio 4 in the Today *programme on 25 April 1973, the centenary of the birth of Giles's grandfather, the celebrated poet Walter de la Mare. Robert Robinson was interviewing Giles's father, the poet's son, Richard, and had asked him what sort of books his father liked to read.*

de la Mare: Among his favourites was certainly Thomas Hardy, who I think influenced him to some extent and who was a friend of his as well.
Robinson: Did he share Hardy's interest in death?
de la Mare: Well, in a curious way he did, yes. He felt it was the great adventure at the end of your life and that it was something in a way to be looked forward to – as a great adventure. I mean he firmly believed in some sort of life after death. I haven't any doubt about that at all.
Robinson: I'm very much addicted to his ghost stories and I think of the grotesque Seaton's Aunt and the appalling Mr Bloom . . . Did anything ever happen in real life of a vaguely occult nature?
de la Mare: Well yes. I wouldn't use the word occult but perhaps telepathic would be the better word to use. More than once, yes. There was one occasion I remember vividly because I was involved in it personally. We were going to look at antique shops. He collected furniture and china to some extent, in a rather desultory way; but it was an amusing thing to do, to go and look at antique shops, and very often I would go with him. This particular day, we got on our coats ready to go when a friend turned up who wasn't expected and whom he didn't particularly want to see but he felt he must stay and talk to; and we were prevented from going –and he was disappointed. Well, that afternoon two other friends of his went to this particular shop that he visited regularly and while they were looking in the window the wife suddenly ran away from the shop in some sort of distress and her husband went after her and said, 'What on earth's the matter?' And she said, 'Well, I'm worried about Mr de la Mare because I could see him in the shop, but he wasn't there because I could see a bureau through him . . . '

There is an interesting coincidence in connection with this anecdote:

Giles de la Mare remembers his father telling him that the woman who had seen the apparition of the poet in the shop heard later that her own mother had died that day.

Through Children's Eyes

A child's account of conversations with figures invisible to the adult eye is usually dismissed as the product of a lively imagination, as we have seen. These tales indicate that young children may have the ability to see and perhaps communicate with ghosts without a fear of the unknown such as is normally acquired at a later stage in their development.

Mrs Margaret Rowe, a primary teacher in Victoria, Australia, is a 'sensitive' who has contributed a number of her own remarkable experiences to my current research into coincidences and precognition. Here she recounts an incident involving a relative, who refused to discuss it. Mrs Rowe had heard the story from her father's cousin, who was the mother of the young wife and mother that it featured.

'She and her family had bought an old house in Brighton (Victoria, Australia) and were being disturbed by footsteps at night for which they blamed their children, then aged four and two. The children denied it and said that it was a nice young man who came and held their hands when they were afraid of the dark. The older child, a girl, started to draw pictures of what looked like a man in an old-fashioned uniform.

'The parents then found out that the old couple who had originally owned the house had lost a son in the First World War, he had the same name as the one the children used' [when speaking of the figure they saw at night].

Mrs Pamela Barford of Staffordshire says her father was born at the turn of the century and always believed very firmly in ghosts.

'He explained to me that when he was a small boy living in Walton le Dale, near Preston, Lancashire, this little girl used to come and sit on the end of his bed and talk to him or sit with him. She visited him for years and one day, when he was about ten, he told his father about the little girl (his mother had died when he was six).'

Mrs Barford's grandfather scoffed at his son, who nonetheless insisted on the reality of the little girl, describing her clothing in detail, although he could not give an accurate account of her colouring. But he was able to remember one curious characteristic she possessed: he told his father that on her left hand were three moles in the shape of a triangle.

'Grandfather was horrified, and explained to my father that it was his sister Annie, who had died from smallpox five years before he was born, and because his parents were so upset about her death at the age of seven, they had never told my father about her.'

Mrs Juliet Mary Whicker of Sussex writes:

'When my daughter was a tiny girl she used to talk of a little old man who used to come into her bedroom and sit on her bed. I don't know if he spoke to her. She didn't seem at all worried about it and, as she had a vivid imagination, I thought nothing of it.

'Just recently her eldest son, aged about three years, was staying with me and sleeping in his mother's old bedroom. He spoke casually of a little old man who came into his room!

'I have never seen this friendly little old man in the twenty-two years we have lived here, and no one else has said anything, so presumably he prefers tiny children to talk to.'

And this story comes from Mrs Brenda E. Goatham of Devon:

'When our son was not quite three years old he came running out to me in the kitchen where I was preparing tea. He tugged at my skirt and said "Mummy, come! There's a white-haired old lady!"

'He led me into the dining-room. "There," he said, looking towards the chair his grandmother used to sit in, but as he looked he added sorrowfully "Oh, she's gone!"

'His grandmother had been white-haired, but he wouldn't have remembered her. She died when he was eight months old.

'We are practising Anglicans and do not believe in ghosts. But our son was too young to be playing tricks, and I'll never forget the sorrow in his voice, or the look on his face' [when he discovered the old lady had gone].

Mrs Mary M. Watson (usually known as Mollie) lives in the West Midlands, but was born in Scotland where her family talked for decades about the eerie adventures of her twin boy cousins.

The twins' father was a gamekeeper in the early years of the century working on the vast estate surrounding Rosehaugh House near the fishing town of Avoch in the Black Isle, a peninsula between Inverness and the Cromarty Firth in Ross-shire.

The house was the 'ninth wonder of the world', according to Mrs Watson, covering many acres of ground and extravagantly furnished with gardens, swimming pool, tennis courts and shooting moors. Decorative stone and marbles from all over the world were used in construction of the house, together with valuable woods for the wall panelling.

The owners, Douglas Fletcher and his wife, were childless. When the master of the house died, his widow remained there, using only two rooms of the vast mansion. Mrs Fletcher died in the 1950s and the house was subsequently demolished, all traces of it disappearing except for a unique laundry.

In 1909 the Fletchers were abroad and their servants, except for a skeleton staff, were on leave. Taking advantage of the opportunity to relax their supervision, the remaining servants allowed the gamekeeper's twin sons to play inside the house. Mrs Watson describes what happened to them:

'The twins [then nine years old] were playing in the house, and mounting the grand staircase arrived on the huge landing. Stepping off one wing of the staircase were two little men no more than eighteen inches high. They were oddly dressed in loose tunics and small pointed hats. And they were grey-haired and bearded.

'The four confronted one another and, to the amazement of the twins, the two little people walked past them and disappeared into the hall below.

'There was talk around at the time of sightings of fairies or elves or "the little people". Later on a bootlace which could not be accounted for was found by one of the housemaids preparing for their master and mistress's homecoming – a strip of leather without any metal fasteners.'

On another occasion the twins were outside playing.

'Looking towards a long thick growth of trees they beheld a railway engine and carriages moving above the tree tops, silently and at speed.

'Some weeks later the announcement was made that the track for the Black Isle railway was to be cut, running right through the woods where the twins had seen the vision. They had been thought quite mad when they talked of what they had seen.'

The twins lived to a ripe old age, the elder dying quite recently aged eighty-four, and his brother predeceasing him by six years. Throughout their lives they swore to the truth of these adventures.

Mrs Watson adds that within the family the twins were assumed to have the gift of second sight.

'Dear Madam,' wrote Mr T. E. J. from Wales, who prefers to remain anonymous, 'I am moved to set down the following experience . . . Although far removed from the realms of enthralling tales of headless horsemen and wailing apparitions, it has, I assure you, the merit of being true.'

T. E. J. hits the nail on the head: most of the experiences contributed for possible inclusion in this book are more likely to puzzle than shock, especially where readers have had no similar experience. But they do ring true.

'My only apparent contact with supernatural manifestation occurred when I was a small boy and now, at the age of seventy-three, I can still remember it quite vividly.

'Our house was lit by gas in those days and although my parents were the first tenants, my mother always said in later years that the house was haunted.

'My brother and I slept in the middle bedroom and the gas light which was on a wall just inside the door was always left burning on a low level.

'I awoke with a start very early one morning. I assumed it was morning because of the circumstances. I then saw a hand and an arm, bare to the elbow, brown, and covered with black hair, just like my father's, appear from behind the door (which was always left ajar) and turn out the light. I assumed that it was my father going to work and thought no more of it, although I did wonder about the arm being bare because it was a cold winter's morning.

'Nothing was said until father came home from work when he denied turning out the light. Brother and I promptly got told off for, and warned of the dangers of, playing with the gas light. When I related my story of the bare arm the subject was dropped like a hot coal. It appeared that father was buttoned down to the wrist in any event.

'It was not until years later when my mother voiced her opinions about the house, saying that the built-in cupboard in their bedroom used to vibrate at high speed on occasion in the early hours, that I connected my experience with anything supernatural, although mother had done so.'

Lucy, the daughter of Mary Outhwaite (see p. 32) experienced something strange in their fifteen-year-old house on the edge of Dartmoor, but learned how to handle the situation.

'She was looking out of the window one day and said she could see a figure of a man coming up the drive dressed all in blue in a doublet and hose and wearing a hat with a blue feather. She could hear his feet on the gravel of the drive. My mother and I happened to be looking out the window at the same time and yet we saw nothing. Sir Francis Drake was born a few miles away and a neighbouring farm had a sign of his keys impressed over the doors, so obviously the neighbourhood had some connection with him. Could this have been the figure Lucy saw?

'At the same time as Lucy saw the man in blue she seemed unable to sleep at night and kept complaining of the face of a little girl leering down at her while she was in bed, pulling horrible faces at her which terrified her.

'I suggested she should pull a face back at the child, and once Lucy started doing this, the face disappeared and the child never came back.'

Ghosts of Pets

The manifestation of ghosts of animals, particularly beloved pets, is by no means unusual, although it may not be the former owner who reports seeing the creature in its ghostly form, as the first story illustrates.

Mrs Mena Wade now lives in Hertfordshire. A former highly qualified nurse, she tells of her experience as a young woman employed in a private nursing case in Winchester in 1930.

She had been engaged by an elderly lady, Miss Anthea [*name changed*], to care for her maid, Bella [*name changed*], who had been with Miss Anthea's family for many years and was now elderly herself. Mena Wade takes up the story:

'This was in the days of coal fires and Bella was feeling the heavy work load too much. So they got a girl to come in daily. Unknown to everyone she was a diphtheria carrier.'

Miss Anthea succumbed to the disease but recovered. Bella was not so fortunate. She became very ill with diphtheria, and it was then that Mena Wade was engaged as night nurse to look after her in what proved to be the last week of her life.

One night Mena Wade came on duty and went up to Bella's room to check her patient.

'She was unconscious, quite peaceful, quite a good pulse. There was nothing I could do for her so, leaving the light on and the door wide open, I went downstairs to the sitting room which was a large room with french windows at the far end opening on to the garden.

'I fetched the book I had brought with me, made sure the door was wide open and got a chair, a hard one (prevents one falling asleep) and set it against the door so that I had my back to it. I polished my glasses and started to read, when round from behind my chair came a brown dog who walked the length of the room and vanished among the floor-length curtains.

'I jumped up in some alarm, saying to myself "Surely those doors aren't open?" and rushing across the room pulled the curtains away – no, every one of the doors was fastened. Where was the dog? No trace of him. And also no way out, although I knew very well he had to pass me to get out of the room. I felt very uneasy. I searched under all the furniture and eventually the whole of the ground floor, without success. I had been there a week and didn't know there was a dog in the house.

'At that stage I thought I must go and see my patient. She was just as I left her, but she was gone. No pulse, no breathing.

'Nurses have a little check of their own. When circulation ceases, all the blood settles into the lowest part of the body. If the patient is lying on his back, the blood collects in the back tissues, therefore the nose is the first thing to lose its blood supply and warmth. We touch the nose with the back of the hand. If the patient is living the nose is warm, if dead it's like touching a piece of marble. There is no mistaking it.'

Miss Anthea had retired to bed long before the dog appeared, and Mena Wade went to rouse her with the news of the death of Bella. She was told to leave everything until the next morning, which she did. But before she went off the next day the nurse asked Miss Anthea if she owned a dog. 'No,' replied the mistress of the house, 'there are no dogs here.' Mena Wade then said she had seen one the previous night, describing the animal as being 'a dark brown, rough-haired dog, about the size of a border terrier. He had a parting down the middle of his back, as if he had been brushed and combed,' and she told Miss Anthea how the dog had disappeared through the curtains of the drawing room.

Miss Anthea was amazed. 'We had a dog just like the one you describe!' she cried. 'It was years ago. He was my dog, but he never bothered with me, it was Bella he loved! They were devoted to each other, and were never apart. Bella was heart-broken when he died of old age. He came to fetch her, I am sure of it!'

Mena Wade, now in her eighties, was much perplexed by this experience. If the dog came back to fetch his beloved mistress, why did she, the nurse, see him, and not Bella the maid? she asks. And why, if spirits can pass through walls, did the little brown dog bother to walk through the sitting room? Was it, she wonders, to let her know her patient had died?

Mrs Hilary Boxall lives in the south of England where she is group chairman of the local Women's Institute. In November 1987 she called on a member to help arrange the Institute's group carol service to be held later that year. Although she was acquainted with the member (we'll call her Mrs Stern) from occasional contact at meetings, Mrs Boxall knew absolutely nothing about her personal life or indeed about the house in which she lived. Mrs Boxall writes:

'I called on Mrs Stern at 2 p.m. on a very sunny day, and knocked on the door. She opened it and I entered a bright, extremely well cared for home – in fact nothing was out of place, and everything shone.

'There was a glass door leading from the hall to the kitchen and I followed Mrs Stern through. As I walked just behind her and went through the door a magnificent golden retriever/Labrador came up to me. I bent down to stroke the dog and as I did so I said, "What a beautiful dog!" Mrs Stern thereupon said, "We haven't got a dog!" When I turned to the dog, it had gone. I asked quickly whether it was a friend's dog, and Mrs Stern said she disliked dogs and had never had one in the house. I was rather taken aback as the dog was a real as a dog could be.

'I looked round the kitchen later, thinking I may have seen a golden duster or something which may have made a trick of the light, but the kitchen was just stainless steel, and the only colour was blue. As I've said previously, not a thing was out of place.

'Not knowing Mrs Stern well I made light of my "mistake", but I know I saw this dog.'

Mrs Boxall was so mystified that she decided to do a little private investigation. Mrs Stern's spotless house proved to be only ten years old, but an interesting fact emerged: the building had been erected in the garden of a much earlier house. Had the handsome golden dog Mrs Boxall saw belonged to the property in the past?

'There you are,' concludes Mrs Boxall. 'A very strange story, but absolutely true!'

Mrs Patricia Fairhurst's encounter with the manifestation of a dog might be a comfort to Mrs Boxall. Mrs Fairhurst lives in Lancashire, but her story is set largely on the Isle of Man.

'A number of years ago friends of ours, Peter and Janet Brown [*names changed*], had a Pekinese dog called Mr Mobo. On occasion he stayed with my husband and me when his owners went on holiday. We had a poodle of our own at the time, called Tammy, and they got on very well together. Mr Mobo became one of the family, sitting on my knee or laying his head on my foot to go to sleep. He was a lovely little dog, and we were very sad and sorry when he died. He was buried in his own garden in which he had been very happy, complete with inscribed headstone.

'A few years later Peter and Janet went to live in the Isle of Man, and in September of that year my husband, daughter and myself went to stay with them for ten days. The Browns were to go on holiday for a week in the middle of our stay, leaving us on our own in their bungalow.

'Peter and Janet met us off the boat, and drove us to their home. As we went in through the front door Mr Mobo came running down the hall, happy and excited, towards me. I bent down and stroked him and patted his head, and he was so pleased to see me.

'Mr Mobo followed me everywhere over the next ten days, both inside the bungalow and out in the garden. He sat next to me on the settee, or would lie on the floor resting his head on my foot, just as he had in life. I talked to him, patted him, stroked his lovely soft silky fur, just as I had always done. Mr Mobo was there when I got up in the morning and stayed until I went to bed at night. Every time we went out he was sad, and each time we returned, he was so excited.

'Oddly, though no one else saw him, no one thought it strange that I did. It was a very sad day for Mr Mobo and me when I left.

'I haven't been to the Browns' since. My husband has, but as on the previous occasion he saw nothing. I don't know whether Mr Mobo is still there or not.'

Mrs Fairhurst regarded the experience as a happy one though a strange one at the same time, and she asked me the following questions: 'If I had seen Mr Mobo in his old home here in Southport, or even in our own home, I could have understood. But why should he have gone to a strange home in the Isle of Man? Perhaps he went with the people he loved, but then why should I be able to see him, and not them?'

Eva Barnes the 'Poetess' (as she likes to be known) lives in Lancashire. She claims to be psychic, as was her mother. She writes:

'A few months ago I was washing up in the evening. It was still light. My husband was in the bakery where he works regularly at night.

'I was suddenly drawn to look up at the window. There before my eyes was my lovely pussy cat, Beauty, a ginger-coloured cat which died over twenty years ago. Beauty caught a disease when only four years of age. We had to have him put to sleep, which deeply hurt me.'

She had never seen a manifestation of her beloved cat before.

'He looked almost real to me. He stared at me. I was just going to say "Hello love!" when he disappeared in a flash. I couldn't stop thinking and wondering why he appeared like that. He looked just as young as when he died.'

Among Mrs Shelah Newman's many psychic experiences are two which feature animals, a cat and a dog. Of the first she says: 'It still fascinates me today. I have no fear of the cat in question, incidentally.'

The story begins in her home in South Yorkshire with a stray kitten she decided to rescue.

'It had been pitiful to see the pathetic little creature struggle to survive in the depths of a bitter winter. So one night I lurked with intent, armed with an old bag lined with a warm blanket. It was all far easier than I had anticipated.

'The dirty little face peeped out over the top of the bag, offering no resistance to the new situation in which he suddenly found himself . . . apparently resigned to whatever fate might have in store.

'Treatment and proper care wrought a big change and by the spring an alley cat had been transformed into a beauty, very meticulous over his appearance. But there was something decidedly uncanny in the way he regarded me with his long almond-shaped eyes.

'Alone with the newcomer one bright morning, I watched him at play, going round the room at a great rate, leaping, rolling, tumbling. Then I saw him pawing at another cat which, as I watched, melted away into the furniture. As I watched over a period of time I realized beyond doubt that I had acquired a ghost cat.

'I see it all the time now, as an entire cat, but sometimes only in part, as the mood dictates. The complete picture finally emerged of a lovely jet black, part Persian cat with a tail like a fox's brush, offering an occasional glimpse of topaz eyes. Full of mischief, it has been known to go into the cat flap by melting through it – or having meowed at the house door, comes in conventionally, only to disappear immediately afterwards!

'A cynical visitor once commenced a lecture . . . "No such thing as a ghost cat, indeed!" when suddenly he faltered, turned pale, and announced his intention of leaving: the cat had sprung out of the wall and vanished at his feet. The visitor exited so rapidly I doubt if he heard my assurance that if the cat so desired it, it could quite easily accompany him home.

'Some of the elderly ladies who live in the area have recalled that as children they would visit the occupant of the house who was a dressmaker, organizer of children's concerts, an animal lover, teller of fortunes by crystal ball (offering remarkably accurate predictions) and a medium.

'The ghost cat is around constantly, both inside and outside. I try talking to it and wish it were possible to try to stroke it, too.

'I did not readily jump to any immediate conclusions about the appearance of the cat until I had made sure no logical explanation could be found. But after a lifetime of encountering odd experiences I realize that if something cannot be proved, it does not mean to say that it does not exist.'

The dog whose ghost Mrs Newman occasionally sees in her house is a will o' the wisp, bits of him appearing momentarily from time to time, offering her a glimpse of fur one day, an impression of energy charging around the room the next. Interestingly, she has only seen the complete dog on one occasion, in late November a few years ago.

'I was in one of the upstairs rooms when I became aware of a drop in temperature. The light was on. It would have been about 9 p.m., and as I turned around facing the door, I became aware of the dog spinning around, apparently chasing his own tail and entirely surrounded by a pale greenish light. It was all over in seconds, when things returned to normal.'

The ghost dog is still in evidence, and Mrs Newman's own living dog shows no reaction at all to it.

Rosemary E. Hutchinson of Northumberland is used to animals: she is a professional rider married to a farmer and they live in an old house, one section of which dates back to the 1500s. She says that the farmhouse is home to a ghostly visitor which seems to confine its appearance to the dark hours of the night.

'I have for many years now been a person who awakes during the night and sneaking downstairs will tuck into cornflakes or ham sandwiches.

'I have discovered, however, that during these nightly trips to the kitchen I am never alone! It happens that as I walk along the upstairs hallway past the orange bathroom there sits a large, dark and very friendly cat. It will follow me to the kitchen and sit beside the remaining empty wall before walking quietly back up stairs, where it is again in position upon my return to my bedroom.'

Rosemary Hutchinson is not the only person to enjoy the company of the ghostly cat – another member of the family is quite familiar with it.

'The cat is a regular visitor to my daughter's room. She will often ask about the dark cat that walks through the doorway. My daughter is now three and a half years old.

'We have four small house dogs and three cats of our own, none of which seem to notice anything.'

H. W. R. Stevens, known as Roy to his friends, lives in Hampshire. He is a retired schoolmaster. During the Second World War he served abroad with the RAF.

'We stood at the entrance of a German air-raid shelter near our tents in late December. The shelter was quite deep, having been a refuge for the Jerries who had worked at this storage depot at the edge of the airfield at Benghazi. There was another entrance but it had been blocked by all sorts of rubbish – wood, boxes, iron bars, barbed wire – before we, a small advance party, had moved into the site.

'From where we stood, a steep-sloping passage led down about twenty feet to a long narrow room lined with planks, braced with timbers to prevent the sides and roof falling in in the event of a bomb's near miss. It was very dark down there.

'On this particular night it was very dark outside too, when all was quiet. There was no moon and the enemy was making the most of it. Their bombers' engine noise grew louder and the air was suddenly rent by the crash of anti-aircraft fire, 4.7s and Bofors, the muzzle flashes lighting the ground and the bursting shells adding noise and stars to the heavens. The bluish beams of searchlights reached up, seeking out the raiders and, as the bombers came over the town, the thunder of guns, bursting shells and crashing bombs became intense.

'Peering from under the brims of our tin hats we watched the barrage of exploding shells and strings of tracers move back and forth across the harbour, lumps of jagged steel thumping into the ground as the barrage came over us. As an unlucky bomber was caught by one of the searchlights, the other beams converged upon it and it became a small bright cross in the sky, weaving like a bird trying to escape from a cage of tracer bars. Then it was going down, down towards the sea.

'At that point an Airedale dog padded out of the shadows towards us. The gunflashes and reflected light from the searchlights made the night bright enough for us to see its curly brown coat as it trotted between us, close enough to touch, and entered the shelter. Somebody said "He knows where to go, doesn't he!"

'At that moment an enemy bomber glided in low and we heard the bombs swishing down. We all dashed down the slope into the underground room. It was pitch dark. A match was struck and the flame illuminated the bare earth floor and wall boards of the shelter.

'"Where's the dog?" somebody asked. We all looked, but it wasn't there!

'It had not been seen before this incident took place and although we all kept an eye open for it in the next few days, it was never seen again.'

Roy Stevens adds that five or six other men saw the ghost of the Airedale dog as well, but no one was able to offer any explanation for its manifestation on that war-torn battlefield in Libya.

One of the most notable features of our relationship with animals is the loyalty often displayed by pets. Stories of families saved from fire or drowning by dogs are legion, but the following incident which occurred when Jack Read was a boy is exceptionally moving. Now retired and living in London, he was brought up on the Isle of Wight. The beach at Ryde, his favourite playground, provided the setting for the drama he describes.

'When the tide was in the beach was covered, except for a small area called the West Beach. Near the sea wall the water was three to four feet deep, ample for diving and swimming but at the tide's ebb it went out for nearly a mile, leaving a flat sandy beach on which to play.

'Although the sand appeared quite flat, there was a bank which was slightly higher and this bank extended some 600 yards from the sea wall, about half a mile seaward, and it was some 250 yards wide. A kind of channel extended right round it which filled when the tide started to come in so that you had to be careful not to be marooned on the bank. This was not normally dangerous, but if you left it too late, the only way to get ashore was to wade or swim back.

'One day "our gang" decided to travel along the beach to Puckpool Fort and play among the casements there. The fort had been built during the First World War to protect Portsmouth Harbour. On the way we met two girls from our school, Molly and Eileen, who said they were going out on the bank to get a closer look at the large liners passing. We went on our way, while the two girls made their way on the bank to the water's edge to see the large Cunarder sailing on her way to America and a couple of battleships and their destroyer escort making their way to Portsmouth.

'Ships take longer to pass than one thinks and the girls, not noticing that the tide had turned, were searching for shells. They forgot about the time while the water silently flowed into the channels until the bank was surrounded.

'Suddenly, the girls were startled by the barking of a dog. Not far away was a middle-sized dog which had black fur except for its paws and left ear, which were white. They called to the dog but it just barked and ran to and fro as if trying to get them to follow. Eventually they chased after him and as they got nearer, he renewed his barking and running towards the shore.

'Molly then noticed something odd – "Look, Eileen, that dog's not leaving any footprints!"

'"Don't be silly, that's because the sand is wet now that the tide's coming in." Then, realizing the danger, she said, "Oh, Molly! We've been cut off!"

'The dog was barking even more excitedly, and drew them to the channel. As they followed, he ran across the water while the girls watched in amazement, for the dog seemed to be running on top of the water – no ripples or splashing!

'They were very lucky the water did not come above their knees as they carefully paddled across to the shore and, looking back, saw the black dog bark as if to say "Now you are safe" and run off in the direction of the lane (an opening leading to the sea) from a nearby farm.

'On our return we met the girls who told us how the dog had saved them. "He didn't leave any footprints in the sand and walked on the water!"

'"Don't be silly – you're kidding us – wait till we tell them at school!"

'They were teased a great deal when the story got around and though they tried to convince everyone about what they had seen, no one believed them.

'Time passed and the story of the dog was forgotten, until we had a new Sunday-school teacher who told us about strange happenings and asked if we knew any.

'"Yes," we said. "Ask Molly, she has seen a dog which walked on water!"

'When Mr Drysdale heard the girls' story, he said, "Next Sunday I will tell you something interesting about this tale."

'And this is what he told us: "In a local paper dated 1898 was a story of three girls, Emily, Barbara and Mary, who went with their dog, Nigger, out to the Bank. The weather was fine but windy and the sea rough. They were aware of the dangers there but, sadly, they went out too far and played too long, so that when returning homewards they found the tide had come in faster than they had expected, and the water near the shore was very deep. None of them could swim and no one was around to call to for help. The eldest girl, Emily, took five-year-old Mary on her shoulders and started to cross. The water was chest high and, unfortunately, in the deepest part they both fell and Mary was carried out to sea by the strong current.

'"Nigger paddled quickly after her and, gripping her clothes in his teeth, he tried valiantly to swim with her towards the shore. The current was too strong; they were being carried out to sea but Nigger never gave up the hold on the struggling girl and would not leave her.

'"Some days later their bodies were washed ashore. Nigger was still gripping Mary's clothes and her arms were wrapped around him.

'"Mary's parents wanted Nigger buried with her, but the vicar refused to allow this and the dog was buried on the right-hand side of the lane."

'We were all very silent when he told us the description of Nigger – it was the same as that given by Molly of the dog that helped them!

'Local people say that Nigger guards the bank to this day.'

Nancy Cadwell of Essex wrote the following story about the experience during the Second World War of a close member of her family. [All names have been changed.]

'Rosie Allen lived in what once had been the village of Corsten, now a suburb of a large, grubby town. All that was left to remind people of the old rural way of life was the old lane and the canal bridge. Children dangled home-made fishing lines into the water below the bridge, just as their fathers had done . . .

'Rosie's grandfather had come to Corsten from Lancashire to buy the village shop, now called the corner shop. With his wife and son he was soon accepted in the village and was well respected. When his wife died, his son and daughter-in-law came to live with him. On his death they took over the business. The last squire of the village sold his house and land but left the old lane in trust for the people of Corsten to use as a bird watching area. No one took advantage of this privilege, but the children played on the lane and Rosie, now running the shop, walked its length every Wednesday when she visited her friends, the Winsters.

'A less imaginative woman than Rosie Allen would be difficult to find . . . At the age of ten she had been knocked down by a car. Her right leg was badly injured leaving her with a very ugly limp which stayed with her for the rest of her life. Her loving parents were over-protective . . . preventing her from becoming independent, and she grew up successfully avoiding anything that was not part of the routine of her days.

'Part of the pattern of Rosie Allen's life was her weekly visit to Stella and Bert Winster. Every Wednesday she closed the shop at one o'clock, added up the takings, ate her lunch and at three o'clock precisely started her walk to 12 Crawford Road . . . Her journey took ten minutes longer than necessary because she went via the old lane . . . which reminded her of her childhood. Few people used the lane, and those she met were usually of her own generation who knew her well enough to greet her with a cheerful "Hello Rosie", knowing she would smile but would not stop to talk with them. She would limp onwards, happily anticipating the pleasure of being with her friends.

'On the second Wednesday in November 1943 (a day Rosie said she would never forget) Stella greeted her on her arrival with the news that Bert was in bed suffering from pleurisy. "Go up and see him," said her friend. "He's worried about you."

'As she mounted the stairs Rosie wondered what there could be for Bert to worry about. She found him propped up on pillows looking slightly flushed. Patting his hand she commiserated with him and asked if he was in much pain. "No," he replied, "and I shall soon get better, but I'm worried about you going home without me to see you to the bridge. I want you to stay here and go home in daylight."

'Rosie had never slept away from the shop in her whole life and the thought was alarming. Also she was puzzled by Bert's anxious concern. "You see, Rosie," he continued, "it wouldn't be very nice in the winter even in peacetime, but with the war and the blackout . . . " his voice tailed away and he gazed at her with troubled appeal. Smiling brightly she patted his hand again, saying, "What is there to worry about? Who would want to bother me, a middle-aged woman with a limp and a face like a piece of suet?"'

Bert appealed to Rosie to take his warning seriously, urging her to borrow his torch when he realized she had no intention of staying overnight. But, disregarding Bert's premonition and warning, Rosie said goodbye to her friends and set out alone for home.

'Walking along Crawford Road where the street lamps were dimmed and the houses showed no sign of life behind darkened windows, Rosie . . . hobbled along until she came to the main road which she crossed before going into the old lane. It had never entered her head to do as Bert had advised and take the shorter route home. Habit was not something that she could easily break. In the lane she was at once struck by the sudden darkness that enclosed her . . . If only she had remembered the torch . . . Bert had always carried it on dark nights and they had shone the light up into the trees hoping to see an owl which they sometimes heard hooting. Walking with Bert and the torch had been fun. Now the darkness seemed to grow more dense as she limped slowly forward, moving the damp leaves underfoot and finding comfort in the familiar noise of the rustling hedges and trees.

'Suddenly she stopped, straining every nerve to assure herself that she had not heard the sound of footsteps . . . Standing stiffly with head raised she waited, but all she heard were the sounds special to the lane. "Don't let your mind run on such things!" she murmured aloud, and limped forward. The footsteps also began to move nearer. Now she was certain that there was someone else in the lane. She called out "Who's there?" But no one answered . . . Fear urged her to hurry. It was not easy to move swiftly with her staggering gait and even as she increased her pace she was aware that whoever was behind her was also walking faster. Oh Bert! . . . If only she had remembered the torch! The thought of a light only made the dark seem more dense.

'As the footsteps came closer . . . she lost control of her shaking legs, stumbled and fell. The footsteps stopped, and she heard a stifled cough. Her pursuer was only a few yards away. Panic brought to her lips a cry of terror and she called out "Rover!" Rosie was too demented to wonder why she called that particular name, but almost before her cry faded a dog appeared. He circled her as she lay, then rushed back along the lane. She heard him growl, and immediately heard the words "You bloody thing! You've bitten me!"

'The dog came back to her and stood at her feet with tail wagging and mouth open. The sound of retreating footsteps brought Rosie . . . to her feet. She called to the dog but he did not move and not until she began to move forward did he run beside her. Each time she stretched her hand to touch him, he was always a few inches out of reach. Talking to him as they made their way to the canal bridge brought Rosie a sense of comfort and by the time they reached the shop Rosie felt tired but, for some reason she could not explain, very happy.

'In the light from the open shop door, Rosie could see that the black and white sheepdog was in excellent condition. She tried to persuade Rover to enter the shop, but he insisted on staying outside the door, and every time she reached out to touch him, he moved away. She had to content herself with putting out food and water before locking up the shop and going upstairs to bed.

'Next morning she got up early. She went downstairs and found the food and water untouched, and no sign of Rover. Sadly, she returned to the shop and she later opened it up. In spite of her many inquiries to her customers – the postman, the baker and anyone else who might know of a dog fitting the description of Rover – she was unable to obtain the slightest scrap of information which might lead her to his owners.

'She was greatly mystified: she had no idea why she had called out the name "Rover" when she fell to the ground. She had never owned a dog called Rover, and she had not been acquainted with anyone who had a dog of that name.

'Automatically she performed the tasks that she always did on

Thursdays but her movements were part of a routine, while her thoughts were strange and alien to her nature. Before retiring for the night she went to look out into the road . . . There was no sign of the dog.

'The next morning the postman came with a letter from her cousin Stanley who lived in Chester. They had not met for thirty years. Unlike Rosie, her cousin belonged to one or two local organizations such as the chapel, cricket club and a choir. From time to time he would enclose with his letter a photograph of some event that had taken place concerning one of his diversions. On opening the envelope on this occasion she saw between the pages of the letter a coloured snap which she removed with interest.

'As she looked at the print, her hand trembled. Staring at her from the picture was Rover! Bewildered, she read the letter. There was a postscript. "You never knew my old dog and now it is too late because he died two months ago," wrote Stanley. "A better friend a man could not wish for, and I know that I will never have another dog like Rover."'

Pets' Reactions

Pets cannot be relied on to react to the presence of a ghost in any specific way: some show fear, some ignore the phenomenon. It is tempting to conjecture that, like their human companions, some pets simply refuse to believe in the paranormal, while others are remarkably sensitive to it.

Thomas Henry Walker, retired, lives in Yorkshire. He remembers with clarity an incident which occurred when he was about twelve or thirteen in 1931–2.

'One Saturday evening at about 10.30 p.m. my father decided to take the dog, Sandy, for a walk. It was November and rather foggy.

'On our way back home around 11.30 p.m. we were approaching the ginnel [lane] as it was known, when suddenly Sandy stopped dead in his tracks, his hackles up, ears pricked and tail straight out. I asked my father what was wrong with the dog. He told me to be quiet and not to move.

'Suddenly, from the lane, an outline of red appeared, walked across the road and disappeared towards the River Foss, which flows alongside of Huntingdon Road.

'On our way up the lane and down the street my father explained the apparition's appearance. Before any houses were built in the area, he said, it was open, boggy land leading into the river. The ghost, when living, had been drinking rather heavily. He lost his way, and was drowned opposite what is now the ginnel.'

When Mrs Rosemary Fedrick and her family left their home in Berkshire for a day's outing some years ago, they got more than they bargained for at the site of a Roman villa in Oxfordshire.

'This is not just *my* experience,' Mrs Fedrick emphasizes. 'It's a family one, and includes the dog!

'Some twenty to twenty-five years ago with my husband, our two daughters aged about eight and twelve, and our spaniel dog, I visited the remains of a Roman villa near the River Evenlode, near East End, Long Hanborough in Oxfordshire (Ordnance Survey No. 397154). The villa was then being excavated.

'It was late afternoon in early autumn, September, I think. The villa was in a valley, about a quarter of a mile or so from the road, down an earth track. A wood lay to the right with fields and high hedges around. The river was presumably at the end of the track, though not visible. We could see no hard surface near by.

'At the entrance to the site was a hut, but presumably due to the late hour the caretaker had gone home, so on our own we walked around some recently exposed paving, in what would have been the courtyard of the Roman villa, with various rooms opening off it.

'Suddenly a thick mist rolled out of the woods near the villa, heading towards the river. It was a weird mist – I've never seen one like it before or since.

'Then we heard the sound of horse's hooves galloping towards us from a distance. We couldn't tell from which direction they came, but the sound became increasingly louder as it approached the villa. The "horse" clattered close to us, as if on paving stones, then abruptly stopped, as if the rider had pulled up.

'We all felt what I can only describe as terrified. Without a word to each other we all ran as fast as we could away from the villa.

'The odd thing was the dog's behaviour. As soon as we heard the noise his hackles rose, and when the "horse" entered the courtyard, he started growling. He led us at speed back to the car – when we got there he was shaking, like the rest of us.

'Later inquiries suggested that a new-born baby's skeleton had just been found buried in the corner of a room off the courtyard, a common practice I believe with still-born babies in Roman times.

'Could the "horseman" have been a distraught father rushing to his wife in labour?

'Incidentally, when we reached the car there was no sign of mist and it was still quite light.'

VARIETIES OF GHOST

Sarah Winthrop [name changed] now lives in a remote village in Lincolnshire. Earlier in her father's town house, which had been passed down the male line of the family for generations, the presence of her dead grandfather had been obvious to her and a number of other people.

'I recall in the years just after the Second World War . . . I had been baking and, waiting for something to cook, I sat by the kitchen fire with a cup of tea, and my dog. Father was out. Suddenly my dog sat up, wagged her tail and gave her soft "wuff!" as she did in greeting. She was looking through the kitchen door into the back hall and glancing that way I saw through the door window a dark shadow come down the stairs, cross the hall and enter the dining-room.

'I thought Father had come home, so I went to see if he wanted a cup of tea. But there was no one in the dining-room and my dog, who had trotted in gleefully, flattened her ears against her head, dropped her tail and crouching, walked backwards out of the room. Then, with a yelp, she ran to the kitchen.

'But I saw nothing, so I went into the drawing-room (next to the dining-room) expecting Father to be there. No one was in there either. So I went upstairs to find him, still convinced that Father had come in. There was no one anywhere in the house and feeling brave no longer, I went back to the kitchen to find my dog sitting behind my chair trembling. She jumped on my lap – making it very awkward as at that moment I was not sitting down! I calmed her eventually. But for some weeks afterwards we saw the dark shadow come down the stairs at the same time, 3 p.m., and enter the dining-room. My dog always jumped on to my lap, or tried to, even when I was standing up.

'I told no one about this visitation and it stopped quite suddenly. A day or two later Father had a visit from an old family friend whom I had never met before. I went out to the kitchen to get the tea tray and returning to the drawing room heard Father say, "Oh yes, my father always came down from his bedroom at 3 p.m. every afternoon except Saturdays and Sundays." (I realized they were the two days I had never seen the shadow.)

When David Stevens, a schoolmaster from Somerset, was a teenager, his family's black cat was run over.

'Some weeks later I was coming downstairs and a black cat shot past me and vanished into the bedroom. Mother called out in surprise to ask if I'd seen it.

'We searched in vain both upstairs rooms and just as we were concluding that we must have imagined it, the cat darted past us down the stairs.

'I had time to notice that it seemed to be only the outline of an animal, and we never saw it again. But when taking the dog for a walk later we opened the hall door to go outside, and the dog froze in terror. She could obviously see something invisible to us, and when tugged on the lead, she gazed fixedly at one spot, edged round it, and shot off in a panic. We concluded that she probably saw the cat.'

Part Two

GHOSTS HEARD, SMELLED, FELT AND PERCEIVED

Ghosts have been seen and recorded so frequently throughout history that we tend to think mainly of visual encounters if we think about such matters at all. But documentation of the other human senses registering the unseen is equally ancient; there is only one sensory experience missing from the record – no one appears to have *tasted* a ghost. But from the beginning of time men – including figures like Socrates – have heard (and heeded) voices from invisible sources; men of all cultures have sniffed and marvelled at sweet or nauseous odours in unexpected places; and they have experienced the alarming touch of an unseen hand. Through four of the five senses, the ghostly experience is common to all nations, primitive and sophisticated alike.

Voices and Sounds

Sounds attributed to otherwise invisible ghosts are frequently reported. They include voices, footsteps, knockings or rappings, and breathing.

Michael McParlin is a retired council labourer who lives in Tyne and Wear. He worked as a dustman for his local council for twenty-two years.

Saturday morning was known to the binmen as salvage day, when they visited local shops and factories to collect empty cardboard boxes, waste paper, rags etc., delivering them in the wagon to a depot where other workmen pressed the material into bales for recycling and subsequent re-use. After emptying the load of salvage at the depot, the bin-wagon was washed clean, ready for use the following Saturday. One Saturday morning, however, this routine was broken. Michael McParlin describes what happened:

'This particular Saturday morning my mates and I were unloading the salvage from the bin-wagon and carrying it inside an old house used as a depot or storage place . . . situated in Engine Square.

'On entering one of the rooms with a bundle of cardboard in my arms I heard a voice from somewhere, not from a human, say distinctly to me, "In here, Michael! Come in here!"

'Immediately I dropped the cardboard boxes I was carrying and rushed through two rooms in a sort of panic, but still this voice kept saying "In here, Michael! In here!" On entering the room, what confronted my eyes was a large concrete slab, which I learnt later was used as a temporary morgue during the Second World War. No dead bodies were on the morgue when I saw it – a good job for me, as I would have died from fright.

'Later I learnt from fellow binmen that the body of a person who had drowned in the River Wear near by had lain on the slab I discovered.'

VOICES AND SOUNDS

Such voices can be helpful though. Mrs Margaret Hopwood of Tyne and Wear tells the story of her sister, Mrs White [name changed], whose son wanted to become a butcher.

To help her son achieve his ambition after he had completed his apprenticeship, his mother gave up her own business and extended her living quarters to create a butcher's shop for him. After several years' hard work he succeeded in establishing the butchery, but then, quite tragically, he died at the age of thirty-two.

His mother, nearly out of her mind with grief, decided that there was only one course to follow: she must carry on the trade. But how? She had not the faintest idea how to proceed. Mrs Hopwood recalls what happened next.

'She stood at her son's butcher-block with his tools in her hand and said "Son, show your mother what to do and guide my hand." It paid off. He did just that and, I may add, my sister turned out to be a fine butcher. It may seem to be a far-fetched experience, but every word is true.'

Mrs Margaret A. Maguire is a college lecturer who lives in Devon; but five years ago she lived with her family in a three-storey Victorian house in Hale, a 'village', as she describes it, in South Manchester.

'There was my husband, two daughters and Sam, our hairy old yellow Labrador dog, and me.

'It was about 10.30 p.m. The family were out, the dog had gone walkabout as hairy old male Labradors are wont to do most of the time. I was sitting in the lounge struggling with the last two words of the *Telegraph* crossword – the "big" one for which one requires a funny brain!

'Suddenly I heard the sound of children singing – lots of children singing loudly, no particular tune, but very close. Maybe it's Trick or Treat, I thought, so I went to the front door and looked out. No, nothing and nobody there. I came in again and shut the door. The singing continued, even more loudly. I looked up the long stairwell which soared to the very top of the house and realized that the sound came from there, from the playroom which we only used for trunks, cases and the general storage of family rubbish. I hung about in the hall, looking upwards and listening. The singing continued for about ten minutes – then very gradually it faded away. Silence.

'Maybe I should have been scared, but oddly enough the voices sounded so happy, they were only children, and I just felt they were having such a jolly time!

'I didn't tell the family – I thought they would think I was loopy and I certainly didn't want to scare the girls. I did go up to the top room the next day, but everything looked just the same.

'I never heard those children singing again.

'Months later we were having a dinner party – just two couples and our younger daughter, Mary [*real name*], who was about twenty years old. After dinner we all trooped into the lounge for coffee and brandy. Then the conversation turned to ghosts, the supernatural and so forth.

'Suddenly Mary said, "We have ghosts here in this house, you know."

'Calmly I said to her, "Oh, what sort of ghosts?"

'"They're children who sing," she replied. I was absolutely riveted.

'"What do you mean sing?" I asked.

'"Well, there must be loads of them because it's quite loud," she replied. "I've only heard them once, but they're at the top of the house. No particular tune and they sound very happy. I wasn't scared because they were obviously very happy and having a lovely time."

'"How long did it go on?" I asked.

'"Oh, I suppose about ten minutes, then the singing very gradually faded away."

'Then I admitted I, too, had heard the children singing.'

This story comes from a young man, an Irishman called Michael Monaghan, a floor tiler now living in Newcastle. At the time of the incident, he lived in Divismore Park, Belfast, where back gardens of houses border a footpath running along the banks of a river dividing two estates.

Michael Monaghan was courting a girl called Rita and in mid-July 1970 they were sitting together on the river bank below the garden of one of those houses, in an area lit by the glow of street lamps at the top of the estate.

'A hedgerow divided the garden from the footpath and there was a grassy patch in which we sat. We talked for a while and I gave Rita an affectionate kiss, closing my eyes. I literally could not believe my ears when I heard a baby's voice saying "Mammy" in my ear. My immediate reaction was to jump up, and I held my ears, wondering what had happened. My first thoughts were that one of my friends had crept up, having a joke.

'I tried to speak to Rita and found myself stuttering. In my confusion I thought it was my friend Max, and I called his name. Rita asked what was wrong and I said that I had just heard a baby crying in my ear saying "Mammy". I asked if she had heard it. She said, "No! I didn't!" She took to her heels and ran . . . When I caught up with her she asked me to take her home.'

Much perturbed by the experience, Michael Monaghan told people about it and put up with their varied reactions – some were sympathetic, some mocked in disbelief. A few months later he made a new friend, Chris, and mentioned the ghostly baby voice to him. To Michael's surprise Chris told him that he knew people who had lived in that house with the garden bordering the river. They were convinced the building was haunted by a baby. He offered to take Michael to meet them, explaining that the family had moved to a new address. Michael agreed, and the two friends called on Gerry and Margaret. Although Michael had known about the couple living in the neighbourhood, he had not met them before. Margaret was at home.

She explained that when they had lived in the house she had played bingo regularly, leaving Gerry at home to mind the children. One night he had had heard the children crying, and on going upstairs to investigate, he found them all fast asleep. Another evening the same thing happened, only this time something, an unseen force, had pushed him against the wall of the room. Gerry became very unhappy about staying in the house alone with the children, eventually arranging for two local girls to act as babysitters when his wife was out. One of them was Bernadette, the sister of Billy, a friend of Michael Monaghan's.

'One evening,' Margaret told Michael, 'while the two girls were sitting with Gerry, there was a sound of a baby crying and moaning. The sounds drifted downstairs and into the hall. When the girls found there was nobody in the hall, they both ran outside into the street, screaming.'

Margaret said to Michael that they had requested the priest from the nearby Corpus Christi Church to visit and exorcize or bless the house on three separate occasions. But the disturbances continued and eventually Gerry declared he could not continue to live there. He moved the family to another house, a few streets away.

Reassured by Margaret's down-to-earth acceptance of what had happened, Michael was by then sure that the sound he had heard on the river bank below the garden of the haunted house had been the spirit of a dead child, crying for help.

'I became more curious than frightened about what I had experienced,' he says, and he decided to investigate the matter further. He talked to Bernadette, and she confirmed Margaret's description of the ghostly crying of a baby that had driven her friend and herself from the house. 'I was totally convinced,' Michael remembers, 'as she is a level-headed, serious type of girl.'

A few months later the subject was brought up again by two of his friends, Martin and Tommy.

'We made an arrangement to meet and go together to the footpath at the rear of the garden in the early hours of the following morning. By this time the river was being piped in; there were large piles of earth everywhere.

'We made ourselves as comfortable as possible. I found a breezeblock on which to sit; the others found similar objects. It was a calm, still night. We talked. Martin was nervous, but laughing and cracking jokes ... I did not feel frightened at all. I do not know why. Tommy was quiet, but as we discussed local happenings we became more at ease. I was sitting in the middle.

'After approximately half an hour, I heard a moan from the back of the house. I stopped the conversation for a second and then continued. Neither of the other two appeared to have heard this. I did not know how or why, but felt that one of them would hear the baby, and that it was *not* going to be me again.

'All of a sudden Martin stood upholding his ears and he ran.

Tommy saw the state of Martin and he also tried to run. I held on to him as long as I could, but had to let him go as it was like holding back a charging elephant. I did not feel afraid, and walked after them.

'When I caught up with them, Martin was standing staring at the sky and gasping. I asked him whether or not he believed me and he gasped "Yes!" He was stone white and appeared to be in a state of shock.'

Too upset to go home, Martin stayed with Michael until morning.

And that was the end of the story. For Michael was unable to pursue the matter further because of the 'Troubles' in Belfast.

Some of the most moving stories included in this book involve the ghosts of children. Mrs Moreen Organ, who is a private secretary and now lives in Essex, tells of her own encounter with one.

About fifteen years ago the Organs, together with their son, two daughters and Mr Organ's father, travelled up to Norfolk in the middle of summer to spend two weeks in one of a pair of houses close to the sand dunes on the coast. (Mrs Organ has supplied the address, but requests that the house remain unidentified.)

'It was a fairly large house. There were two double bedrooms and one much larger room on the first floor, with two attic rooms above.

'One night quite late I was still awake in the room I shared with my husband. My father-in-law was in the other double room on the first floor and our son was in a single bed in the large room backing on to the wall immediately behind my side of the bed. Our two daughters were asleep in the attic rooms.

'I was lying on my right side and could hear quite clearly in my right ear the crying of a child. I got up and went to see if our son was all right. He was sleeping quite soundly, breathing deeply and gently. So I climbed the stairs to the attics where our daughters were. They too were sleeping very quietly. I stayed a while but nothing changed and I could not hear any sound other than the sea and a slight breeze. I went back to my room and got back into bed.

'As soon as my head touched the pillow I could hear crying again. So I went back into the large room and knelt down by our son's bed.

He was still sleeping very quietly. I knelt there for some little while trying to think where the crying could be coming from. I remember feeling that it sounded like a small girl rather than a boy.

'I realized that one wall butted on to the house next door and went over to listen at the wall, but could hear nothing at all. I went up to the attics again, but with the same result. I wandered round the house listening and puzzling it out. I went back to my bed.

'When I laid my head on the pillow I could again hear the crying. And so, without really consciously thinking it out, I sat up, arms round my knees, and said clearly but softly, "Stop crying, darling. You are quite safe. Mother's here." And the crying stopped.'

Some years ago Mrs Hester McNeill of Cumbria shared an odd experience with her daughter.

'I lived in a very old house in the Lake District at Crook. I heard footsteps round the landing at night, but the family thought it was imagination. I'd never said anything about this to my daughter aged about six years.

'One night she slept in my bedroom as the house was full of friends. She woke me up at about 2 a.m. and said "I don't believe in ghosts but I've just seen one! It walked round the foot of the bed and I thought it was a burglar, and then it walked through the wall!"

'Some time later I sold the house, and after a while the new owner rang me up to ask if I'd ever seen anything strange in the house, as she had heard footsteps. I said "Yes. That's our friendly ghost!"'

Mrs Rita Gambrill of Coventry is a secretary. At one time her husband was a cinema operator, who caught one of the last two buses home each night at the end of the show, arriving at the family's house at either 10.55 p.m. or 11.10 p.m. Mrs Gambrill's peculiar experience was apparently connected with her husband's late working hours.

'For several weeks I would hear footsteps coming down the garden path and the key being put in the lock and then no more (unless my husband had caught the 10.55 p.m. bus), then at 11.10 p.m. the same thing would occur, but this time my husband would come in the door.'

Not wishing to upset her four children (aged seventeen, fifteen, eight, and two) Mrs Gambrill never mentioned the puzzling sounds to them, to her husband or to anyone else. But in time she learnt that she was not the only person in the family who heard them. She had been hearing the footsteps followed by the sound of the key being inserted in the lock for months when one night – after she had heard them again and her husband had failed to appear – her eldest son spoke to his mother.

'He said he, too, had heard the noises several times but didn't mention it in case *he* frightened *me* ! We compared notes and found that neither of us was ever frightened, and if we happened to be alone at the time, we had often opened the door,' – but they found no one there.

After discussing the matter fully, mother and son discovered that their dog, although often looking up and pricking his ears at the sounds, had never growled when the noises occurred. Then, to Rita Gambrill's surprise, the house produced another mystery.

'One day, about 4 p.m., I was coming in with my smallest child in the push-chair when I saw "something" go through the living-room door and through the wall into my neighbour's house. When my eldest son came in a few minutes later I told him, and we tried several ways of coming into the room to see if it was a trick of the light, but couldn't find any explanation.

'The amazing thing about this event was that the next day my neighbour (who was alone in bed the previous night as her husband was abroad), told me that she'd had an awful scare. She said she woke up and "felt" someone at the side of her bed. She kept her eyes closed and after about ten minutes she knew the "presence" had gone.

'When she told me about it I told her of our visitor and laughed, saying "Poor thing! It's been trying for ages to get in our door and when it does, it finds it's in the wrong house!"

'The other thing about this story is that from that day on, we have never heard the footsteps or the key!'

Sydney Ernest Cooper is a retired civil servant now living in Hertfordshire. As a young lad in 1926 he emigrated to Australia, where he found his first job on a small farm three or four miles from a little town called Armadale, south of Perth in Western Australia.

'The farm was up in the foothills of the Darling Ranges, the nearest house was a mile away, while the farmhouse itself was the ordinary bungalow with a wooden verandah running all round it. The farmer and his wife, a Mr and Mrs Bowles [*name changed*], used to run the farm between them with me as a general help. A narrow road ran past the farmhouse, which stood back about forty yards from the road. Being a sparsely populated area, there was very little traffic on that road; a path from the roadside gate led to the house. It was the custom for us to have our meals by the kitchen, out on the back verandah facing the hills.

'One day in 1927 the three of us were having our midday meal on the verandah as usual, when we heard footsteps come down the path towards the house, step on to the verandah, continue round the front to the side, then cease suddenly about half-way along. I looked at the boss and his wife, saying, "It sounds as if we've got a visitor. I'll go and see."

'I got up and walked round the corner of the verandah from where I could see the whole length of it, but nobody was there. Puzzled, I went to the front path and looked around, but nobody was in sight, neither was there a car, horse, or pony and trap. I went back to the others and told them. They were as puzzled as I was, because each of us heard those footsteps, firm and heavy as a man's, yet there was nothing there to explain them.'

Charles Hughes of Birmingham and his brothers and sisters were very happy when, as a result of bomb damage to their house during the Second World War, their parents moved to a three-bedroomed house in a new area. The extra space meant that the two daughters had a room to themselves. Their three brothers occupied a small room, while six-month-old baby Carol shared a room with her parents. As far as the boys were concerned life was wonderful, Mr Hughes remembers. Until one night in November 1951.

The three boys shared a large four-poster bed and that night they were startled by the sound of loud knocking coming from the region of the dark attic stairs. It was an eerie and frightening experience. The eldest boy was only nine at the time.

In the welcome light of dawn the three brothers rushed to tell their parents about the knocking noises they had heard and were dismayed to find that no one else in the large family had heard a thing.

Reluctant to return to their bedroom the next night, the boys huddled together for comfort. For the next six years they endured similar disturbances, working out between themselves that the three knocking noises that were involved always started at twenty minutes to eleven each night. The eldest boy had become fifteen. He and his brothers were pleased with themselves because they had learnt to live with the phenomenon, but while they were no longer terrified by it they still found it worrying.

The time came, however, for the house to be demolished to make way for high-rise tower blocks. The boys' mother was sad to leave what she described as a 'very lucky house', but her sons were delighted – it was a relief to them to see the removal van pull up outside.

On the day they moved into their new house, their mother told the family that when she was saying goodbye, a neighbour had told her a secret. As the secret was revealed the hairs on the back of the eldest boy's neck stood on end. According to the neighbour, long before the family had moved in, the house had been occupied by an old man who had made a promise to his very old wife: if she died before him she was to knock on her coffin three times while she was being carried out of the house. He promised her he would then follow her to the grave a short time later.

The wife died at twenty to eleven one night. While her corpse was being taken through the front door to the hearse three loud knocks were heard coming from the dark oak coffin. One week later the old man died, as he had promised.

'This was a traumatic experience for the fifteen-year-old,' adds Mr Hughes, now a carpenter and joiner, 'but he survived pretty well, and is still going strong in 1988!'

GHOSTS HEARD, SMELLED, FELT AND PERCEIVED

Mrs Helen Brighty describes an event that took place at her home in Kent.

'I sat in my living room finishing the last pages of my book about Sir Francis Chichester sailing around the world. My husband and two young children were in bed. I know my husband was not asleep.

'While I was reading I became aware of somebody breathing, a heavy slow sound as if the person was taking air through the mouth. The breathing grew louder and took over the room.

'I sat for a short time, a little puzzled, and felt concerned for my family. I then went into my kitchen adjoining the living room, took a knife from the drawer and went back into the living room thinking somebody had come into the house. The door of the living room leading to the hall was shut tightly and would not open, and the breathing was becoming more regular and louder.

'I was shaken but not really frightened. The breathing seemed to be growing softer until it eventually died away. I put the knife back into the drawer in the kitchen and went back to my seat in the living room. Eventually I rose, went to the door, and this time I was able to open it easily.

'I went to my bed and I did not mention this incident to my husband who was by then asleep.'

Helen Brighty says that the house was quite new at the time, and after four years' occupancy the Brightys sold it. In the twenty years it has existed, the house has been owned by many people.

It is difficult to find a logical explanation for an experience of this kind. Many people will dismiss Mrs Brighty's story as the product of an overheated imagination, or offer the theory that she fell asleep for a minute or two and dreamt the incident. And they might be right to do so. Only readers who have had a comparable experience will sympathize with the bewilderment such an incident causes.

Many contributors have indicated that they had dismissed out of hand stories of the paranormal *until* they had experienced incidents like the one described by Helen Brighty. But it may be difficult even for them to overcome a lifetime of prejudice and accept the possibility that there is an extra dimension to life as we know it. All the same, such people do at least appear to be willing to keep a more open mind on the subject.

Ghostly Odours

Unfamiliar to me personally until very recently, aromas of this kind appear to mark the presence of a ghost, otherwise invisible, and trigger a response ranging from fear to enjoyment (in my own case reassurance) (see p.118).

Paul Helmn bought more than he bargained for when he purchased a run-down farmhouse in Lancashire in 1985. The property had been allowed to fall into a serious state of dilapidation by the previous owner and its tenants. The final occupants had been squatters who had removed the slates from the roof and sold them, along with fireplaces and fittings ripped from the rooms.

Faced with a slateless roof and no water supply, the Helmns decided to demolish the most recent part of the house, built after 1890, and retain the earlier buildings; and they subsequently cleared away tons of rubbish.

One evening, just before sunset, Paul Helmn was laying sewer pipes from the house to a septic tank when he had a strong feeling that he was being observed from behind. He was also aware of the pungent smell of pipe tobacco. At the same time he felt a strange chill in the atmosphere. He made a thorough search of the area, but found no one.

It was the first of a number of visitations by the 'invisible smoker', now identified as 'Henry', who invariably made his presence felt (or smelled), Paul noted, in the vicinity of the barn, built sometime before 1700, or else near the site of the old house, which also dated from that period. (The present house was built between 1700 and 1740.)

Delving into the history of the house, Mr Helmn discovered that it is situated on the old packhorse route between west and east Lancashire. To the north and south of the property, and within a mile or two of the farm, are the remains of the Roman road that ran from Wigan to Lancaster.

Commenting on the presence of the pipe smoker, Paul Helmn was aware that 'He comes and goes, keeping an eye on the old place, which used to be called Wright's Tenement. The former estate agent for the sellers would not visit us, and *never*, he said, would he spend a night there, as the place gave him the creeps, a haunted feeling. He was responsible for the tenants who let the place fall into rack and ruin! So I suppose Henry disliked him.'

After Paul Helmn had encountered 'Henry' several times, some one suggested asking a medium to investigate the situation. The medium duly arrived at the farm one cold day in February 1986. He had been given the address of the property, but no other information.

The medium detected a male presence, whom he described in detail and, like Mrs Bathurst (p. 60) then even sketched the figure he saw. He wrote down and gave to Mr Helmn the information he elicited from the spirit called Henry. This follows, unedited.

> Person more concerned with his earthly environment, spends a lot of time around Valley Farm. Man. Likes Mr Helm's (*sic*) presence, would be willing to share home. Other people [from the spirit world] there, not all the time. Friends and relatives, they are trying to encourage the man to take up permanent residence away from the physical plane. Aware of our thoughts, no objections. Inspired drawing. In spirit world a long time. Died on farm, 92 age. Passed his property to a friend, a male, Henry Becket. Owned cottage himself. Willed to him from his family. In family quite a long time. February passing 25th 1852. Date of birth 1760, December 29th. 1744 house built. Henry born there. Young girl his daughter died before him. He planted a rose in memory of this girl. Magdeleine (*sic*).

There the matter rests. Paul Helmn lives in harmony with his invisible companion, and his wife is quite untroubled by Henry's pipe-smoking presence, as she has never encountered it.

At the time this manuscript was going to press, I myself had a similar experience.

Barrow Court, the home of a friend, is a handsome Elizabethan house situated a few miles from Bristol. It contains imposing panelled rooms and decorative plaster ceilings, and boasts a well-documented history going back to the thirteenth century when the first building on the site, a nunnery, was erected.

Staying there on Saturday 13 May 1989, I was reading in the master bedroom, formerly a Justice room where local cases were heard, when I smelled pipe tobacco wafting all around me, although there was no sign of smoke in the room. My friend joined me after about twenty minutes but he couldn't smell anything. Neither of us smoke, and we were alone in the house.

Left by myself I continued to read, surrounded by the strong aroma, and in my mind's eye (I could see nothing unusual) I was conscious of the presence of a Victorian figure dressed in a black frock coat and trousers, and a grey waistcoat worn with a white stock at the throat. Heavily bearded and with an amiable expression, this masculine presence seemed to offer me reassurance and protection. As a result I felt calm, and in no way worried by the experience.

After twenty minutes or so I left the room to join my friend in the solar at the front of the house, and to my surprise the scent of tobacco smoke followed me along the landing corridor, down the stairs into the main hall, and up another flight of stairs leading to the solar. There it surrounded me again, a very strong aroma, although my friend, sitting next to me on the sofa, could smell nothing at all. After about half an hour it suddenly disappeared – one second it was there, the next it had vanished.

I had always been uneasy and troubled by something intangible when staying at Barrow Court, but the protective presence of the unidentified 'Victorian gentleman' changed my attitude. After the experience I felt accepted by the house and, for the first time, safe within it.

On a holiday tour of Devon accompanied by her friend Stella [name changed] *in the very hot summer of 1976, Mrs Irene Howarth of Yorkshire stayed at King Arthur's Castle, a hotel in legendary Tintagel. Never a sound sleeper, Mrs Howarth was woken up one night at about 2 a.m.*

'I felt this very slight draught of perfume pass my face and vanish through the door. My bed was very close to the door, in a long narrow bedroom with the hand-basin well down on the opposite side. It disturbed me a little because I knew it wasn't my perfume, which is always Estée Lauder. I got up and sniffed my soap, but it wasn't that, and I knew it couldn't be the bathroom because it was much too far away. So I couldn't place it; but mind you I never thought about ghosts, or I would have gone next door to my friend.'

The memory of the incident remained vividly in Irene Howarth's mind for the rest of her holiday. After she had been home for some weeks she happened to read something about ghostly manifestation by aroma, and for the first time linked that knowledge to her own experience in Tintagel. Did that whiff of perfume passing in the night indicate a ghostly presence in King Arthur's Castle? All she can add to the story is that, for some unknown reason, her friend Stella had also had a very unsettled night – but in Mrs Howarth's opinion Tintagel 'was enough to unsettle anybody!'

Mrs Jean Riding is a retired nursing sister living in a small cottage in a village in Lancashire. The village was purpose-built around 1840 to provide homes for mill workers. To this day the houses bear names related to their former occupants: Cloggers Cot (shoemaker), Readers Cot (schoolmaster), Drapers Cot, Bakers Cot and Apple Cot. Jean Riding describes her cottage, and its aromatic inhabitant.

'As far as I can discover my home was never used for any kind of business, yet I have something here. Periodically there is a strong sweet smell of what I would describe as fudge or toffee apples, most often apparent in my bedroom situated upstairs in the front of the house.

'When it appears, it may be around for days or weeks, but it can be absent for similar periods. I have only smelled it downstairs occasionally. A few weeks ago my daughter was visiting me. After I had gone to bed, she remained in the sitting room watching TV. She told me next morning the smell was all around her when she was sitting on the settee.

'Whatever it is, it is not malevolent. I've christened it "Mr Candyman" and I say hello to him when I smell the sweet aroma. The only time I've felt uneasy was on an occasion when I was cleaning out drawers in the bedroom. My Siamese cat, Kimi, was sitting on the bed watching me. Suddenly I heard her purring very loudly. When I looked at her she was lying on her back as though someone was tickling her tummy. When I called out her name she stopped purring and sat up.

'The lady I bought the house from was "frightened of something she couldn't explain". Personally, I felt that this was going to be a happy home right from the start.

'Well, there you are, is it a ghost or not? Whatever it is, the sweet smell, the two cats and I live very happily here.'

Another atmospheric condition is occasionally reported in connection with these experiences: vapours.

Mrs Karen Alderson of Avon tells of her mother's experience after the death of her husband.

'My father recently died very suddenly, an event which came as a tremendous shock to my mother, sister and myself. He died late on Sunday evening in January [1988], so very little sleep was had by anyone on that night.

'However, the following night my mother went to bed in their room and, waking in the early hours, thought the house was on fire because the room was full of mist just hanging in the air.

'Not being able to smell smoke and feeling really rather calm (and not hysterical as one normally would be if one thought one's house was on fire) she put on her bedside lamp and instantly all the mist disappeared. The dog who sleeps in the same room didn't even wake.

'My mother isn't at all the sort of person given to hallucinations and being taken in by anything paranormal. She has a very strong character and is most determined. It was quite a few days before she related this experience to us, thinking we would suspect her of being a bit loopy!'

However, the same smoky, mist-like substance seen by Mrs Alderson's mother in the house in Avon also features in the following story.

Anthony Vardy of Derbyshire, an accounts office supervisor, writes:

'For many years my parents looked after a man who suffered with a mental disorder and was unable to look after himself properly. In due course he died in the house, and then in 1979 my father died, and in 1980 my mother died. I was left with the problem of sorting out the house. My wife tells me that often a figure could be seen standing behind me, watching me as I sorted out, say, a chest of drawers. The figure would smile and then pass through the door back on to the landing and disappear.

'One evening I had to go up to the house on my own to repair a light fitting downstairs. Just as I had finished there was the most unearthly crash from upstairs and something told me to get out very, very quickly. I did this, slamming the door behind me. I did not stop shivering and I did not get warm again until I got into Belper nearly four miles away.

'I had for a period of time someone who slept at the old house mainly to protect it prior to my selling it, and also to help him by offering him somewhere to stay. He knew nothing of the history of the house, but was often woken up in the night with a feeling of unease, to see a figure standing by his bed, and to see what looked like smoke filling the room.'

A common experience in connection with ghosts is what feels like a sudden chill, as we have seen elsewhere.

Eva Barnes 'the Poetess' (see p. 87) writes:

'There is a ghost in the bakery where my husband works. His boss won't believe it because he hasn't seen it. My husband and other workers have. The ghost appears in a grey form.'

She thinks that the ghost was associated with the building long before it became a bakery. Over a hundred years ago it was used as a towel-weaving mill and a young man is believed to have died on one of the machines in the factory. Her husband senses a marked drop in temperature whenever the ghost appears in the bakery.

Ghosts Felt

An alarming sensation connected with ghosts is that of being touched, gripped or shaken by unseen hands.

Mary Outhwaite (see p. 32) has had a number of odd experiences. The one described here took place after she had moved to Devon with her husband, daughter and parents. They lived in a large house built only fifteen years earlier, on the edge of Dartmoor.

'My parents occupied the upstairs section and we lived downstairs with Lucy, aged three, having a bedroom at the top of the stairs. The first strange thing about the house was that everything started to go right for us – we had been having some pretty bad luck.

'I had always wanted to play the piano and John bought me one with which I was very thrilled. I started to have lessons. My parents found all the scales etc. very tedious and once a fortnight they used to go and visit friends for the day; so I spent that time practising.

'One summer's afternoon I was sitting alone in the house. Lucy was at school, my parents were away and I was playing the piano – a piece of Chopin, a musician I greatly admired.

'Suddenly I felt a poke in my back and turned round quickly. The french window was open, but there was no one there. It happened again and again, always when I was alone, always on a Thursday, always when I was playing the piano. I never saw anything, but just felt this strong pressure on my back.'

Mary Outhwaite was heartened to learn that she was not the only one to suffer the inexplicable poke in the back by an invisible hand.

'My Aunt Alice also experienced it when she was walking along a corridor in the house with my mother following her. She suddenly stopped and asked my mother why she had poked her in the back at that moment. My mother was carrying a tea tray at the time and could not possibly have done so.'

Jacqui Hine is a freelance cookery writer who lives in Surrey. With her two young sons she was invited to stay with friends who owned a small hotel in Batheaston, just outside Bath. It was summer time, and the two children slept with their mother in a room at the far end of the corridor.

'On the second night I just couldn't get to sleep and didn't want to disturb the children with a light. Eventually . . . I snuggled down on my side and slid my left hand under the pillow, a natural position for me.

'As I slid my hand under the pillow it was held by another hand – a warm, chubby, motherly hand which held mine loosely, in a comforting manner. It was a very real hand and I had no thoughts or conception of anything beyond the elbow. It never occurred to me that there was a person beyond the hand. My eyes were open and I could see the room, but I was paralysed.

'I took a deep breath and told myself to relax, then moved my legs. My hand was still being held. I then slowly withdrew my hand and rolled on to my back. I felt no other "presence" in the room.'

When she related the story of the disembodied hand to her host and hostess next morning, they were not surprised. Jacqui Hine's friend told her that she often felt the presence of a little girl watching her when she made the beds in that particular room, and she and her husband regularly sensed the presence of people in the hotel when all the guests were out and no one was about.

'Somehow the "motherly" hand and the little girl seemed to make sense,' concluded Jacqui Hine, adding that this was the only experience she has ever had of anything remotely connected with the paranormal.

Miss Brunell [name changed] *is a retired ladies' outfitter now living in Somerset. She told me this:*

'Approximately ten years ago I lived in a very old cottage adjoining a large house which was originally an old coach house where travellers stopped on their journeys to rest their horses and to have food and drink. My cottage was originally the stables.

'One night I was awakened by my bedroom door slowly opening.

A figure draped in black and carrying a torch gradually moved towards me. I was terrified. I sat up in bed and screamed. (My friend's bedroom in the large house was beyond the dividing wall and my screams wakened her.)

'I threw out my arms to push the apparition away, and in so doing knocked over my tea-maker, water and milk. The figure then turned and slowly walked out the door.

'On another occasion when asleep I felt someone shaking me as though to waken me. On both these occasions it was very real and I have never forgotten the sensation. I must admit I was not so happy living in the cottage after this and soon moved away, although I understand the present occupants have also reported unusual happenings.'

Mrs Margaret Hopwood and her husband live in Tyne and Wear and were looking forward to visiting Mrs Hopwood's widowed aunt. On the first night after their arrival, the travellers went upstairs to bed, tired, happy and looking forward to a good night's rest. But that, alas, was not to be.

'We were kept awake all night long,' Mrs Hopwood recalls. 'It was just like cobwebs going over and over our faces.'

In addition to the sensation of sticky cobwebs engulfing them, Margaret Hopwood was beleaguered by a movement which she could only describe as that of a cat jumping on her bed. But there was no cat in the room! Terrified first by the cobwebs and then by the invisible cat, Mrs Hopwood was profoundly upset.

'My husband tried to console me, but I was afraid the cat would get on him too!'

Next morning the couple went downstairs, exhausted by the events of the previous night, which they described to their hostess. She told her niece that the room in which they had slept was the room in which her husband had died, and it was there that he had been laid out and placed in his coffin.

Shortly afterwards, Mrs Hopwood's aunt continued, while the family were all sitting downstairs, they had heard an awful bang. When they went up to the room (empty, apart from the body) they had found that the lid had somehow lifted itself off the coffin, and was lying on the floor. As everybody in the house was gathered together downstairs, no one could offer a rational explanation for the removal of the coffin lid.

After hearing this tale the Hopwoods were not prepared to endure another night in the haunted room.

'Needless to say my husband and I left as soon as we had had breakfast. This is really a true story and one awful experience.'

Sensitivity to the supernatural may run in Margaret Hopwood's family. See page 107 for a description of her sister's experience following the death of her son.

Mrs Hopwood is not alone in reporting the sensation of having a ghost cat landing on her bed. Five years ago James N. Byrne of Tyne and Wear was living alone with only his beloved cat for company. To his great distress the cat died.

'About eight or nine months after my cat's death I was lying in bed thinking about papering the walls of the front stairs when I felt the cat jump on to the bed. Funny, but I was fully aware of everything: how he slowly stepped over my ankles, turned round and slowly settled down and started purring. I could feel his weight. I could hear him purring, but I could not see him. This lasted for about twelve to twenty seconds.

'The second time he visited me I was sleeping in the room in which he died. This was approximately four months later. I was awake at about 2.30 a.m. looking at the moon and stars when bang! I felt him land on my legs. It was so sudden that I started kicking out with my feet as I shot to a sitting position in bed, then he was gone.'

James Byrne's experience is matched in the following story, sent to me by David H. Palmer of Northamptonshire.

As a teenager he lived with his family in an old farmhouse built in 1694, the home of a tabby cat called Tiger. Early one morning when he was sixteen, he was woken up by a cat which came into his bedroom and walked all over him as he lay in bed.

When he got up he told his mother how Tiger had woken him. But the family soon established that it could not have been Tiger who had been in his bedroom that morning because he was known to be somewhere else at the time.

The ghost cat continued to visit David Palmer. It appeared so often that he began to keep a written record of its nocturnal visits. Like James Byrne, David Palmer never saw it, but always felt it jump on his bed and walk all over him. Fearing ridicule if he mentioned the matter, he kept the information to himself, recording the visits of the cat over a period of twenty years. On average it called on him four times a year.

When he moved to a new house, he wondered if the cat would accompany him. After he had been living in the new building for a year, the ghostly visitor called on him. Once more, he decided to keep a written record of the visits.

'It happened three times. The last time something said to me that it would not visit me again – that was twenty-two years ago.'

And David Palmer never again felt the ghost cat jumping on to his bed. But he raised an interesting point: that part of the old house in which he slept as a boy has now been pulled down. Was the demolition of the cat's old home connected with its failure to appear again on his bed?

Presences

Ghosts may be 'felt' in intangible ways, as if they are presences, picked up by some sixth sense.

Mrs S. M. Woodyatt of Devon has already reported the experience of some friends (see p. 20). She herself has always been very sensitive to the atmosphere in houses. During the Second World War her husband was in India when her father-in-law, who had broken his wrist and could not handle his car, invited her to drive him to Colyton in Devon and stay with him for a week's holiday in a guest house.

'We duly arrived at Colyton Cottage, a delightful L-shaped thatched cottage looking beautiful on a golden summer's evening. I carried the luggage in, and my left arm suddenly went dead up to the shoulder.

'My father-in-law was given a little room at the back of the cottage and I was shown into a large room in the front with an enormous old-fashioned fireplace, and a door next to it. The moment I entered the room I realized I couldn't stay in it, as I felt it was haunted. The landlady said that that was nonsense, and that there was nothing at all in the room.

'I asked her particularly about the door and she assured me it was just a cupboard. I voiced my fears to my father-in-law (who claimed to be psychic) but he said I was being foolish and there was nothing at all to worry about.

'We went down to dinner and again I went stone cold, so I asked the landlady to tell me whether the house was haunted, as I felt I could probably cope with it if I knew what it was. She eventually conceded that there were a few Elizabethan spirits about, but that they were perfectly friendly. My father-in-law still refused to change rooms so I went to bed; I got under the blankets and felt absolutely rigid with terror.

'A long while afterwards (perhaps I had fallen asleep and had woken up again) I became conscious of the sound of bells tolling across the meadow, which was very strange and most unusual as it was wartime [when church bells were silent] and there seemed to be no explanation for this sound. On going down to breakfast I told my father-in-law that unless he would agree to change rooms I would have to go home. He refused, so I packed up and left, asking him to try and find out more about the house. Two weeks later he wrote to me saying he had managed to get the whole story from the landlady.

'Apparently my bedroom had been the court room for Judge Jeffreys [best known for his infamous conduct of the Bloody Assizes of 1685 at which many of Monmouth's supporters against James II were tried and hanged] when he was holding Assizes in the area. The door in my room (which I had tried to open and could not), had been the entrance down some stairs to the condemned men's cell; the prisoners were hanged outside my window.'

About ten years later, when Mrs Woodyatt and her husband had decided to leave their home in Berkshire and go and live in Devon, they invited a young couple, new to their village, to supper. Mrs Woodyatt discovered that the husband, Richard [*name changed*], had lived in Devon as a boy, in a cottage called Colyton Cottage; it turned out to be the very one she had stayed in. Mrs Woodyatt immediately asked him if it was haunted.

'He said that it definitely was. They had had a French governess who had run screaming from the house never to be seen again. He described the bedroom I had occupied and said it was used as his night nursery when he was a little boy, and used to have a grand piano across the door I couldn't open. He described how he had seen a ghostly figure walk through the grand piano but he said he had never felt frightened in the room.'

Mrs Mary Outhwaite encountered her first ghost when she was in her mid-twenties (see p. 32). The unnerving episode described here occurred a little later, when she was living in Croydon.

One day Mary met a young man called Winston [*name changed*] who, only two weeks earlier, had lost his mother to whom he was deeply attached. His father, a doctor, had died when he was three years old and his mother had remarried. Her second husband was also a doctor who lived in a large and handsome house in Coulsden, in which he ran his practice. She and her son had joined him there after the marriage and it was to this house that Winston invited Mary when she offered to help him complete urgent paperwork after his mother's death.

For five or six weeks Mary visited the house regularly, typing letters and generally assisting Winston in clerical tasks.

'One evening we went up to the house intending to cook some supper and to finish off the typing. We were in the kitchen and Winston went into the hall to answer the telephone, leaving me alone in the kitchen holding a piece of raw steak in my hand, which dripped blood into the sink.

'Suddenly I felt this terrible feeling of hatred being directed at me as though his mother was there despising and loathing me since I came from a very ordinary background, not moneyed and privileged like her son. I was aware of a sensation of opposition and hatred that I was seeing him, and it was frighteningly apparent that I was just not good enough for him.'

Mary froze, holding the bloody steak at the sink until she felt impelled to say out loud: 'Don't worry, I will never marry your son!'

'The terrible feeling then gradually vanished, and Winston came back into the room.'

On an earlier occasion Winston had taken Mary on a tour of the large house. 'When we came to his mother's room he walked in expecting me to follow, but it was as if there was a barrier across the door, a strange and horrible feeling': Mary could not enter the room.

'We went out together for a long time and Winston did eventually propose to me; but although I wanted to accept, I just felt I couldn't. Eventually he married someone else, but the marriage was not happy and they divorced. He remarried and had two children, both of whom were deformed. His whole life seemed full of unhappiness, broken asunder.'

Presences, suspected or sometimes not suspected, may be caught by a camera.

In Old Deer, near Mintlaw in Aberdeenshire, some thirty miles west of Peterhead on the east coast, lie the ruins of Deer Abbey, originally founded by Cistercian monks. Not much is known of the history of the abbey, but apparently in the sixteenth century the community numbered about twelve. The ghostly form of a female figure dressed in grey has been seen in the area from time to time. Locally she is known as the 'Grey Lady'. It is said that she was romantically involved with a monk at the abbey, and later disappeared mysteriously.

Friends of Mrs Ann Wood of Banffshire visited Old Deer in September 1987, Mrs Wood says that Tom Banks [name changed] *is a keen amateur photographer.*

Enchanted by the autumn colours in a birch wood near the abbey ruins, next to an old graveyard, Mr Banks wandered round taking photographs of the landscape. He was accompanied by his wife.

When his prints had been developed, Mrs Banks was surprised to see a figure lurking in the background of one of the photographs. Looking at the picture more closely, Mrs Banks suggested to her husband that he had accidently taken a photograph of the ghost of the Grey Lady! They were both astounded, because there had been no one visible in the viewfinder when the picture was taken.

But there does seem to be the image of a woman in the centre of the photograph, between two V-shaped trunks of silver birches.

Is the figure the result of a double exposure? Is it some form of chemical reaction, or a fault in the film? Or is it indeed the image of the Grey Lady of Old Deer?

John D. Aldous of Essex is a qualified surveyor, and so a member of a scientifically based profession. Mr Aldous had regarded the paranormal with suspicion. He offers this information to provide 'a background to an event I experienced and which shocked me into a more sympathetic approach to metaphysics'.

'About forty years ago I was employed as an assistant in the Architects' Department of a local authority and as such belonged to the appropriate trade union, NALGO. They ran their own holiday centre (and still do) at Croyde Bay, North Devon. As the West Country has always been my favourite holiday area in England I soon took advantage of the centre.'

John Aldous and his friend Richard [*name changed*] took a holiday at Croyde. It was excellent weather and mid-week they travelled by bus to Lee near Ilfracombe.

'A perfect day, sunshine, white-crested breakers dashing on a rock-bound coast – click went the camera,' (an old Box Brownie, he recalls: he had reason to remember using it).

'One week later, back at work and the holiday only a pleasant memory, on my way to tea at Martin and Mary's [*names changed*] (my married friends) I collected the photographs from the chemist.

'When I arrived at their home Mary was alone, so over a cup of tea we decided to look at my photographs – my usual mediocre standard of typical holiday subjects, until we came to the one taken at Lee Bay. We looked at each other and again and again at the photograph. There were the waves dashing on the rocks as background, but in the foreground was a massive mooring post and imprinted on the post, as clear as any photograph of a living being, were two villainous faces, one below the other, wearing headscarves absolutely typical of the North African pirates. The faces were so clear, and even now I can see them in my imagination or memory. I must admit both Mary and I were a bit scared. So much so we agreed not to show the photo to her husband as he was and is of a rather nervous disposition.

'I had little sleep that night. I took the photo to work but decided to show it to no one else. Eventually I tore it to shreds and put it in the waste-paper basket.'

There was a sequel to John Aldous's story: 'I was talking to the curator of the little museum at Ilfracombe about ten years ago. Without prompting she told me how North African pirates used to lie in wait in the Bristol channel ready to hit . . . the more ponderous merchantmen. The lateen rig of the pirates' boats enabled them to sail much closer to the south-westerlies and thus make their getaway with the loot.'

Mr Aldous says that his friend Mary, the only witness to his story of the photograph of the villainous pirates, is willing to confirm his story, and he ends his account with this comment: 'I still believe in rational explanations, especially since Einstein has taken us so far beyond Newton, and we know that each particle in space has its own clock. Perhaps time gets displaced sometimes.'

The view that our conception of time may need revising is one commonly held by contributors seeking a rational explanation for apparently inexplicable events.

Mrs S. M. Woodyatt was puzzled by one of her photographs, too, but her camera was aimed at a Canadian scene.

Some years ago Mrs Woodyatt and her friend Rosalind toured Canada by car. At one stage they were driving along a lonely stretch of road which felt strange and desolate to Mrs Woodyatt, who stopped the car to take photographs of the endless empty space, 'so that people at home could see that there were miles and miles of nothing still left in the world.'

The road stretched ahead for miles, empty as far as the eye could see. Surveying the road through the viewfinder, Mrs Woodyatt took several photographs and had them processed into slides which she subsequently projected on a screen.

'To my utter astonishment there was a figure walking down that road and it appeared to have an aura around it, almost a fluorescence; it looked rather like the figure of an old Indian chieftain in all his war feathers.

'I mentioned the matter to an old doctor friend who was a very good photographer, telling him that I thought I had taken a picture of a ghost. He was sceptical but on looking at the slide he agreed it was very strange and that there was certainly a figure there. He suggested that I should get it enlarged but this proved to be too expensive so I did nothing about it.

'However, at the time I was a sort of seaside landlady doing bed and breakfast, and a very nice family came to stay. It transpired that the husband was a director of Kodak. I mentioned my photograph to him and he asked to see it, together with the slides from the whole roll of film in case he could detect a fault in the film or camera. He also thought it most extraordinary, agreed there was something there, and asked permission to take the film back to Kodak to have it enlarged.

'This he did and it was examined closely by all the experts at Kodak who could find no faults on the film or with the camera, and could not account for the image of the Indian at all. There seemed to be no logical explanation.'

Possession

'Possession' of the body by an unseen force occurs from time to time when an individual loses physical control and is 'possessed'. This must be the most frightening of all sensory experiences.

Mrs Mary Jacobsen of Tyneside wrote down her experience immediately after the event. 'I was so shattered,' she confesses, 'that I had to record what took place, without any thought of ever showing it to anyone. I sincerely hope that such a brush with evil – and it was evil – never touches me again.'

'The day was beautiful. Vivian and I started out for East Woodburn in the highest of spirits. It is always nice to get away from the "brick jungle" and out into the country. Our route took us over the Whannie Moors. Clouds were scudding across a blue sky and all was right with the world. We arrived at East Woodburn full of the joys of life.

'After being entertained by a dear old lady of eighty-eight we went along to see the village show. Set out in the village hall were all the exhibits on which much love and care had been lavished: leeks looking more like ship's masts, carrots of immense proportions, flowers lovingly arranged, jams and cakes displayed with pride. Children were running round, parents greeting one another, the vicar beaming proudly, and outside the local men were throwing horse shoes over a stick in a sort of quoits game. Then it was back to the house and a lovely country tea by a roaring fire. Our hosts packed the boot of our little car with farm produce and we started back on our journey home, a journey which I am not likely to forget.

'By this time it was raining slightly, a fact which didn't worry me; I've driven through all sorts of conditions and the prospect of driving over a few miles of lonely moorland did not bother me in the slightest.

'Vivian and I chatted away, when suddenly I was conscious of something beside the car – I had a wild desire to accelerate to get away from it; but common sense told me to keep to a reasonable speed as the road over the moors is wild, and there are no cat's-eyes to guide one. The feeling of tension mounted within me and I felt the hair on my scalp tingling; but at least I was still driving the car.

'We did not talk; Vivian fell silent, smoking furiously. I tried to fight off the rising sense of fear – to tell myself that I was just imagining it all – when suddenly the thing was in the car.

'A sense of evil pervaded me. "It" seemed to be laughing, as it quietly took over the wheel. My hands tightened, attempting desperately to keep the car on the road. The battle was on. I prayed as I have never prayed before. "God, what are you doing to me? We will be killed!" But the grip on the wheel just became stronger, forcing us into the side of the road.

'I managed to stop the car, making the excuse that I could not see very well. The Thing just sat there; I sensed that it was waiting – there was nothing to do but go on. Trying desperately to get a grip of myself, I started the car.

'Now, my car had easy steering, but the wheel was held tight with a demoniacal hold. It took all my strength to keep us out of the wild moorland ditches. I never thought that one could fight it out with something one could not see, but I felt it was the Thing or me. By this time my hands were wet with sweat and my body icy cold, although the heater was blasting forth.

'The headlights swung drunkenly from side to side as I tried to get the better of the Thing. The thought uppermost in my mind was "God, I've heard of queer things happening to people, but it can't be happening to me!" The Thing was gloating over my terror. I tried I tried to talk to Vivian but the words struck in my throat; my mouth was dry with fear.

'By this time I wasn't driving. I was just holding the wheel. The stupid thought came into my mind that if the local policeman saw me he would breathalyse me on the spot. I wish to God that there had been a policeman there – it might have brought back an element of everyday sense.

'By this time my feeling of the evil in the car had risen to the point where I felt my faith in God was being put to the test. My feet were paralysed. I kept my foot on the brake, but still the car went on swaying from side to side. I no longer had control – the Thing just drove. I didn't dare say a word to Vivian, who fumbled with her seat belt, a thing she has never done before in all the miles we have driven together.

'Never have I thought that anyone can be possessed – but I was at that time possessed by the Thing which had got into my car, and me.

'As the lights of Newcastle Airport came into view, suddenly the Thing left us – the wheel became loose and I was driving. I was my old confident self, although badly shaken.

'This experience is true, and it happened to me. I don't know any ghostly presences on the Whannies and nobody has told me of any happenings there, and I don't dare ask.'

An article by Charlotte Rastan published in the Independent *on 13 February 1989 featured comparable incidents on Dartmoor.*

'The road between Two Bridges and Postbridge slices across the very heart of Dartmoor, through some of its most barren and beautiful countryside . . . In such country it comes as no surprise to learn that one of the chief hazards of the Two Bridges–Postbridge road is not the freezing fog which can descend like a blanket from nowhere, cutting off travellers, but a large, hairy pair of disembodied hands which wrench motorists off the road, sometimes to their deaths.

'One of the first recorded victims was Dr Ernest Helby, prison doctor at nearby Princetown who, in 1921, was travelling along the road on a motorbike, ferrying the deputy governor's two children in his side-car. Suddenly he yelled to the children "Jump!" and the motorbike swerved violently off the road, killing him instantly. The children survived to report an extraordinary tale: just after the accident they had seen a huge pair of hairy hands on the handlebars.

'Sceptics say it was probably his driving gloves – but that would not explain an incident two months after Dr Helby's death in which a young army officer was flung from his motorbike on the same stretch of road. The *Daily Mail* of 14 October 1921 reports him saying: "Believe it or not, something drove me off the road. A pair of hands closed over mine . . . large, muscular, hairy hands." There is now no trace of the officer, to whom the newspaper refers only as "Captain M", but the story of the Hairy Hands is far from being a dead and dusty legend; there are people living on Dartmoor today who have had the unfortunate experience of a hairy handshake.

'Theo Brown is an author and folklorist who lives in Broadclyst, on the north-east edge of the moor. Theo was just nine when, in 1924, she and her parents pitched their caravan at Powder Mills, the site of a former gunpowder factory, close to the haunted road. One night her mother was awoken by a scratching sound and saw a large, bristly hand clawing its way up the side of the caravan. Convinced its intent was evil, she prayed for protection and slowly the hand sank down out of sight.

'"People who have these rather alarming experiences don't like to write them down," Theo says. "They think people would laugh."

'Many years after the event, she persuaded her mother to record the grisly encounter, and she now has her handwritten testimony, but she never saw the malevolent mitt herself . . . It could be said that Theo Brown, as a folklorist, has a vested interest in the story, but the same is not true of the Dartmoor prison officer who recently had a wrestling match with the Hairy Hands and described it as "the most frightening experience of my life". The officer, who asked not to be named, was driving along the road when he felt a massive force wrenching the steering wheel towards the ditch. He fought with it for some time until he finally regained control.'

Northumberland and Devon are hundreds of miles apart, and yet the descriptions of the unseen force that took control of vehicles on isolated stretches of road running across barren moors in each county are surprisingly similar.

In June 1975 Lionel Geoffrey Jaekel was paying his first visit to the Orkneys when, quite by chance, he stumbled upon haunted territory.

'On the Sunday after my arrival I set out for a walk along the cliff beyond Stromness (on Orkney) where I was staying. It was a cloudy day with only intermittent sunshine. The area was totally deserted.'

The isolation did not worry him. He stepped out confidently, determined to enjoy the wild beauty of the island. He followed a path along the sheer rocky cliffs rising straight from the sea, which varied in height from 360 feet at Black Craig, the highest point, to about forty feet.

He walked slowly for about half an hour before suddenly becoming aware of a peculiar atmosphere he could only describe as one of complete and utter depression.

'But what really scared me was a feeling of compulsion to go to the cliff edge and look over. I can't stand heights and knew that if I did so I'd get an attack of vertigo and go over. I had literally to fight to keep about ten yards from the edge.'

The nightmare of the compulsive force which appeared to be propelling him to the edge of the cliff continued for about half a mile before he walked out of the affected area when, to his immense relief, it evaporated.

He continued his walk along the cliffs in relative peace, but was nervous about his return. It proved to be uncomplicated. 'I walked about a hundred yards away from the cliff edge by the same route, but without any trouble whatsoever.'

On leaving the Orkneys and returning home, Mr Jaekel could not shake off the memory of his terrifying experience and resolved to find out more about the area. His research revealed that that particular clifftop area was haunted.

'Over the following weeks this business played on my mind so much I wrote to the *Orcadian*, the local newspaper, to see if it were known if anyone else had had a similar experience.'

He was intrigued by the response. 'Apparently somewhere about the 1860s two farmworkers at a certain farm in the area (which I could see away on my right, the only building visible) fell out over a woman, and one killed the other with a hay flail. He hid the body until dark and then slung it over the back of a white horse, led it to the cliff edge and heaved it over.

'I had a reply to my letter published in the newspaper from a Mr Terry [*name changed*] stating that a visitor to Orkney in the July following my own visit had been scared out of his wits by the appearance of a white horse, which vanished at the cliff edge. Without seeing anything, I was thoroughly frightened.'

Blood

What appears to be human blood occasionally signals the presence of some ghostly activity. It is a disturbing experience for people who see it.

Eric B. Raybould, an ex-RAF pilot, and retired management consultant, lives in Cornwall. In his first letter to me he wrote: 'I enclose an account of the one experience of my life for which I have never been able to imagine any explanation compatible with the clear and contradictory evidence . . . Every detail of the A25 ghost is as clear now as on the day it occurred.'

'In the sixties I lived in the southern outskirts of London. I was employed by a major chemical company, usually in a consultancy role to work with teams set up to solve specific technical problems. Thus my attitude could reasonably claim to be scientific and objective. I had little belief in magic. My duties frequently involved travel around the country to other company sites, and whenever the journey was short and the weather favourable, I much preferred to travel by motorcycle. This has a bearing on what follows because from the saddle one has a completely unimpaired view and feels much closer to one's environment. Sounds and smells are much sharper.

'One of my regular routes was along the A25, that narrow, winding, congested but very pretty road that runs through a whole series of picturesque villages below the North Downs between Reigate and Guildford. It was a fine dry afternoon in early summer. Just beyond Westcott in the Dorking direction the road rises slightly with scrubland and a small disused sandpit on the right. To the left are widely spaced houses of the well-to-do, set back from the road in mature gardens. The boundary fences are again set somewhat back from the footpath bordering the road on that side.

'Half-way up the rise I came to a queue of slow-moving vehicles. I wondered which of the usual causes was to blame, most probably a farm tractor, possibly roadworks or perhaps an accident. I moved out to the middle of the road for a better view, but the traffic continued unbroken over the crest of the rise, so I dropped back, intending to wait for the better view from the top of the hill.

'I then noticed some fifty yards ahead a woman vigorously sweeping the pavement. She was very unremarkable. Middle-aged, tall, slim and dowdily dressed as many affluent countrywomen are when busy in the garden. A moment later the reason for the traffic hold-up became clearer. A few feet out from the kerb where she was sweeping lay a huge patch of fresh blood, quite two feet across, certainly a pint of spillage and probably more. A trail led to the kerb and on to the pavement as if the victim had been dragged from the road.

'The sheer volume of blood was shocking. It must have been a deer or a pig or a very large dog – or a person. The horror of the sight was slightly blunted by the curious lack of the usual signs of an accident: no shards of broken glass, no twisted chromium trim, no deposit of fine powdered mud from crushed wheel arches; no skid marks on the road or the verges, no police, no ambulance, nothing – except the blood.

'And then an uncomfortable thought struck me. I had clearly seen at least a dozen cars ahead of me pass through the position of the blood and yet it had been completely fresh and undisturbed. Normally one would expect tyre marks leaving a repeated pattern like a revolving printing wheel. It was not impossible for every car to straddle the patch; but they were too close, nose to tail, to get advance warning, and I had not seen any take avoiding action.

'Once past the incident, the traffic accelerated off towards Dorking, leaving me behind to go slower and slower as I tried to work out what had happened. A few hundred yards later I had come to a halt, much exercised in my mind as the old writers used to say. The cold horror of the blood was giving way to bewilderment. I could propose no scenario that would be compatible with all the evidence. There was nothing for it but to return; easily enough done, even in such a narrow road, when on two wheels.

'I was back at the scene within five minutes of the first occasion. I almost missed it. There was no woman sweeping the path and no patch of blood. I stared in disbelief. It must be the wrong house. I drove on, right to the outskirts of Westcott before turning back again. Approaching from the original direction I knew I had not been mistaken. I stopped and got off. I examined the road surface closely for fifty yards in each direction. It was bone dry with not the slightest stain. The pavement was coarse asphalt and would have been impossible to clean in a few minutes, if at all. The gutter was dry and colour-free. There were no signs of movement in the house or garden.

'I lacked the effrontery to knock on the door and inquire whether there had been an accident when there obviously hadn't. Or even worse, I might be intruding just after a loved member of the household had met a violent death. So I just restarted my machine and continued slowly homeward.

'And there the matter rests. Some romantic epilogue would be pleasing – that I saw a glimpse of some past carnage. Not all that I witnessed belonged to the same standard of reality, however. The location was absolutely real and has changed very little some twenty-five years later. You can easily identify it from this narrative.

'I cannot now believe that the blood and the woman existed on that summer day. The line of cars ahead of me? I am not sure. They all slowed down to a walking pace at the spot when the view from the top of the hill immediately afterwards revealed no acceptable reason for doing so. They must have seen something.'

After many years of considered thought, and in spite of his scientific and objective attitude, Eric Raybould concludes that 'The supernatural is more likely than the miraculous cleansing of the road in five minutes in spite of passing traffic.'

George Hauton of Lincolnshire is an ex-Hell's Angel. He is also a packing-line operative with aspirations to be a writer. He tells this story in his own words:

'On the A607 about seven miles south of the city of Lincoln stands a little church on a hillside overlooking the Witham and Trent Valleys . . . There is nothing unusual about this church from the outside . . . but it is supposedly haunted, by whom I never really found out.

'I was a Hell's Angel at the time (before becoming a born again

Christian) and nothing nor anybody ever scared me! But this tiny church did – I wasn't scared, but petrified.

'One November night in 1971 I and several of my biker friends decided to investigate this place after getting fed up to the teeth by all the stories we had heard from mates who lived near the village and who had dared us to go inside.

'The night we picked was rather cold and cloudy but with no trace of any fog you associate with ghost stories. After going to a nearby pub to get our courage up, we parked our motorcycles by the church hedge and crept inside the building.

'In those days it was very rare to find a holy building locked and we had no trouble at getting inside. While one of our number decided to try and find some Communion wine to drink, the rest of us climbed the tower to where it was said that the ghost haunted.

'Half-way up, one of my mates began swearing loudly as he thought he had put his hand in some wet mildewed stuff but when I switched a pocket torch on, to my abject horror I found it was blood trickling down the steps.

'I said to one of the lads in front that we ought to get him to a doctor, thinking he had caught his hands on something sharp and torn the flesh open. When we stopped to examine ourselves, however, there wasn't a trace of any injury, and the blood was still trickling slowly down the stone staircase.

'As one, we all panicked and in the rush to get out of the building I dropped my crash helmet. After about ten minutes of agonizing, and with all the gang reluctantly following behind me, I went to retrieve it.

'I think that night was the worst of my life and I was literally shaking with fear. I felt sick and weak and I couldn't stop my legs from shaking. Worse still, there was a freezing sensation down the length of my spine.

'I found the helmet all right but nothing else! Despite a hurried search with a couple of heavy duty torches, no trace of that oozing blood could be found anywhere – although we bravely climbed to our last known position in the tower. Consequently, a very frightened gang of Hell's Angels soon departed at high speed from that church.'

Part Three

HAUNTINGS

Haunted buildings are the commonest source of ghost stories, ranging from new council flats to ancient country houses, and from shops, offices and factories to theatres and churches.

Wider areas such as complete towns, airfields, stretches of roads and parts of the high seas have also been found to be haunted.

Historic houses

Britain appears to have more ghosts per square mile than any other European country. Many of them inhabit ancient abbeys, castles, and manor houses, which acquire the reputation of being haunted after repeated reports of sightings. It is fertile ground for myths, and it is a mistake to take too literally the traditional historical connections frequently bestowed on ghosts which are said to be those of illustrious former residents.

Simon Reynolds is an art dealer who lives in London (see p. 28). As a student at Heidelberg University, he took the opportunity of travelling widely in Germany. On one occasion he visited Schloss Neufraunhofen in Bavaria, where his host introduced him to his brother-in-law, Count Preising.

The count, who was then in his mid-thirties, told Simon Reynolds about his student days, when he was befriended by Prince Maria Emanuel of Saxony, the eldest grandson of the last King of Saxony. In 1944 the count stayed with the prince and his father, Friedrich Christian, Duke of Saxony, at their hunting castle, Schloss Moritzburg near Meissen.

The visit was to be an informal affair, the boys looking after themselves, as the entire castle staff was away contributing to the German war effort, and had left the duke and his son virtually isolated in this vast and historic royal palace.

The duke himself met the boys at the local station and, on arrival at the castle, the party of three entered the Great Hall. Lying face downwards on the floor was a small picture. The duke stopped abruptly, picked it up, scrutinized the painting, a Renaissance portrait, hesitated, and, turning a pale and anxious face to the boys, asked them to make their own way to their rooms on the upper floor of the castle.

Two days passed uneventfully while the boys explored the castle and their host, much preoccupied, rarely appeared. On the third evening, as dusk was falling, the boys sat reading in Prince Emanuel's room, midway along one of the four wings of the house. The connecting doors at each end of the room were securely closed to preserve what heat could be retained in so many cold and uninhabited rooms.

Simon Reynolds records the count's description of what happened next. 'The profound silence was suddenly shattered by the steadily approaching clatter of opening and slamming doors and soon footsteps, moving briskly from one of the towers, became ominously audible. From the direction of the approaching footsteps came inarticulate cries of a man in evident distress. The boys let fall their books and all eyes were directed towards the approaching clamour.

'One of the two doors of the room flew open and in strode a young man, short in stature, wearing a green doublet and close fitting hose; round his neck he wore a white ruff, dark hair lay lank on a puckered brow, the face was white, almost opaque. As the figure stormed through the room within a few feet of the astonished boys, its anguished cry echoed from wall to wall: *"Vater! Vater!"* [Father! Father!]

'Terror gripped the face of the intruder and enveloped the boys, unwilling spectators as they were. The stranger wrenched open the opposite door of the room, slamming it behind him, and the anguished voice, footsteps and slamming doors receded into the distance. A tomblike silence fell once again on the darkening room.

'Much alarmed, both boys ran to the duke's room and, stammering and interrupting each other, they related their tale. The duke listened in silence before leading the boys to a distant audience room where a number of family portraits dating back to the early days of the Wettin Dynasty hung in the gathering shadows of evening.

'"Look," said the Duke, "tell me if you recognize him."

'The boys wandered from portrait to portrait. Both halted, riveted in their tracks, before an identical likeness of the young man in green. There was anger in the eyes that met theirs, defiance mingled with a heartrending desperation.

'"Yes," said the duke, "it was he you saw, or rather his restless spirit which still roams this ancient house. It was in the tower nearest to your room, Emanuel, that he murdered his father many generations ago. But his cry of anguish, *'Vater! Vater!'* still echoes among us."'

The duke revealed to the prince and the young count that that was the portrait which had been found lying on the floor on their arrival in the Great Hall – although when the duke had left the castle the painting had been locked in the castle safe, the only key being in his possession. Aware that the Russians were driving the German soldiers before them through Silesia towards Saxony, the duke knew his family's heritage was threatened both from without and within. He showed the boys how a small crucifix had been placed behind each picture or ornament decorating the walls of the castle.

He commented sadly: '"Were it not for this spiritual protection they would run the risk of being smashed on the floor. Behind the beauty of this beloved house there lurks a presence or presences that bode us ill. My family has not ruled for so many centuries without leaving its imprint of good and evil . . ."'

Some years later Simon Reynolds visited the haunted Schloss Moritzburg on a grey day in winter. Snow lay thickly on the castle park, the moat was half frozen and the four massive fortified towers threw black shadows on the frosty waters below. The great silent rooms opened into one another, devoid of corridors, leading from tower to tower around the square Renaissance courtyard. By then in communist hands, the haunted castle was instantly recognizable from the count's description, and little seemed to have changed since the autumn visit of the two schoolboys towards the end of the Second World War.

In 1940 Mrs Louise Mary Sayer (see p. 62) was at finishing school in Paris when it was evacuated from the danger zone to a castle near Stirling in Scotland, where the headmistress was English but the rest of the staff were French.

'The castle was very beautiful but rather eerie. I shared a bedroom with a very nice girl called Melissa [*name changed*]. Our room was called the Rose Bedroom, a room with a lovely view . . . situated down a long passage. One of the French mademoiselles slept in the bedroom next door to us.

'We did cookery classes every morning in the old kitchens of the castle where there was a dear old Scottish cook who had worked in the castle for many years. (The owners had left after leasing the building to the finishing school.)

'The first strange thing that happened was that Melissa, who was very musical, told me that she kept hearing someone playing the piano in one of the rooms at the top of the castle, but that when she went up there no one was in the room. She eventually plucked up courage to tell the mademoiselle who was in charge of her music lessons, who told Melissa that it was probably all in her imagination.

'However, one of the staff of the castle heard Melissa's comments. She said Chopin had stayed there and his music was often heard in the room in which Melissa had heard it. Melissa confirmed that it was Chopin's music that she had heard. They then looked at the date of Chopin's visit to the castle and found that it was exactly the same day of the year that Melissa had heard the piano playing. I thought at the time that it was all a bit weird but I did not really believe it. However, something equally weird was going to happen to me which changed my attitude entirely.

'One night about midnight when Melissa and I had both been asleep for some time, quite suddenly we both woke up at exactly the same moment. Without saying anything to each other we both rushed to the window, opened it and leant out to breathe the fresh air as we both had smelled the most appalling smell of gas. I shall never forget it. We got out our gas masks (which, in those days everyone kept close by in case of a gas bomb being dropped by the Germans) and ran next door to tell mademoiselle about the gas. She came into our bedroom but to our astonishment she could smell nothing, and told us that we were being silly, that it was all in our imagination.

'We felt very stupid but knew in our hearts that we were right, and although we went back to bed again, exactly the same thing happened twice more during the night. However, we did not wake the French mademoiselle again, but just rushed to the window and breathed in the fresh air and felt very frightened.

'When we came down to breakfast in the morning we were very

upset because the mademoiselle had told some of the other girls about how we had woken her up in the night, and they all laughed at us and we felt terribly embarrassed. Even the headmistress had heard the story and she laughed too, and told us that there was no gas installed in the castle, adding that she didn't think the Germans would bother to bomb a glen in Scotland with gas. So we felt very stupid. We decided not to mention it ever again and to put it out of our minds.

'However, that same morning when we were down in the old kitchens preparing vegetables for the cookery class, one of the girls in our class started to tease us.

'"Whatever got into you, waking mademoiselle and telling her you smelled gas in your bedroom last night?"

'We said we didn't want to talk about it any more but suddenly the old cook, Bessie, who was cleaning the kitchen range, looked at us and said, "Which room are you sleeping in, miss?"

'We told her we were in a room called the Rose Room. Suddenly there was a fearful crash — Bessie had dropped an iron on top of the kitchen range. She wiped her eyes and looked terribly white and shaken. Then she told us that she had worked in the castle for thirty years and that the bedroom we were sleeping in was where the son and heir of the family who owned the castle always slept — before he was killed in the First World War. He was gassed at the front and died the following day, 11 October 1917.'

The two schoolgirls stared at the old woman as they realized the implication of her words: the smell of gas, filling the Rose Room and making them choke for breath, had occurred the previous night, the night of 11 October!

'After that we never mentioned it again, but it has always haunted me, and although it happened such a long time ago, I know I shall never forget it.'

The following tales must remain anonymous at the request of the person concerned, a close friend of mine whose name I have changed.

Diana lives in a most attractive ancient house, parts of it dating back to the twelfth century. It is one of those charming old houses full of nooks and crannies, sloping polished wood floors, steps and stairs in unexpected places and a painted chamber decorated in the sixteenth century, with a biblical text over the great open fireplace and flowers painted in the days of Elizabeth I glowing on whitewashed walls.

This room, known as the 'solarium', is used by visitors, who sleep in a bed so high it is like climbing Mount Everest to reach its snowy summit, crowned with fresh lacy linen. The room is large and well proportioned, and opening off it at the end opposite the hall doorway is an attached dressing room. There is no other exit from the suite of rooms.

When Diana's two children were small they used to play in the painted room until one day the younger child, Emily, came running to her mother crying that there was a man in the room who would not go away. She said he was dressed all in black, 'with a frilly thing at his neck'.

Diana assured her daughter (who was then about three years old) that no one was in the house but themselves. She took her by the hand and led her back to the painted room. But Emily was so frightened she refused to enter the room, and would never play there again. Indeed, even today, grown up and independent as she is, Emily prefers not to enter that room, and absolutely refuses to sleep there.

Some time after that experience, Diana's husband developed influenza and, reluctant to keep his wife awake, decided to sleep in the painted room. During the night he was woken by a chilly feeling, and struggling up to lean against the pillows he saw, sitting by the fireplace, the figure of a man dressed in black with a ruffle at his neck.

Several years later, when Emily was about six, Diana received a visit from the local vicar, a friend, who brought with him a portrait of a man.

'I thought you might like to have this engraving,' he said, handing it to Diana. 'This chap was a church warden who used to live here in this house in the early part of the seventeenth century.'

At that point Emily came into the room, spoke to the vicar and demanded to see the portrait. Her mother showed it to her and Emily cried: 'That's him, Mummy! That's the man who was in the painted room.'

When Diana's husband returned from London that evening he

confirmed Emily's identification: the portrait depicted precisely the features of the man he had seen sitting by the fire in the painted room.

I spent Christmas with the family recently, and I slept in the painted room. It was the third or fourth time I had stayed there, and on each occasion I had found the atmosphere in the room slightly uncomfortable. I would go to sleep quite happily and with no problems, but wake up feeling icy cold for no apparent reason. I would put on the light immediately and then be extremely reluctant to turn it off again. To tell you the truth, I didn't turn it off, and if Diana's electricity bill rises whenever I stay with her, she will now know the reason why.

Nothing else happened while I was at the house on that occasion, but shortly after I returned to London Diana telephoned me. 'I've had an awful problem since you left,' she said. 'I can't get into the painted room.'

'What do you mean you can't get into it? Have you locked yourself out?'

'No, nothing like that,' she replied. 'I mean I can't physically get beyond the step.'

She told me what had happened. Wanting to find a home for a Christmas present, she had decided it would look best in the painted room. So, with the ornament in one hand, she climbed the wooden stairs leading to the first floor, crossed the upper hall, and climbed the two or three steep steps to the closed door of the painted room. She opened the door with her free hand and moved to enter. But she could not get past the doorway.

'It was as if a solid wall stood between me and the room beyond,' she told me. 'I tried desperately to get through it, but I simply couldn't. Don't ask me to explain it. I can't. All I can tell you is that there was a physical barrier preventing me from going through the doorway into that room. But it was invisible. I could see absolutely nothing there except the open doorway. When I set foot on the step and tried to enter, my body could not go past some kind of unseen obstacle.'

Alone in the house, for several days she struggled to get through, becoming more frightened on each occasion. At the same time the atmosphere in the house seemed to have become highly charged in some way which was difficult to describe. In the end she rang me again to tell me that she had called in her friend the vicar, and he had organized a ceremony designed to exorcize the building.

The vicar and his assistant arrived and the ceremony was conducted outside the door of the painted room. At one point in the service Diana was requested to take a large brass cross from one of the participants and hold it in her hands.

'The most awful thing happened,' she told me on the phone. 'When we reached that part of the ceremony and the cross was held towards me, I couldn't move to take it. My hands and arms were paralysed, just as my body had been when I tried to enter the door. Try as I might, I simply couldn't take the cross.'

Eventually one of the clergymen held the cross over Diana, and the service was concluded. It was effective in allowing her entry into the room again but the presence, whatever it is, remains in the house and although she prefers not to talk about it, Diana is always fully aware of it. Emily and other members of the family still avoid entering the room, and refuse point blank to sleep there.

The history of Bradshaw Hall near Bolton in Lancashire dates back to 1074, according to Mrs Irene Heaton, whose family, the Deakins, were local landowners. Mrs Heaton, who now lives in Dumfries-shire, was a close friend of the last owner of the hall, Colonel H. M. Hardcastle, and often visited him there.

One room in particular was considered to be of great historical significance: it was the room where the death warrant for Charles I was drawn up and signed by Thomas Bradshaw and five others before being sent around the country for the addition of the rest of the necessary signatures.

The strip of lawn in front of the hall was believed to be the scene of a famous duel between Bradshaw as a young man and his sister's lover, whose identity was then unknown to him. At the climax of the fight, the stranger was disarmed and Bradshaw, sword in hand, was about to give the *coup de grâce* and run him through, when the beaten man cried out: 'Hold! Would you kill your king?' Bradshaw lowered his weapon and after a pause, while the identity of his adversary dawned on him, he is supposed to have replied: 'Not this time, but when next we meet, then!' When that historic meeting took place, Bradshaw was the judge who condemned Charles I to death.

First Mrs Heaton describes an incident concerning a friend of her parents, a Major Ryan [*named changed*] who was invited to Bradshaw Hall to shoot.

'He arrived late and was shown up to his room immediately and offered a bath before changing for dinner. Everyone changed for dinner at Bradshaw in those days! Tired and travel-stained, he accepted gratefully. On his way along an oak-panelled, dimly lit passage he saw a figure, also clad in a robe, enter the bathroom before him. Assuming this to be another late-comer who had beaten him to the tub, he returned to his bedroom to wait his turn, leaving the door ajar. After a frustrating delay he crept to investigate, and finding the bathroom had been vacated in total silence, he took a quick dip, somewhat chagrined.

'Descending in due course, he found his host awaiting him by a roaring fire in the dining hall. Enjoying a welcome pre-dinner drink, he noticed the table was laid for two people only. To satisfy his surprised curiosity he made some remark about a supposedly fellow-guest hogging the bath, to which the colonel replied: "There is no other guest! Just you and I!"

'Mystified, Major Ryan took his seat, as did the colonel, to await the arrival of the soup. Startled, he became aware of the same robed figure suddenly appearing directly behind the colonel's chair.

'"But there is the gentleman I saw upstairs!" he exclaimed.

'The colonel turned his head. "Where? Who?" he asked.

'"There!" was the cry. "Standing behind your chair, now!"

'Again the colonel turned his head to have a look. Then he said with some amusement: "I never *can* see him! Much as I would like to! It's our monk, you know! I find it so disappointing – I have not got the gift of "second" sight! You *would* have seen him upstairs – the bathroom used to be a priest-hole. He often appears there, and on the staircase, but never for me, sad to say!"

'Colonel Hardcastle told me personally that he would "give his right arm" to see the monk. He had considered having him exorcized but as he did no harm, he let him alone. He did not appear to be in any way an evil spirit, and only gave the odd guest or two a heart attack (and they never died of it!).

'Several appearances of the ghost in Bradshaw Hall were witnessed in my day, once on the staircase during a fancy dress party when the monk was taken for one of the guests. This resulted in a fainting fit, but was well worth it, as the lady concerned became the heroine of the hour. It was said she was the life, and the monk was the soul, of the party!'

Mrs Heaton adds an interesting rider to her story: 'Curious to relate, Colonel Hardcastle did not lose an arm, but he did lose a foot after being bitten by a tarantula spider on safari in Africa.'

Mrs Heaton also recounts details of another legend closely connected with Bradshaw Hall and her friend Colonel Hardcastle.

Near Bradshaw Hall many years ago lived two young people who were determined to marry although their union was bitterly opposed by their families. Choosing death in preference to life without each other, the lovers committed suicide. The scandal was hushed up and the bodies buried in unconsecrated ground in the vicinity of a certain Tinkerbottom's Farm, Bradshaw, where possibly one of the families then lived.

A long time passed, and years later human remains were dug up during some excavations. They proved to be the crown of a male skull and a piece of a female skull. For a time they were kept on display at the farm. However, in due course they were disposed of unceremoniously in a hole in an adjacent field.

That same day a series of fearful disturbances started: ceaseless knockings and rattlings set the nerves of the workers at the farm constantly on edge. It was also alleged that a poltergeist created havoc at night.

This mysterious activity caused a considerable stir in the local community, especially when it was realized that the disturbances had occurred only after the skulls had been cast out of the farmhouse and into the field. Consequently they were retrieved, and peace was at once restored.

A few years later Tinkerbottom's Farm was due to be demolished. A request was made to Colonel Harcastle, who agreed to take responsibility for the skulls.

Mrs Heaton continues the story: 'Because the piece of the woman's skull was so small, he had a silver stand made for it and placed it with the crown of the man's skull, beautifully polished, on the Hardcastle family bible at Bradshaw Hall.

'One day, while the colonel was away hunting in Scotland, a housemaid knocked the little mount over, denting the silver. Instructions were given by the colonel to his housekeeper that it was to be forwarded for repair to Manchester and, without a second thought, the female skull was sent away.

'At once terrible disturbances of a hair-raisingly violent nature occurred. Colonel Hardcastle was again consulted and remembering the old story (which he had always believed), he ordered the woman's skull, on its mount, to be immediately reunited with the man's. The noises ceased. Since that time the pair have never been separated.'

Colonel Hardcastle died in 1948 and his ancient hall was demolished, to the distress of many local residents as well as Mrs Heaton. There was some consolation in the fact that many items from his treasured collections of objects of all kinds, including the skulls, were taken to the museum at Turton Tower. This building dates from 1420 and had close links with Bradshaw Hall. Indeed many locals believed the two landmarks had been connected by an underground passage.

Mrs Heaton was able to examine again the objects she remembered from her visits to the hall, when she had listened enthralled to the stories Colonel Hardcastle had told her about them. On a visit to the museum late one afternoon some years ago Mrs Heaton and the caretaker's wife strolled through the rooms together.

'I spent the time in nostalgic contemplation of the relics from Bradshaw Hall, all of which were familiar to me. The caretaker's wife had come with her husband from Scotland not long before and naturally I asked her how she liked living at Turton Tower. She said it was "all right now". I pressed her to tell me what she meant and she said that when they first arrived they had occupied a dark old bedroom in which she had been quite unable to sleep. The face of an unknown man had kept appearing in her mind's eye, haunting and frightening. Eventually she persuaded her husband to move to another room, where all was peace.

'Several months later they were sorting the contents of a massive chest of drawers in which were stacked piles of unframed old drawings and paintings of men and women, mostly head and shoulders, fairly large in size. Leafing through them one by one with a duster in hand, she was suddenly startled to find herself face to face with her night visitor, the spectre who had haunted her dreams and robbed her of sleep.

'I asked her if she had been able to identify him. She replied that she had not, neither had she been successful in unearthing any event of a sinister nature which may have taken place in that old, dark bedroom at Turton Tower.'

Taking a last look at the skeletal remains of the lovers, Mrs Heaton returned home to Scotland, determined to keep herself informed about the fate of the Bradshaw Hall collections in Turton Tower.

Recently, she learnt from local sources that Turton Tower Museum was in danger of being boarded up because the local council had withdrawn financial backing.

The national press picked up the story, highlighting the tale of the Lovers of Bradshaw Hall: 'The most bizarre items in the museum,' announced the *Daily Telegraph* on 5 March 1986, 'are fragments of two skulls kept upon an ancient bible . . .'

There is a well-known Elizabethan mansion in Lincolnshire which a former employee claims is haunted. She is so convinced of the presence of some spirit in the house that she has specifically requested that neither her name [we shall call her Dorothy] *nor that of the house should be revealed.*

The huge and magnificent building described in this story has been occupied continuously from 1600 to the present day. Fortunately it remains exactly as it was when originally built.

Dorothy was employed as one of the cleaning staff. One Monday morning six years ago she and her friend Amy were busy polishing the thirty-foot floor of the gallery at the top of the hall. They chatted together across the expanse of waxed floorboards dividing them, each planning what she would cook for supper that night.

'Suddenly the gallery door opened and closed as though a window had been left open and it had caught the draught,' remembers

Dorothy. 'At the same time, there was a noise of a baby crying, as though it was locked in a cupboard.'

The two women were so frightened that they ran out of the room and on to the landing before recovering themselves sufficiently to investigate. But they found nothing to explain the opening of the door, or the sound of the crying baby. After examining every cupboard within the vicinity of the gallery without success, they checked the windows, only to find them all locked.

'Everything seemed so quiet and peaceful, except that Amy and myself were shaking. Eventually we went back in the gallery. In there it felt quite eerie, as though all the paintings had come to life and were watching us. After we had calmed down, we polished the floor side by side, and finished in record time!'

When the house opened for the summer in 1988, many visitors reported a peculiar, icy atmosphere in the area leading to a certain room located immediately below the gallery. The story of the room is well known to the staff. About 150 years ago a maid was chased through the house by a young man intent on having his way with her. She jumped out of the window of the room, landing in the shrubbery below and died from her injuries. The ghost of the Grey Lady, who is often seen after midnight near the church next to the house, is presumed to be the spirit of that poor girl.

Dorothy writes: 'Four years ago a hairdresser came to my house to set my hair. We were talking about different things when she brought up this strange story of when she was driving through the village past the hall and past the church. She slowed down approaching the corner, and suddenly this outline of a woman in grey floated past from one side of the road to the other. She was very startled and could not get home fast enough to tell her husband.'

Another time, when all members of the family living at the house were away on holiday, the housekeeper made one of her regular visits to check that everything was safe and sound. She was working in the kitchen when all at once: 'She felt someone pinch her bottom. She swung round to tell the person off, but there was no one there!'

Dorothy and the rest of the staff believed the mischievous ghost responsible for that little episode was one of the original family who had lived in the house and who were well-known for their love of practical jokes.

On another occasion, also when the family was away, a forestry worker was out walking his dog one night when he heard music coming from the hall. He walked closer and identified the sound as the grand piano being played. Knowing the family were not there he searched for the cause, and found no one in the house: the rooms were as dark and silent as the grave.

It is not unusual for a ghost to remain active in a historic house long after it has been converted to commercial use.

When Mrs Pamela Barford (see p. 78) was asked by her daughter recently if she believed in ghosts, she replied firmly that she did, and had very good reason to do so. This is her story, told in her own words:

'In 1971 I was living with my husband in Barnet, Hertfordshire, and for a treat I was to have a weekend at a local beauty farm housed in a lovely stately home . . . near Potters Bar. It was owned at the time by a "rough diamond" who, I understand, was an ex-safe breaker who had been flown over enemy lines during the last war. A film had been made about him but I only remember his name as Eddie – can't remember any more.

'On the Friday afternoon I duly booked in for my peaceful weekend. I was staying on my own as my husband had to be at work. My room was the first room up a beautiful staircase, turning left at the top. It was a typical antique-furnished room with a dressing-table opposite the bed which had a small side chest to the left of it.

'In the middle of the night I woke because of a noise in my room – a figure of a plump lady dressed in calico with lots of petticoats and a lacy mobcap was opening the drawers in the dressing-table opposite me. She searched frantically through my belongings then, leaving them untidy, would close the drawer and open the next. I could see in the mirror of the dressing table her clothes and outline, but I could not see any face. Backwards and forwards she went through the dressing-table drawers, and then came towards the bed. Her clothes were rustling against the bedclothes and made a noise I have never heard before or since – I have never seen calico in my life.

'She bent down to the side chest to the left of me and started rummaging once more. Over and over she went, then she returned to the dressing-table where again she searched frantically. She eventually left (without opening the bedroom door), only to return later to continue her search, when she woke me up for the second time. My feelings throughout this? I was terrified! I could not speak, I could not move, I just sat and stared, praying she would go away.

'The following morning I mentioned to the staff that I was exhausted and told them why. They just looked at each other and then turned away.

'The following night the whole procedure was repeated. On the Sunday morning I telephoned my husband, explained everything to him, and he suggested that he would come over and that I should ask for a double room for us both, which I did.

'Obviously nothing happened in our new room, but I now believe very firmly in ghosts and I am still frightened by the thought of them.'

Don McKeown is a telecommunications engineer living in County Durham.

'For years Beamish Hall near Stanley in County Durham was occupied by the National Coal Board No. 5 Area and used as their administrative headquarters. I was responsible for maintaining the internal telephone system within the historic building. The office staff used the main banqueting hall, complete with minstrels' gallery, as their canteen in those days. I was part of the fixtures and often joined the staff for lunch, where a popular topic of conversation was the haunting of the premises by the Grey Lady, a little old lady who haunts the hall to this day.

'On one occasion a car had swerved violently to avoid her on the main drive which twisted through landscaped grounds *en route* to the grand pillared entrance hall. A very large "pub-type" ashtray had, on another occasion, crashed on to the parquet floor from an empty desk.

'Some employees had always taken these "apparitions" with a pinch of salt until the day several of them left the banqueting hall after lunch, heading along one of the many oak-panelled passages that eventually ended up at the main general office.

'A couple of typists were some twenty yards ahead of the group and out of sight, having turned a couple of corners. The second group arrived back at the office to find the two typists in an agitated state, to say the least. As they were on the "home straight" and approaching the main office door, an old lady was seen coming towards them from the opposite direction. She stopped momentarily, then entered the general office.

'The two girls commented that "the old dear must have lost her way". But on entering the office themselves, they were astonished to find it completely empty. If my memory serves me right, the brandy bottle came out that day – for purely medicinal purposes, of course!'

Churches and Colleges

Not surprisingly, churches and their graveyards are also traditional settings for ghosts.

Messing is a delightful and so far unspoilt village near Colchester in Essex. Charming old cottages jostle for room next to a cosy pub, and the church boasts an ancient lineage.

But on the day George Bush became President-Elect of the United States in 1988, the world discovered Messing: international headlines identified the sleepy little village as the original seat of the Bush family. Will it ever be the same?

Recently, a young married woman, a friend of mine who lives in the village, offered to arrange the flowers in Messing Church. When she arrived she heard the organ playing. Putting her flower basket down in the church porch, she went inside to check with the organist that it was a convenient time to decorate the church.

To her dismay she found the organ locked, and the church deserted.

She has had the same experience on several occasions more recently.

In 1964 Victor Neville-Statham was working in London in the Ministry of Technology. After a discussion about ghosts, he and three of his colleagues decided to spend the night at the site of what has been described as the most haunted house in Britain, Borley Rectory in Suffolk.

The house itself had been burnt down over forty years ago; the foundations had been removed for use as infill during construction of an airstrip during the war, and nothing now remains of the haunted building. The nearby church, however, still stands and is also believed to be haunted.

CHURCHES AND COLLEGES

The intrepid young men from the ministry, Victor, David, Christopher and George, clubbed together to hire a car and were driven down to Borley by a friend of Christopher's, determined to spend the night in the porch of Borley Church. They did so, finding it conveniently furnished with bench seats on which they passed the long hours, ears strained for any noises.

At dawn Christopher returned to the car parked in the lane outside the church to talk to the driver, who had been in the vehicle all night. The two men stayed together until the party reassembled some minutes later.

Victor Neville-Statham describes what happened to the other three men who had remained in the church porch after Christopher left them: 'David announced his intention of going down the lane a way to see the sunrise. The other man, George, a somewhat sceptical Scot, stayed with me in the porch, complaining that the outing was a complete waste of time. I must confess to being disappointed in not experiencing any phenomena.

'Suddenly George pointed towards a tall fir tree by the churchyard wall, some twenty to thirty yards distant. "What's David doing by that big tree?" he demanded. I looked, but could see no one, and said so. George was most emphatic. He said that David was standing by the tree sporting a big black beard, a pipe in his mouth, and wearing a long black coat, buttoned at the neck.

'I still couldn't see anyone. George lost his temper and stormed over to the tree. (I must point out here that David was clean shaven and a non-smoker.) I watched George over by the tree . . . calling on David to stop mucking about and show himself. At that point David came through a gate at the opposite end of the churchyard.

'Reaching me, he asked what George was doing. Meanwhile George returned and demanded to know where David had hidden the beard, etc. I said that David couldn't have brought them with him because we all would have seen the package. (None of us had taken anything with us.)

'I walked over to the tree and noticed an old gravestone nearby erected to the memory of the Reverend Bull, a former vicar of Borley . . . I suggested to George that perhaps he had seen a ghost. He denied this, insisting that David had dressed up to play a trick on him and adding that if any ghosts were about, then I should be the one to see them since I believed in them. He did not, he said.

'As I have said, I saw nothing. I later got hold of a book about Borley and in it was a photo of the deceased reverend, sporting a big black beard, a pipe in his mouth and, of course, wearing a cassock (the long black coat).'

Mr Neville-Statham told me that he was surprised George had seen the figure when he, Victor, had not, because he had had a number of psychic experiences throughout his life, while George had had none previously, and was quite emphatic in declaring his disbelief. When I questioned Victor about the whereabouts of Christopher and the driver of the car at the moment when the figure in black was seen by George, he assured me that the two men had remained in the car and knew nothing of the incident until Victor, George and David returned to the vehicle and told them of it – before they drove off to a nearby town for breakfast.

According to local legend the Thursby Grey Lady was the mistress of a wealthy family man named Brisco who lived at Crofton, six miles from Thursby (which lies between Wigton and Carlisle).

Brisco resided in Crofton Hall with his wife and family in the eighteenth century. He housed his mistress in a lodge near by. When she died, Brisco wanted to have her body interred in the family vault, but as the family was scandalized by this suggestion, he had the corpse placed in a grave beside the church door, surrounded by a black railing. However, the ghost of the mistress was restless; she roamed the churchyard ceaselessly until the locals opened up her coffin and hammered a stake through her heart.

'To this day,' writes Mrs J. Reay of Cumbria, 'an evergreen tree grows out of a grave' on the left-hand side of the church in Thursby. Black railings surround the grave but the inscription on the headstone can no longer be read, being deliberately concealed by the tree, according to Mrs Reay, who reports that local people believe that anyone who chops the obscuring branches away will be cursed.

Even now, in the twentieth century, this Grey Lady still haunts

Thursby church. Mrs Reay, who was married there twenty-three years ago, writes of her sister-in-law's experience: 'The vicar and his wife at the time told of how they were visited by a lady ghost dressed in a grey dress and bonnet. My sister-in-law, visiting them, was there to put her children's minds at rest because of local talk concerning the ghost.'

'As they sat on a wooden locker in the church discussing this, a draught and rustling noise went past them, as though someone in a long skirt caused the disturbance.

'The most outstanding thing in my relation's mind at the time was a strong smell of lavender. She turned to the vicar's wife who nodded and said, "Yes, she just went past us then, leaving her usual smell of lavender perfume behind her."'

Mrs Hilary J. Cameron is a secretary in Scotland. In July 1974 she and a friend set out to visit Traquair House at Innerleith, Peeblesshire, reputed to be the oldest inhabited house in Scotland.

'At the end of our tour we visited the small family chapel situated in a remote wing of the house. Before it was built, the family celebrated Mass in secret in a room at the top of the house known as the "Priest's Room". With the passing of the Catholic Emancipation Act in 1829, however, they were able to worship openly and the chapel dates from that time. Its interior was a haven of peace with its white marble altar and statue of the Virgin Mary with a bowl of flowers at her feet.

'It was with a sense of surprise that I suddenly became aware of the chanting which was like the sound of many voices in repetitive singing. It came in uneven waves as though carried on the wind. At first I thought that a Catholic Mass was being broadcast on a radio near by, but there was only the tearoom next door. I could even hear the rattle of teacups. I was convinced the ethereal singing was not coming from that direction but was at a loss to pinpoint its source.

'To my relief my friend heard it too. There was nothing unusual to be seen; nothing to cause the slightest alarm. Yet somewhat shaken, we left and were glad to exchange the gloom of the chapel for the sunshine outside. On reflection, we agreed not to tell anyone about our strange experience. Neither of us relished the prospect of being laughed at as a pair of amateur ghost hunters.'

Mrs Cameron was relieved to discover some time later that their experience was, in fact, a fairly common supernatural phenomenon. She concludes: 'I keep an open mind on the subject of ghosts but think a better solution lies in Marconi's theory that no sound is lost but merely travels out into the ether. In this way a permanent record is preserved for those with the psychic ability to tune in on the correct wavelength. Had a hundred and fifty years of Roman Catholic devotions had such an effect on the atmosphere of Traquair chapel? If so, it may be an echo of the past that we heard on that summer day thirteen years ago.'

Academics, and scientists in particular, are notoriously reluctant to admit to a belief in ghosts. Colleges in Britain's ancient universities might be expected to harbour one or two apparitions in their cloisters, but very few have been recorded. St John's College in Oxford is an exception.

Mrs Eileen Stamers-Smith contributes the following story written by her late husband and published originally in the St John's College Society Notes for 1973–4 (a publication restricted to members of the Society). Mr H. A. Stamers-Smith had been a Rhodes Scholar at St John's College in 1924. He was prepared to admit publicly that he had seen something inexplicable in St John's but his colleague at the centre of the sighting was not willing, later in life, to be associated with it. Was his earlier claim a hoax, as he suggests, or was he deliberately trying to conceal his contact with the paranormal? This is the account as it appeared in the journal:

'Anthony D. Hippisley-Coxe's recent gazetteer of ghosts, *Haunted Britain*, records only one Oxford ghost – ours: "St John's College is haunted by the ghost of Archbishop Laud, who was beheaded in 1645. Some say he bowls his head across the Library floor."

'Who "some" are is anyone's guess. The more usual College version is that the ghost (unidentified) retains its head but has its feet protruding through the floor of the Library. This, it is claimed, was raised at some period, and the ghost, accustomed to walking on the old level, declined to changed its habits.

'But has anyone ever seen the ghost? Mr H. A. Stamers-Smith, now resident in Woodstock, has supplied the Editor with a gripping account of a sighting, which we print below. The undergraduate referred to in the account as L— is, in fact, still alive, and the Editor recently wrote to him to procure his version of the events. He replied:

'"I remember the incident in question and the names of the people you mention but at this length of time I have no recollection of anything further . . . I think the incident of March 1924 must have been one of those huge undergraduate jokes."

'This seems to bespeak a wish not to be associated with the sighting, and for that reason Mr Stamers-Smith and the Editor have agreed to conceal L—'s identity. Mr Stamers-Smith writes:

'"The following account of apparitions seen by myself and other undergraduates of the College is based upon my own memory only, as I have never before attempted to describe them in writing. Since very nearly fifty years have passed, I can make no claim for exactness over the date of the first apparition, or the identity of the fourth member of the auction bridge four who were disturbed at their game that evening. In other respects the events were so strange that they remain as vivid to me as they were then.

'"The three other undergraduates in the bridge four were myself, C. H. V. Talbot and C. H. J. Rawstone: the fourth was either M. B. Foster or W. G. Bird, probably Foster. We were playing in Talbot's rooms on the ground floor of the staircase that then led up to the Junior Common Room and the College Library. The time was about 11 p.m. on a Saturday night in March 1924. I cannot remember the exact date. The weather was fine, although decidedly cold.

'"In the middle of a game Talbot's door was suddenly burst open and an undergraduate named L— staggered into the room, knocking violently against Rawstone's shoulder as he pitched forward: his face was pale green and he was in a state of terror. My first reaction was that he was drunk, but I immediately dismissed that idea as I knew he never drank and was in fact a very quiet and studious scholar. He had evidently been in his bed as he was clad only in pyjamas and his feet were bare: between gasps he seemed to be saying, 'Oh, the feet, the feet . . . Oh, my God! . . . the feet in the ceiling . . .' We propped him on a sofa and gave him a drink of water and wrapped him in one of Talbot's blankets.

'"When he had calmed down a bit, he told us that he had been to bed and was awakened by a brilliant light in his room, followed by a cold blast of air that made his hairs stand on end with fright, while the light was seen to be coming from two vivid legs and feet that marched beneath his ceiling and came nearer each second until he hurled himself out of bed and fled along the Quadrangle, scarcely knowing where he was going.

'"While Foster stood watch over the still-terrified L—, we other three went out into the Quad to investigate, walking first towards L—'s room in the next staircase towards the Garden Front. All was quiet at that late hour, and at first there was only starlight to be seen, but suddenly we all perceived a light moving along the Library over the Garden Front and then turning towards us as it moved in the direction of the Library entrance.

'"While the light was quite vivid, it flickered a little as though it was a candle, and its movement could have emanated from a person walking rather slowly along the Library floor. Feeling sure that there was someone, most probably Dr Stevenson, working late in the Library, I ran back and mounted the staircase to the rather massive door into the Library only to find it securely locked: nor was there sign of light or any sound.

'"There could be no doubt that we had seen a light, or that it had been moving, so our next move was to summon Henry Payne, the Head Porter, to explore the Library with us. He was positive that its door had been locked by Dr Stevenson and the key deposited by him in the Lodge at 10 o'clock. He lifted it down and we all made a thorough search of the Library that was by now illuminated with its electric lights. We found nothing unusual, nor any sign of any occupant, mortal or otherwise.

'"During the whole of my residence I was fortunate enough to remain for three years in the suite of rooms on the Buttery Staircase with windows facing St Giles': this part of the College was formerly the Monastery of St Bernard and had extremely thick walls and very small windows and at that time was divided into a sitting room and a bedroom, the latter having one window on St Giles' and another facing the Main Gate.

'"Twice during these years I was awakened in the early hours by an apparition not unlike that other; the same brilliant light and the same blast of cold air; also the same prickling of hair and a feeling of ghostly terror. The only difference was that I dared not open my eyes, so cannot to this day record whether there were feet beneath the ceiling!"'

Theatres

Unlike universities, theatres have provided a rich source of ghostly tales, and many a theatre in London's West End and across the country is proud of its resident ghost.

Bath is an excellent hunting ground. Special evening tours for visitors are devoted entirely to tracking down the best-known haunts of the most famous apparitions. Another Grey Lady, who inhabits the Theatre Royal, is one of them.

This young woman has been seen many times over the years by theatre staff and by celebrities appearing on stage, including the legendary ballerina Anna Pavlova and the actress Dame Anna Neagle.

One of the ghost's familiar features is a strong scent of jasmine associated with her. She is believed to have been an actress in the 1880s who became involved with an admirer, who watched her from a box in the theatre every night. But her husband, a member of the same company, learnt of the affair and challenging his rival to a duel, pierced him through the heart. The woman appeared on stage for the last time that fateful night wearing a long grey dress with a headdress of grey feathers. The following morning her body, clad in the same costume, was found hanged in her room at the Garrick's Head Hotel next door.

Whenever she is glimpsed in the theatre she is seen wearing her death robes, and she leaves behind her the haunting scent of jasmine.

Recently a well-known clairvoyant and ghostbuster spent hours in the theatre, sitting in the box in which she has been seen repeatedly over the years, waiting for her to appear. But although he reported sensing a strong, stubborn and uncooperative presence he saw nothing, and this Grey Lady continues her restless haunting of the charming Theatre Royal building in Bath.

Hospitals

As might be expected, these institutions abound in stories of ghosts, and a hospital is the setting for one of the most impressive anecdotes included in this collection.

The event described below was witnessed by two nurses who were deeply shocked by it; and acknowledgement of it having occurred was given by senior staff at the hospital. Mrs E. Christine Jones, a vicar's wife now living in Hampshire, tells the story:

'I was a nurse in a London hospital going on night duty at 8 p.m. When I reported at sister's office the staff nurse told me to do my first round of all the beds, noting treatments due etc., as she had not finished writing up the day report. After this I went to the lotions cupboard on the corridor, to fill my trolley for the night, when staff nurse came out to say she was ready to give me the report.

'But just then we heard a man's footsteps coming up the stone stairs and we saw a man in chauffeur's uniform who said: "I have come for my wife." As this was a male ward, we told him to go down to the office to inquire and he would be told where to go, although no patient would be discharged at that time of night.

'My night sister was late in coming around. She said she had waited by a patient's bed, as she was dying. This lady had been brought in during the morning, unconscious. The police were trying to trace her husband.

'I asked who was going out of that ward that night and told her about the chauffeur. She went down to the office to ask about the matter but was told no one had been in to inquire; and the lift man standing in full view of the stairs said he had not seen *anyone* in any uniform.'

Puzzled by the nurse's story of the visiting chauffeur, the night sister was determined to clear up the mystery; so she visited the nurses' home to ask the staff nurse about it. She confirmed every detail of Christine Jones's story. The night sister then reported the strange visit to the matron.

'Next morning while I was at breakfast a message came from the matron that I was wanted in her office. I wondered what I could have done amiss! She told me that the police had found out about the unknown lady who had died.'

Christine Jones was then told that the husband of the dead woman was chauffeur to a private family. Early on the previous morning he had set out on a long journey with his employers. But the car had been involved in a serious accident in which the chauffeur was killed.

When he left home early that fateful morning his wife was apparently quite well and looking forward to spending a day in town with a friend. The friend called at her house to collect her, and she was surprised to receive no answer to the doorbell. Lifting the flap of the letterbox to call her name, she saw the woman lying on the floor of the hall. A neighbour called the police and an ambulance took the chauffeur's wife to hospital where she failed to recover consciousness and died in the evening.

At this stage no one knew of the whereabouts of her husband, the chauffeur. The police had failed to contact him, unaware that he had been killed in a road accident five or six hours before his wife died in the hospital.

When this information eventually came to light, Christine Jones and the staff nurse were left with the chilling knowledge that the man in the chauffeur's uniform had been dead for that period when he had spoken to them in the hospital corridor.

As the matron of the hospital commented at the time: 'It can only be assumed that the spirit or ghost of the man had come for his wife just at the time she died.'

Christine Jones is quite definite in her recollection of the chauffeur-ghost: 'There was nothing in the man's appearance or speech that was not ordinary and normal – except the way he said, in a very "flat" voice, all on one note, "I have come for my wife."'

Angela Moody is a young woman living in the north of England, who occupies a senior position in the nursing profession. Several years ago she was working as a nurse in a hospital in Surrey when she and a colleague were transfixed by an extraordinary sight very early one morning.

'I was working night duty at the hospital when, on this particular night shift, I was sent to relieve on another ward as they were very busy.'

A little annoyed at the move, Angela continued to work on the new ward until, at about 1 a.m., one of the patients who was very ill died.

'A staff nurse and myself went in to the side ward and laid the patient flat with the intention of returning an hour later to lay the patient out.

'Unfortunately the ward was so busy it wan't until three o'clock that we returned to the side ward. We gave the patient, a pleasant old lady of sixty-eight years, a wash and put on the shroud. Staff nurse Janice was at the foot of the bed preparing a name tag for the patient's shroud and I was putting some towels away at the head of the bed. I turned round and saw Janice in a state of shock, her hair (although I thought it only happened in cartoons) standing on end, and she was pointing. I should think my hair also stood on end, for rising about a metre above the bed was a white smoky haze which seemed to be turning into a mass with each second that passed, although it remained transparent.

'After what seemed like an age but was probably about ten seconds, we could see that the haze had changed into the shape of the lady's body. At this time it is quite truthful to say we panicked and tried to get out of the door (both, I hasten to add, at the same time).

'We told the other staff nurse who was with us what had happened, and she could tell by our pale, trembling bodies that it wasn't a joke. She gave us the remedy to all ailments, a tot of whisky, and phoned the night nursing officer who was very sympathetic.

'As I was leaving the hospital the following week to return home to Cleveland to work I was given the rest of the night duty rota off.'

Gillian Cotton of London is also a nurse. She describes her own frightening experience:

'I was a pupil nurse at St Bartholomew's Hospital in London. On a particular tour of night duty I was in the oldest wing.

'The staff nurse I was on with went off for her tea; this was about 2.30 a.m. I was walking round at about 2.45 a.m. and as I turned the corner of our double-sided ward I saw someone "standing" at the bottom of one of the beds.

'The figure seemed to be floating because I didn't see feet. I was terrified. I stepped back. The thing was dressed in a long black cape and a very large black hat.

'I stayed out of sight for a few seconds, ten at the most. When I stepped forward it had gone. I would have seen it go out of the door if it had done so.

'When I got to the patient she was dead. It had been expected, but still . . '

The following account of the sighting of an apparition was written by Brenda, a State Registered Nurse living in Manchester who wishes to remain anonymous.

'I am a nurse and I work nights. I have seen apparitions floating over the curtains, especially on the medical ward. I once saw a vision of a man with one leg floating about six inches off the ground; he passed right through a pair of double doors leading to the operating theatre.'

The reaction of senior hospital staff to accounts of the paranormal in these stories is intriguing because it was not immediately dismissive, unlike in most cases where contributors have described similar events to colleagues, friends or families.

Does this evidence of sympathetic concern for junior colleagues indicate a willingness on the part of senior staff to accept as normal the occurrence of such phenomena in hospitals? And if so, does that attitude reflect the frequency of paranormal events occurring in hospital wards, particularly those associated with the dead or dying?

Commercial Premises

One of the most unexpected discoveries I made when researching this book was that shops, offices and factories are just as likely as historic houses to be haunted by peculiar noises and by the presence of unregistered staff who appear and vanish at will, paying no regard to the boss or his precious work schedules.

R. H. Hodkinson from Manchester was appointed security officer at Salford University in 1964, and embarked on what was to prove a perplexing and worrying period in his life.

A brand new warehouse was built in Salford by the German firm of Bayer and Co. just before the First World War. It became quite famous as the Manchester Warehouse, or W22 as it was known by the staff of the giant chemist firm, Boots, who acquired it in two parts: the office section in Peru Street, and the warehouse section in Cannon Street. It was never occupied by Bayer and Co. as there was at the time a strong anti-German feeling in that area, the people of Manchester and Salford being convinced that the Germans used their building as a front to conceal German gun emplacements intended for the shelling of Liverpool. Whatever the gossip, the building, completed in 1915, remained empty until Boots purchased it. Then another wing fronting on Adelphi Street was added to it, converting the whole building into a huge oblong, with a motor garage making up the fourth side.

By 1927 the immense and much admired concrete structure housed hundreds of employees who, to the envy of their colleagues in other Boots' branches, enjoyed the latest innovations in office and warehouse fixtures and fittings – including the use of a spacious kitchen and canteen capable of seating two hundred diners. As Boots did not require all the space available, the district manager and clerical staff of HM Post Office Telephones occupied the frontage in Peru Street at this time.

In 1962 the building was empty, and the following year the Royal College of Advanced Technology took it over as an annexe. When the college was replaced by the University of Salford in 1964, the building became known as the Adelphi and was used by students. Today the structure remains much as it was in the days of Boots and HM Post Office Telephones, with the main entrance unchanged, still used as it was sixty odd years ago.

On his first day Mr Hodkinson arrived at 7 a.m. to take over the post from the night duty officer who reported that all was well before departing and leaving the newcomer to begin his duties.

Mr Hodkinson made it his practice to begin his patrol at the top of the building, working his way methodically down to the basement where there was a cubby hole used by electricians as a tearoom. On one particular occasion, a Sunday morning, he found a book on a table and borrowed it to browse through until lunchtime.

Returning with it to his office, he went off to find an electric kettle to make a cup of tea and on his return the book, a copy of *Lady Chatterley's Lover*, had vanished. There was nobody in the building – he had established that on his inspection tour a few minutes earlier – and he was at a loss to account for the disappearance of the book. He checked the security of the building, and searched high and low for it, but failed to find it. The officer who relieved him and all the cleaners were subsequently requested to look for it, but the book was never found.

A year later Mr Hodkinson was on night duty one Saturday from 7 p.m. to 7 a.m. He saw the colleague he relieved leave the building before inspecting the register, which had to be signed by any student given permission by his head of department to work in the building after hours. According to this record the building was empty, and calling control on his personal radio, he walked out into the foyer. As he did so, he saw a man in a blue suit walk along the corridor and disappear from view. Mr Hodkinson heard the intruder open an office door and close it. He gave no sign that he had seen the watchman – and Mr Hodkinson was quite baffled: how had he and the previous security officer overlooked him, and why had a door been left unlocked?

'I went over, turned the door handle to go in and question the man, but the door was locked, and I had to use my pass key to enter, when I found the room empty. I wasn't unduly surprised, merely thinking I had got the wrong office – it must be the next one. But it wasn't, nor the one after that, nor was he in any of the office rooms that lined the corridor. I searched them all, and none had an exit door – where you went in, you had to come out . . . I whistled up the man on mobile and when he arrived he tooted his horn and I let him in.'

Together the two men searched the building from roof to basement, but found no one. The following night, after the day officer had reported nothing unusual had occurred, Mr Hodkinson decided he would track down the intruder in the blue suit. Changing into gym shoes he wandered down to the machine shop.

'It was a big wide room. On the window side, rows of workbenches stretched down to the fire door at the bottom, and dotted about the floor were machines of various shapes and sizes. There was a toilet at the far end, six cubicles with wash-basins on the opposite wall, and fastened above each of them a paper-towel container.'

He stood quietly for some time and was about to move off when he heard footsteps. At first he thought they came from outside the building, but then he realized they were in the corridor. The person he heard stepping along so briskly would have to use the fire door to reach the floor above Mr Hodkinson, which was a passage with a wooden floor. As soon as he heard the fire door open and the footsteps, those of a woman, start clicketty-clacketting along the wooden floor, Mr Hodkinson sprinted upstairs and stood outside the exit door. For a few moments the footsteps were loud and clear and purposeful, but then they stopped in mid-stride. Silence fell. He flung open the door to discover there was no one there.

Mr Hodkinson could find no explanation. He toyed with the idea that the building was haunted: that the man in the blue suit had taken the missing book, that he had perhaps once worked in Boots' workshop; that the footsteps were caused by the restless spirit of a woman who had perhaps worked for HM Post Office Telephones forty years ago.

For some weeks nothing happened. Then, once again on Saturday night duty, Mr Hodkinson was in the inquiry office on the ground floor at 1 a.m. when he heard a thud on the floor of the classroom above.

'There was the sound of a heavy object being dragged from one end of the room to the other, footsteps milled around, the sound of chairs being pushed back as people stood up from a table or workbench – the whole room seemed to be alive with bustling activity, and then came the footsteps that I recognized at once. A chair was scraped back and the quick light footsteps came across the floor, a door opened and closed, and the footsteps began their march down the corridor, through the fire door, and into the passage where weeks ago I had tried to meet the woman responsible for them.

'With gym shoes on I made no sound as I went up the staircase to the floor above. The door of the classroom faced me as I reached the top. I went across to it slowly and quietly, and reached for the door handle. Touching it was like pressing a button – all the noise and bustling activity stopped instantly, and I went in to a silent, empty classroom.

'Standing there in the silence among rows of school desks, the blackboard with its bits of chalk, I suddenly thought that I was an intruder, I had no business to be there.'

Conscious of his intrusion, Mr Hodkinson sensed that the room was crowded with invisible workers of the long defunct Post Office Telephones office, impatiently waiting for him to leave the room before they resumed their tasks.

Later, Mr Hodkinson learnt that in the days of Boots' occupancy the machine shop had been the packing department. In 1927 one of the employees, a morose-looking man, threw down his claw hammer, donned his coat and hat and for reasons of his own, walked out of the job. Three days later his body was recovered by police from the River Irwell, a mere thirty yards from the building.

'The description of him, given to me in 1979 by his brother, fitted exactly the man in the corridor – it fitted the man who used to go into the toilets in the machine shop, in the early hours, to have a wash and brush up. I knew that if I went in I would find nothing. I had tried so many times before – the flushing of the lavatory, the sound of the running tap, the sound of the paper towel, as he briskly dried his hands – perhaps the flush chain would be moving, or a basin would be wet; and what about the paper towel he had used? Would I find it in the bin? No, I never found anything. What I was listening to was of another time – I was listening to the past.

Everything that I heard was an echo back in time. As the years passed, I accepted that theory until, in the year of the miners' strike (1973) the man in the corridor came to see me.'

To conserve electricity during the strike, power cuts were introduced, usually about 9 p.m. when most households were settling down for the night. Many districts were blacked out completely and on another Saturday night when Mr Hodkinson was on duty, he found himself in total darkness in the building with a torch without a battery, and an oil lamp without oil. He radioed to control to explain what had happened, indicating that there was nothing he could do until the lights came on again.

He describes what happened then: 'I found myself an office just off the corridor that I knew had a chair inside to the right of the door and there I sat in the blackness, and pondered on this and that.

'This was Saturday night, the night of the week when the likely lads tottered forth to do a spot of wassailing and dally with a wench or two. My mind shuttled off to the club of which I was a committee member . . . and then suddenly all thoughts of the club left me, as I stared at a round bluish ball that had appeared on the opposite wall – about the size of a tennis ball. It hung there, an electric luminous pulsating blue, that grew bigger and bigger as I watched it, until it was as big as a large football, when it slowly elongated upwards and downwards, and shaped itself into a kind of oblong picture frame – no, not a frame, I was looking through a window and the pulsating blue was space, I was looking through a window into space.

'Sitting in the chair I was rigid, spellbound, every nerve in my body vibrating like a violin string as I stared at the light. Then, in the top left-hand corner of the frame of light, the figure of a man appeared walking quickly towards me. He came towards the bottom corner, getting bigger the nearer he came, and then finally he simply walked off the frame and was gone.

'For a few seconds the frame hung in space, pulsating this incredible blue, then it began to dim and shrink into itself, and then it was gone, and the blackness came back.

'I don't think I was frightened. As I stared into the darkness of the room my mind whirled about trying to assimilate what I had just seen. Somewhere in my mind I could hear a voice saying over and over "The man in the corridor, he was the man in the corridor". And as I stared I became aware of him slowly materializing out of the darkness in front of me, and then I'm afraid I did panic, and I have been sorry about it ever since. I should have stayed instead of groping my way out of the room, desperate to get away. The face I had seen had been a friendly face, the big dark eyes full of kindness. I have thought about him so many times over the years.'

After that episode Mr Hodkinson continued to hear noises in the machine shop for another two years, but the man in the blue suit never appeared again.

With his letter Mr Hodkinson sent me an article about the Manchester Warehouse which appeared in Boots' in-house magazine in 1927, illustrated with photographs taken that year, including several shots of staff working there.

'Look at the picture I have enclosed,' he writes. 'Somewhere among the faces looking out at you is the man in the corridor. Would he be the person who took the book? Was he the man who washed in the toilet at night? . . . And the girl who walked so briskly down the passage to infinity, which one of the girls in the picture is she?'

The Adelphi now houses a school of music. There is some doubt about its future. 'What will happen to these invisible friends of mine if they pull it down?' asks Mr Hodkinson. 'Will the workforce in the classroom still bustle about in a room reduced to rubble? Will the man wash and brush up in a toilet no longer there?'

Lionel Geoffrey Jaekel (see p. 139) had an odd experience after moving in as first tenant of a second-floor flat in Market Place, Kendal, in August 1971. Formerly used as a butcher's shop with accommodation above it, the property was bought by a well-known building society, which converted the upper floors into self-contained flats and used the ground floor as offices.

One Tuesday evening in February 1973, Geoffrey Jaekel retired at 11.15 p.m. and, following his usual custom, read for half an hour before switching off the light.

'Perhaps ten minutes later I was in the pleasant state of limbo between sleeping and waking when I became conscious of a bluish-grey shadow immediately inside the door. I can only describe it as being shaped like a large inverted dunce's cap. I watched it for possibly half a minute when it started to move towards my bed with a juddering movement.

'Strangely, I felt absolutely no sense of fear, although I cannot claim to have particularly strong nerves. The "figure" continued towards my bed until it was near enough to touch, then vanished. I was just reassuring myself that I had imagined the whole thing when there was a heavy thump on my bed, just as though a heavy person, unable to control his weight, had sat on my bed. I certainly hadn't imagined that.'

There was an interesting sequel to the story. 'On the following Friday I was looking through the obituaries in the local paper when the names Brown [*name changed*, former owner of the butcher's shop] and Smith [*named changed*, parents-in-law of Brown] caught my eye. All three had died on the Tuesday night. The Smiths had kept the butcher's shop before Brown, and husband, wife and son-in-law died within two or three hours of one another.'

A photograph of an old building in Birmingham, its brick façade blackened with soot, reminds Cecil P. How of Staffordshire, a retired engineering consultant, of an interesting tale.

In 1951, he acquired the lease of a building at 16–17 Lionel Street, Birmingham, when he bought Rosser and Co., the firm occupying the premises. At that time the building was in a sad state and badly in need of repair.

Rossers undertook factory maintenance work in the region, offering service at weekends and during holiday periods. It was therefore not unusual for Rossers' staff to have keys to the premises to enable them to collect material required out of hours.

The previous owner of the firm, Mr Russell, had died shortly before Cecil How had bought the business, and the new owner started using the old man's office. He remembers clearly the layout of the office in Mr Russell's day, with the old desk and its easy chair, and the old cheque-printing machine which is now kept in Mr How's own home, alongside the original brass door knocker which used to grace the office section of the building and now announces visitors at the Hows' front door.

Late one Saturday night some time after Rossers had changed hands, two of the firm's fitters called in at 16–17 Lionel Street to collect some fittings that were urgently required, and as the key to the gunmetal store was kept in Mr Russell's office, they ran upstairs to fetch it.

Cecil How says that this is their account of what happened: 'On opening the office door they were both shocked at seeing (as they thought) Mr Russell asleep, sitting in his usual chair, and in a great hurry they ran away – they knew Mr Russell had been dead for some time. They would never again go into the office at night.'

Unable to bring himself to believe the fitters' story, Mr How contacted authorities engaged in psychical research in London, but he failed to find any explanation for the incident.

There was, however, a fascinating sequel. In 1958 Cecil How bought the freehold of the building and demolished it, constructing on site a new office block which was officially opened on 25 November 1959 by the Lord Mayor of Birmingham, Alderman Lewis. The remaining stock, furniture and office equipment belonging to Mr Russell's firm was dispersed, but in the new building, Brian Grange [*name changed*], the secretary of Mr How's new business, Froggatt, Prior Ltd, had placed Mr Russell's comfy old chair in his own office.

One day Brian Grange rang down to the general office requesting papers on file to be delivered to him. Half an hour later, when the delivery boy had failed to appear, he rang again demanding to know where the papers were.

Mr How continues: 'The boy then came up to his office with the papers and said that he had been up with them before but, looking through the glass partition, he had seen an old gentleman sitting in the old chair and did not want to go in and interrupt. Brian said that at no time had he had anyone in the office since originally calling for the files, but the boy insisted he had seen someone in the chair. Although quite a newcomer, he gave a description which tallied with the long dead Mr Russell.'

Mr How adds that the haunted chair seems to have disappeared in the various moves and changes made since then, and he hopes old Mr Russell and his ghost now lie undisturbed.

Terraces, Flats, Council Houses

Modern houses and flats are also the scene of inexplicable events, which often feature ghostly sounds.

Miss S. Cartwright who lives in Lancashire shared my own earlier view of the traditional base for a ghost – until her illusions were swept away.

'I always used to imagine a haunted house to look like those in the Vincent Price films,' she wrote, 'a rambling old stone house, standing in its own grounds, surrounded by tall dark trees, not a little urban terraced house like mine, which was probably first occupied at the turn of the century by a family who worked at one of the local spinning mills and who walked to work in clogs along cobbled streets. Hardly the setting for a ghost story.

'There was nothing out of the ordinary about my house – at least I never thought so, until the first of a strange series of events took place.'

One night Miss Cartwright was woken up by a sound on the stairs. 'All houses are known to creak in the night, but this was something different; it was just as though someone was making their way slowly up the stairs. I heard the movements, step by step, until they reached the landing, when they stopped. I waited, holding my breath, listening and waiting, but nothing further happened. It troubled me for several days afterwards, but eventually I put it out of my mind and thought nothing more about it for a long time, deciding I had imagined it.

'It must have been a year or so afterwards that I was awoken again by the same sounds, slowly treading the stairs, only this time they didn't stop when they reached the top. They moved towards the bedroom door, and there was a sound as though someone had brushed against it. I lay motionless, eyes shut tight, frightened of what I would see if I opened them.

'I was sweating, but at the same time frozen with fear, and couldn't move. I waited for something to happen, but nothing did, and eventually I opened my eyes and looked around the room. There was nothing there. I still couldn't convince myself that these were ghostly happenings, always having been very sceptical of such things, even though I could think of no practical explanation.'

Miss Cartwright decided not to tell anyone about her experiences, fearing no one would believe her. But then something rather more unnerving occurred. Once again she heard footsteps. They moved up to the top of the stairs and along to the door of her room. There was no catch on her door, but she heard it open.

'This time the footsteps were accompanied by a heavy, rasping breathing sound ... close to my bed. Suddenly I realized I was no longer frightened. I don't know why, but something made me feel there was nothing to fear. Whatever it was meant me no harm, but was trying to reach me, to be near me. I could feel a presence. Something or someone was there, but when I opened my eyes I could see nothing. The sound of breathing continued ... Someone needed me. Who was it? It vanished as quickly as it had arrived.'

There were times in the months that followed when Miss Cartwright was tempted to confide in someone, but still thinking she would sound foolish, she did not do so.

'In fact I found it hard to believe myself, until something happened that totally convinced me it had never been a figment of my imagination.'

One night when a guest was staying in the house, Miss Cartwright was again woken up. But this time the cause of her abrupt return to consciousness was the voice of her guest whispering in her ear: 'There's someone in the house! Someone is coming up the stairs!'

Arming himself with a shoe against what he expected to be a burglar, the guest, followed by his hostess, made a thorough search of the house without producing any sign of burglars or intruders of any sort. Nevertheless, to Miss Cartwright's private relief, her guest was convinced that some other person had been in the house. For the first time she felt free to reveal her previous experiences.

'Nothing more happened for a number of years, and life

continued as normal. I was attending night school and a friend had dropped me off one evening after a class. It was 3 May, a warm evening about 8.30 p.m., and not quite dark. However, it had just started to rain as I let myself into the house, and I remember thinking I must fetch in the washing from outside before the rain gets heavier. But first I must go to the bathroom.

'I started upstairs, taking off my coat as I went, when I realized I wasn't alone. I stopped, half-way up the stairs, frozen to the spot. Someone was upstairs. Had they broken in while I was out? No signs of a break in ... I stood there, too frightened to go any further ... They are probably in one of the bedrooms! They will have heard me and want to get out of the house! I thought.

'Then a sound which I will never forget came from above me on the landing, a strange sort of groan, a man's voice, a strange moaning sound.

'Fear and common sense gripped me at the same time and at last I found the strength to move from where I stood. I leapt up the remaining stairs two at a time, ran straight into the bathroom, slamming the door shut behind me. Leaning against the door, breathless, I caught sight of my face in the mirror – it was deathly white. I don't know how long I stood there waiting, almost paralysed, for the sound of someone running away down the stairs. But no one did. Or did they? Since then I have never heard any more of my ghostly presence.

'Some time later I confided in a relative who made a very disturbing observation. This last experience had occurred on 3 May. I remember the date because it was a week before the night-school examination. But as my relative observed, it was also the anniversary of my father's death.

'Had he been trying to reach me? Our last meeting before his death was not a happy one. We had not seen eye to eye for a number of years. When he died I could never forgive myself for not making amends sooner ... Was he trying to reach me afterwards to say he forgave me?'

The next contributor, a young woman currently living in Manchester, prefers to remain anonymous, using the name of Sally.

Her father, Peter, was born in Scotland in 1900, and for almost fifteen years before his death he suffered from illness relating to his heart, liver and kidneys. One lung was removed, and finally he succumbed to cancer of the stomach. Because of his condition, Peter always breathed very heavily, dragging his feet when he walked, making slow progress through the family's council flat, and moving in a most distinctive manner.

'He died in April, not long before I was fifteen,' wrote Sally. And she recounted an incident which occurred shortly after her father's death.

One night when she, her older brother and her mother were sitting in the living-room, they heard feet dragging along the hallway accompanied by heavy, laboured breathing. The sound was identical to that of her father making his usual painful progress through the hall of the flat before he died.

'The living-room door was pushed open, although we couldn't see anyone,' Sally recalled. 'I was sitting in the chair behind the door at the time, and felt a cold hand on the left side of my face. My dad always put his hand on my face when he came into the room.'

All the family heard the sounds, they all saw the door open of its own accord, and Sally felt the hand upon her face; but neither she nor any other member of the family could offer any explanation for the incident. They concluded that the presence in the house was the spirit of the man who had recently died.

A few years later, Sally had a little boy who, when four years old, told his mother one morning that he had woken in the night to see a man sitting on the end of his bed looking at him. He had never seen his maternal grandfather, of course, nor had he seen a photograph of him. But when the child described the visitor, Sally recognized the image of her father.

After Sally's marriage and subsequent divorce she was living with her children, two in nursery school and another two in infant school, in a house built over a former graveyard.

'I was in the girls' bedroom trying to tidy it up. I heard a child's voice behind me say "Mam", as if they wanted something. Without thinking I said "Just a minute". Then it clicked: my kids were all in school! It frightened me and I got out of the room fast.'

On other occasions she heard the same call again when she was alone in the house. She heard footsteps in the hallway and thought her son was sleep-walking. When she went into the bedrooms to check on the children, she found them fast asleep. She also saw shadows noiselessly passing her own bedroom door, in the light from the landing fixture which was left on all night to dispel the children's fears of the dark.

'I thought I was going crazy, that it was all in my mind, until one day my son said he wanted to talk to me . . . he told me exactly the same things that I had heard and seen: someone calling his name, shadows passing his door. Even the girls had seen and heard things they couldn't explain . . .

'Finally I had the house blessed by two elders from our church, and I can honestly say there's been nothing since then.'

'Brenda', whose own encounter with a ghost appears on p. 176, contributed the incidents described below which took place in the house of a friend, near Manchester Airport.

'She moved into a council house with three bedrooms and downstairs the room was L-shaped, leading into a back kitchen. One evening she was watching TV when she heard cutlery being rattled. Thinking it was one of the children creeping downstairs she shouted, but heard no reply. Being on her own, she was a bit frightened at going to investigate.

'When her husband came in they both went into the kitchen, and found the table had been neatly set out.

'On another night she was sitting quietly when the curtains at the lounge windows suddenly swished open on their own. She became too worried after lots of strange things happened, and decided to move.

'On the morning she moved out, the lady next door was chatting to her, saying how sorry she was to see her go. My friend asked her who had lived there before, and the neighbour said it had been a couple. The husband had had a stroke before he had died, she said. He used to have his single bed under the lounge window, and every morning he would get his walking stick and swish open the curtains.'

Mrs Mary Cathrine Neale, known as Molly, lives in Tyne and Wear. She says that she is not a medium, but before the events related here she had attended one or two spiritualist's meetings and had been impressed. 'I cannot truthfully say that I've seen a ghost,' she writes. But her experience following the purchase of a modern bungalow was unnerving, to say the least, and demonstrates again the point that haunted buildings are not necessarily old buildings.

Molly Neale and her husband were moving away from Ryton to Redcar as Mr Neale was taking up a new post.

'We looked at several properties without satisfaction until, at the end of a small grove shaped like an atoll, was a lovely bungalow. How could anyone fall in love with a bungalow? I did. We were shown around and decided "This is it!"

'As we left, I felt that someone watched us. I turned back to check. No one was there. But I did say, "Look, no flowers in the garden, privet all around, three lawns and one solitary tree" and I thought it was queer, no flowers, just all green.

'We settled in and were very happy. An aunt and uncle came to visit. Sunday dinner was eaten in the dining-room. It was a lovely sunny day. I brought coffee and cups etc. on a tray from the kitchen and as I placed it on the table a terrible bang shook the table. Dishes rattled like mad and yet net curtains at windows and doors never moved.

'Aunt Mary looked out the front door. Uncle and husband looked out the back door. They searched garden and grove and not a soul was in sight. Aunt, in real *Coronation Street* style, said, "B...y Norah, is the house haunted?"

'I never told her what I'd experienced previously: door handles moved and the door was pushed ajar as if someone was about to come in. I thought I saw a little girl, long hair and yellow dress, run past the window to come to the kitchen door. I'd open the door. No one there. Several times this happened, but I never saw the face because, as she ran, long hair hid her features.

'Once, going to see who knocked at the door, my husband was puzzled at nobody being there, so I told him of my experiences. He just laughed and said that it must be the side effects of new pills I was prescribed for arthritis.

'But one day he was watching TV and I was ironing in the kitchen. He looked over and said, "Did you walk over and put your arms around me?"'

His wife laughed at him and said she had not moved from the ironing board, adding in a teasing tone, 'Who's taking pills now?'

Although Mrs Neale admits she has always been afraid of the dark, she was not scared by the antics of the little girl in the yellow dress. She called her 'my friendly ghost', and often felt her presence in the house. After her aunt's visit, however, Mrs Neale began to consider seriously that her house might be haunted. And then someone else saw the little figure.

'Sheila, who was once my evacuee from wartime London, came to Redcar for a long weekend. She liked a coffee, so I said, "Sit and read the paper. I'll wash the dishes, and we'll both have a peaceful time." (My husband was at work.) She opened the newspaper and called out, "No peace! A little girl has run past the window!" I asked Sheila to open the door. She did so. [There was no one there.] When I asked her to describe the girl she said, "Long fair hair and a yellow dress." I explained to her all that I had felt, and how many times I had opened the door to find no one there.'

When Mr Neale died a little later, his wife's Aunt Mary, her uncle and Sheila attended his funeral at Ryton and drove Mrs Neale back to her house at Redcar.

'It was a Sunday, and as I passed the coffee around Sheila picked up the Sunday paper. She looked at the date and said, "Oh, isn't it strange! It's exactly a year today that I was here, and saw that little girl!"'

No one spoke. The room was suddenly quiet. Mrs Neale says that from that day onwards she never again felt the presence of the little girl, and nobody reported seeing her again.

Molly Neale made inquiries about the previous occupants of the house but, as far as she could establish, no young girl had ever lived there. The house was relatively new. It had been built, she discovered, on land reclaimed from the sea. The only previous owner had been an unmarried sea captain. This information might have been significant, because there was one aspect of the house that had mystified Mrs Neale throughout the time she had lived there.

'The bathroom needed no air freshener. It always had the smell of ozone. And I wonder if my friendly ghost was drowned, or was she trying to tell me I was to lose my wonderful husband and my happy house? I sold the house and moved back here, and often wonder about it all.'

Pubs

Stories of ghosts in pubs are legion, and often received with understandable suspicion. But a remarkable number of them cannot be attributed to over-imbibing.

George Phillips-Smith is a retired railway officer whose home is in Surrey. In the 1970s he lived in a village near Richmond, North Yorkshire, and during journeys to and from the south he used by-roads to avoid the congested A1. One each journey he passed a small wayside inn, The Busby Stoop, at the intersection of the A61 and A167, on the outskirts of the village of Carlton Miniott, near Thirsk.

There were some odd stories circulating about this pub at the time. 'Briefly, it was rumoured that the inn possessed an ancient wooden armchair with a curse on it. It was said that anyone who dared to sit on the chair was likely to come to an untimely end. I never had any occasion to check the tale, being a teetotaller! But I passed the place often enough.

'In about 1975 there was a story in the local press that two young men, in a spirit of bravado (and perhaps too full of spirits), had defied the curse. They were killed in a road accident nearby a few days later. After that the landlord relegated the chair to the inn cellar – he was seemingly afraid to do the obvious, and set fire to it, in case of "repercussions"!'

'About 25 years ago, when I was still on the buses, I had just finished a shift and a half, went home and had a meal, looked at the clock and said to the wife, "I think I'll go down to the Askew Arms (the pub fifty yards from my home) for a pint of shandy and a game of darts",' writes former bus driver James Byrne of Tyne and Wear (see p.127). That decision was to cause him some embarrassment.

'I arrived at the bar about 9.30 p.m., went into the back room, ordered my pint of shandy and started playing darts by myself. Nobody else was in the room. After five to ten minutes I tired of throwing darts and had started playing blind dominoes, still by myself, when through the door that leads behind the bar, the manager, "Big Andy", came and sat at the other side of the table and started talking to me.

'"How are you doing, lad? How's life?" he asked. I told him I was too busy working, had given up drinking, and only had the odd shandy now and then, and that's why he had not seen me in the bar for quite some time. We carried on talking about anything and nothing for about fifteen to twenty minutes when suddenly he stood up and said, "I'd better get back behind the bar or they'll miss me."

'Within twenty seconds of Andy going back behind the bar, seven people had walked into the room one after the other.'

James Byrne knew all the newcomers and when they commented on finding him sitting by himself in the pub he told them he had been talking to Andy for the last twenty minutes. They roared with laughter and began to tease him before calling to Betty, the long-serving barmaid, telling her what he had said.

Betty replied quickly that that was impossible, as Andy had died well over two years earlier. Bewildered, James Byrne insisted that he had indeed been talking to the manager, and he described in detail everything Andy had been wearing, from shirt to slippers, feeling very foolish in the face of the scepticism of his audience. But to everyone's surprise, the barmaid was impressed by James Byrne's description of the clothes worn by the previous manager of the pub.

'Betty said that that was exactly what he was wearing the night he died.'

Mrs Charlotte Bathurst says she is in danger of boring family audiences with the details of the ghosts who appear so frequently in her presence. But on the following occasion she was not alone in seeing an uninvited guest.

Mrs Bathurst and her seventeen-year-old son were sitting in the hall of the Hare and Hounds, a hotel in Westonbirt, Gloucestershire, on a very hot July evening between 6 and 7 p.m. Mr Bathurst was parking the car while a table was being prepared for the family in the restaurant of the hotel.

'We noticed an old man in a black suit with a Gladstone bag sitting with us. When my husband came in we went into the restaurant. We asked the manager who the old man was. He said, "Don't make a fuss. It was probably the ghost. He appears from time to time, with his Gladstone bag!"'

Craig Alexander Godfrey owns The Drunken Admiral, a well-known restaurant on the waterfront in Hobart, and one of Tasmania's oldest surviving buildings. The premises had been convict-built in 1824, and had been used as ordnance and granary stores, soldiers' barracks, and the IXL Jam factory before the Godfreys had bought part of it in 1984, when they had learnt about the Chinese man who was found hanging from the rafters of courtyard buildings at the rear in 1880. Mr Godfrey writes:

'I act as chef in the restaurant, and two years ago a waitress rushed into the kitchen saying she had overheard a customer talking about the ghost he had seen. I went out to chat with him. It appeared that he had worked for IXL Jams and, sitting in our restaurant, he was reminiscing about how the building had looked then, in the 1960s, when he had seen a Chinese man in early garb literally drift across the old courtyard behind the restaurant and disappear into the wall. [That wall had once been part of a room-sized safe which Mr Godfrey had had converted into lavatories.]

'Shortly after we opened the restaurant, our cleaning lady, Betty [*name changed*], who was with us eight years, felt she was being watched and looked up just in time to see a young girl about eight to ten years old, dressed in grey Victorian garb, watching her. The little girl darted behind the bar. Betty was on her own at the time. The restaurant was locked. She investigated, and then realized that she had seen an apparition.'

Betty later said she had felt ghosts 'whizzing' around her in the restaurant, brushing against her, and had often thought she was being watched. One day she heard invisible children singing; on another occasion, shortly before she left The Drunken Admiral, she saw the apparition of a Victorian sailor standing by the kitchen sink.

Mr Godfrey was to learn of a more sinister presence in the restaurant.

'In the last three years Betty was with us, she refused to clean the lady's loo: the aggressive atmosphere in there was too much for her, so she brought her husband in to do this. Then we received two separate complaints about the loo.

'One night a lady told us she was psychic. She had been to the toilet and sensed an asphyxiation, hands around her throat. Knowing how to handle the situation, she said she literally told the ghost to "Bugger off!"

'The second incident was a little more dramatic: a lady had eaten her entreé, then she had gone to the loo. She came back a short time later white-faced and absolutely terrified. She raced over to the Maitre D', cancelled her main course and, before gathering her partner and leaving, told the Maitre D' that she was sitting on the loo when the door unlatched itself, opened and shut again – and then she felt as though she was being throttled. (This seems to be consistent with the Chinese who hanged himself not believing he's dead, refusing "to go to the light" etc., hanging around our toilet and approaching people who are susceptible to such behaviour.)

'The experience really fascinated me, so I called in a couple of mediums who were friends of a friend. I told them nothing: they just knew something weird was going on. Immediately on entering the bar area, one lady said she was being "whizzed past" – a spirit was brushing past her – and she felt that because it was only shoulder high (she was five foot three), it was a child (consistent with the girl ghost our cleaner saw). Then I suggested she go into the loo. I told her nothing. She returned ten minutes later and just looked me in the eye. "Now that is one nasty spirit!" she said. "I think he's Asian!"

'She too experienced the asphyxiation but knew how to cope with it. Later I found out that the Chinese ghost had followed the mediums to their home where they hold regular spiritualist meetings. He turned up at a meeting that evening and half a dozen other ladies in the room could see the medium's throat being indented by invisible hands. Apparently the Chinese ghost refuses to believe he is dead. The medium told him to go "to the light". He refused, so she told him to move on anyhow. "You don't frighten me," she said. "Yes," he replied. "But I can frighten others!" He hasn't been heard of since.'

At the southern end of The Drunken Admiral the Godfreys recently opened Skull-Duggery Inn, a small bar and eatery.

'The staff complained that glasses hanging up over the bar would start a slow pendular swinging movement all of their own and in rhythm they would swing away without any provocation. Other times, glasses literally exploded while waitresses held them. This happened three times but fortunately nobody was ever hurt.'

Mr Godfrey is proud of his historic building and its colourful history. And unlike some owners of haunted premises, he believes the ghosts that inhabit The Drunken Admiral will attract potential customers, not deter them.

In 1986 Craig Godfrey, his wife Leone and their two small children were touring Cornwall during a visit to England. They stopped at the famous Jamaica Inn on Bodmin Moor, hoping for a bed. It was fully booked however, and they were put up for the night at the Inn Farm House directly opposite.

'For some unknown reason our fourteen-month-old baby, Briley, screamed all night, hardly sleeping. Something very wrong and strange appeared to be bothering her. However, I went over to the inn after we had dined to try a pint or two of Cornish hospitality. Under the circumstances I wouldn't have done this, but my wife was adamant that I go, as I had wanted to see the Old Jamaica Inn since I was a child, and it didn't look as though we would ever return to the area.

'When I returned to our attic room at 11.15 p.m., Briley was crying so I put her on a mattress on the floor with me, and cuddled her to sleep. It was a very cold night and our son slept with his mother. (He too was a little spooked.)

'An hour or so had gone by when my wife woke to see a white spectre lifting Briley (now asleep) from me. She saw it carry the child four or five feet with arms outstretched. Leone froze, then screamed, awakening me. The figure placed Briley at the foot of my mattress and vanished through the door. I awoke to find Leone sitting erect, and Briley at the foot of my bedding.'

Airfields

Airfields quite often have their ghosts, which is perhaps comprehensible, since they are from time to time the scene of sudden death.

Harold Webster of York sent me the following story which appeared in the Yorkshire Evening Press *on 16 August 1988, and was later featured in the documentary film* Ghost Train, *produced for the BBC's programme* Forty Minutes, *to which I was attached as consultant.*

It might come as a surprise to members of the public to learn that the RAF takes the subject of ghosts seriously enough to have issued a press release (dramatically headlined TOWER OF FEAR) informing the media of the existence of a ghost at one of their airbases. But that is what happened in the summer of 1988.

As the editorial column of the *Yorkshire Evening Press* commented, the ultra high-tech RAF could be expected to play down the less sophisticated wartime days of lucky mascots, superstition and flying in on a wing and a prayer. Not so: for not only was information about the sighting of the former RAF man made available, but members of the press were specifically invited to meet the people of RAF Linton-on-Ouse who had seen the ghost.

Four people claim to have seen the shadowy, six-foot apparition believed to be W. F. Hodgson [*real name*], born 19 February 1921, who served in the RAF during the Second World War. When his Halifax bomber was shot down over Germany in 1943 he was taken prisoner and held at Stalag Luft 3 and 4. He survived the war, and when he died almost thirty years ago his ashes were scattered on the main runway of the airbase. There have been increasingly frequent sightings of his ghost.

The first report came from air traffic controller Brenda Jenkinson, aged twenty-one, who was on night duty in the control tower when she saw it.

'I was really frightened. I was sceptical about ghosts before but now I believe in them completely . . . I came out of the switchboard room to go downstairs when I saw this figure in the hallway. It was six feet tall – it was a shadow but very distinct. It just moved away.'

Her predicament was made worse by disbelieving colleagues.

'I was really upset. No one would believe me. The next couple of nights I stood in the hallway waiting for the thing to come back.' Then, two weeks later, the apparition reappeared. 'I was coming down the stairs and the same shadow passed a doorway.'

She was relieved when a station security officer and two other women at the control tower also saw the ghostly flyer at night, and provided supporting evidence.

'None of the girls liked to be left there alone,' Brenda told the press. Now working for the RAF as an assistant air traffic controller in Anglesey, Brenda says she will not forget her experience at Linton-on-Ouse, which was treated so seriously by RAF authorities that they are seeking further information about W. F. Hodgson.

When the BBC included this story in the documentary *Ghost Train*, Eddie Burks, a psychic investigator, was asked to accompany the film crew to the RAF base. He met Brenda and other personnel there and was filmed establishing contact with a ghost.

According to Eddie Burks, the ghost suffered pain in his back as the result of an accident. A BBC researcher later discovered that in 1950 an aircraftsman had been knocked down by a petrol tanker on the perimeter of the runway, suffering multiple internal injuries and a fractured pelvis. He was twenty-one years old, and died from his injuries.

The accident victim's symptoms appear to have been very similar to those of the spirit spoken to by the psychic investigator. It seems therefore that two different ghosts may have been involved.

Towns

Individual buildings are not the only places in which ghosts seem to feel at home. Streets and sometimes whole towns are considered to be haunted.

In a letter to me dated 19 April 1988 Ernest Ford of Lancashire, author of Lancashire Tales of Mirth, *puts forward the theory that the most haunted town in the north-west of England must be his own, Westhoughton, which lies half-way between Bolton and Wigan. To substantiate his claim he offers the following account of recent psychic events that have occurred in one particular neighbourhood:*

'Case number one is the strange happenings at the town's Central Labour Club where former steward John Biggy has heard strange footsteps walking through the club when all the customers have left. The swish of a thick taffeta dress has brushed past him, although nothing appeared in any form. These odd noises around the place are confirmed by the present manager of the club who, while clearing away glasses upstairs, has heard the bang of doors closing downstairs when the club was locked up for the night.

'"I was tinkering about on that piano," he said, pointing to the lounge piano which is frequently used, "and I could feel that there was someone there who didn't want me to play."

'All these things appear to happen after the customers have gone and the club is locked up for the night. Strange to relate, there is a certain spot in the club that remains cold no matter what the temperature is outside.

'But the most interesting haunting of all is at the nearby British Legion Club where empty glasses roll upwards and off the table's edge, and it is in this club that a sighting has been reported.

'Fred Kirkman, while serving the club as committee member, has seen an apparition about seven times to date. A ghostly figure of a well-dressed Victorian lady, wearing a bustle and dressed in red, walks cheekily through the concert room, but quickly disappears when the games-room door is opened to gain a better view of the sighting. This ghost doesn't seem to bother Fred but has caused concern to others in his presence.

'At times when the swing doors have opened on to the empty concert room, noises of people chattering and laughing have been heard, as if the room was full of people.

'Back in the 1960s one Hunger Hill family was relieved when the Bolton Corporation took a positive view and rehoused it because the plague of ghosts at the house could no longer be tolerated.

'At the same time as the Hunger Hill incident, David Roberts, working at the Daisy Hill turkey farm, witnessed the ghost of a woman in a wedding dress coming across a field from out of the murky mist. She entered a house next to a church where she stayed for ninety minutes before appearing to wander again across the field.

'Across town now to the disused Palace Cinema, where wooden pallets were made and stacked for the manufacturing trade. Two men passing at night saw a smoke-like apparition throwing pallets and wood around, as if in confusion.

'Mrs F. McMahon, preparing meals in the kitchen at the Red Lion Hotel on Wigan Road, was grabbed by the shoulder, although no one had entered the room. Footsteps had earlier been reported stalking the corridors of this Olde Worlde establishment.

'Just off Wigan Road and about half a mile from the Red Lion lies what used to be Oakes Farm. After the farmer's death it was decided that the farmhouse was too spacious for one family, so it was separated into individual houses.

'In one of these units lives Brenda Chadwick whose dog would only dare to climb half-way up the stairs before making a fur-bristling exit to safer ground. Various things have happened since Brenda took up residence, including the noise from upstairs of someone getting up on her bed.

'Recently a young local artist was commissioned to paint a mural of the battle of Westhoughton Common which took place in 1642 between the Royalists and the Parliamentarians. This splendid mural can now be seen above the entrance to the town's market hall; but the artist discovered a most interesting fact during his research on the project.

'Apparently, a foreign student, lodging in a house overlooking the Commercial fields on the edge of the battlefield, looked through her bedroom window and witnessed the ghostly battle taking place. By the time that a second person could be found to witness the scene, the bloodied spectres had dissolved into nothingness.

'These phenomena have only come to light because the witnesses are not afraid to speak of their experiences,' Ernest Ford comments. (All the individuals mentioned in his report have been identified.) 'Most incidents go unreported because of fear, not only of the supernatural, but of what the unbelieving public might think.'

In conclusion he points out that the ancient town of Westhoughton, dating back to 1199, has had its fair share of tragedy over the years: 'A mill was burned by Luddites of the area resulting in the deaths of three men and a boy of twelve who were hanged at Lancaster in 1812 for the offence . . . and the town was the scene of the biggest mining disaster ever when the Pretoria Pit went up, claiming the lives of three hundred and forty-four men and boys on 21 December 1910. It is any wonder,' Ernest Ford adds, 'that strange phenomena occur here?'

Mrs Joan Read (see page 12) describes another of her supernatural experiences relating to her professional and private interest in historical subjects. On this occasion, the incident was also witnessed by her companions.

'In the early 1960s I conducted a number of walks around Bankside, Southwark, on Saturday afternoons. There were very few people around then as the warehouses were closed.

'One particular Saturday, about a dozen people joined me as it was a fine, sunny afternoon. We walked and talked through the Clink around the rear of the houses on Bankside. The path was narrow, so we had to bunch together.

'We noticed a man walking about forty or fifty yards ahead of us. He stooped a little, making his flat black-brimmed hat appear to rest on his shoulders. He wore a long, black flowing cape; but what attracted our attention was the large lozenge-shaped badge between his shoulder-blades, with what looked like an heraldic device.

'We remarked upon it to one another as we slowly neared

Cardinal Cap Alley. How surprised we were when he didn't turn up the alley – he disappeared through the brick wall which blocked our path just past the alley turning!

'We waited a while, then turned up the alley and continued along Bankside.

'Who was the man? His garb was that of one of the Lord Chamberlain's men. They were a group of players, under the patronage of the Lord Chamberlain, who played at the Globe from 1598 until 1603, and then continued under the patronage of James I.

'The heraldic device would have been the arms of the Lord Chamberlain. Did this player come to an untimely end in one of the many fights which broke out in the nearby stewhouses (whorehouses)? Was he a victim of one of the virulent plagues which broke out between 1602 and 1604?

'We don't know – but we are sure that we saw the black-cloaked man disappear through the wall!'

Fred Hadfield is a bricklayer living in Lancashire. He tells of a fascinating incident which he freely admits frightened him, but not enough to put him off his regular early morning walks with his dog. 'I did not fancy letting a ghost stop me,' he writes. 'Of course no one believes me, but I don't care.' This is what happened in the early morning of 1 November 1987, the night of Hallowe'en:

'Every morning I take my dog Jess for a walk to get a morning paper. It was dark at the time although the street was well lit. I was going to cross the street when I noticed something low on the ground about forty feet away.

'At first I thought it was a white dog. I stopped then because my dog is a bit vicious. Anyway the thing grew to the size of a tall person, and was dancing in a circle. It seemed to be a woman in a shroud, very bright and white, with what I can only describe as tiny bright stardust falling all around her. She seemed to be enjoying herself immensely.

'I was a bit scared by now and more so when the thing spotted me watching it. It then ceased dancing and seemed to be coming over the street towards me, so I went backwards a good few paces. I was very frightened. It then seemed to change its mind and carried on dancing. I managed to pluck up enough courage to carry on past it, and went for my paper.

'After getting the paper I started on my way back, dreading meeting the thing again . . . it was becoming a little lighter and I got my nerve back, a bit. I made my way back up a street parallel with the one with the apparition in it and cut across to the street a little further on, not expecting to see it again.

'It was almost daylight by now and when I did look, it was still dancing like mad and then faded away.

'About an hour later I inspected the place where the thing was dancing and it was all new grass, untrodden by anyone. I swear this is the truth.

'I still take my dog on early morning walks but I avoid the place as much as possible and only dare go past it in broad daylight. I have not seen the thing since, thank goodness, and don't want to!'

Leslie Cruse of Leicestershire is a retired police officer and a former member of the 9th Battalion Royal Sussex Regiment. He describes his sighting of a ghost which had previously been seen by a number of people from all walks of life. There appeared to have been no observable pattern to the sightings. In 1961 Mr Cruse was the village bobby at Thringstone.

'On finishing duty just before midnight on a warm April evening, I decided to take my boxer dog for a walk along the footpath across the fields opposite my home, where now stands the Melrose Road housing estate.

'It was a beautiful night, almost a full moon, and not a cloud in the sky. We had been walking into the field for about a hundred and fifty yards when suddenly my dog gave a deep-throated growl.

'I looked around me and could see no one, or anything to upset the dog. However, he continued to growl and came and stood close to me as if protecting me. I put my hand down to stroke him and the bristles along his back were stiff and rigid.

'A few seconds after this there was a chill in the air and a white form in the shape of a long cloak and hood glided by me and disappeared in a high hawthorn hedge about twenty-five yards from me. When this form went out of sight, my dog quietened down and the chill went out of the air.

'The next day I told my neighbour of this and he said: "You have no doubt seen our local nun, and she could have been on top of the tunnel." On delving into this further I learned that a tunnel is supposed to exist between the monastery and the priory, which is now Grace Dieu Ruins.

'The nun, according to legend, was hiding the treasures of the priory so that the reigning king could not find them. Anyone who sees the ghost of the nun, and where she disappears, will find the hidden treasure.'

Leslie Cruse learnt of another sighting which took place at about 10.50 p.m. on a winter's night, when a bus driver stopped near the Grace Dieu Ruins to pick up a passenger.

'The conductor went to help what he thought was a nun up the steps of the bus,' writes Mr Cruse, 'when the nun disappeared into thin air!

'I know in my own case it could not have been a practical joke, as the hedge was so thick it was impossible for any human being to walk through it.'

Rural Ghosts

The British countryside is famous for its beauty and, if all accounts are true, it is heavily populated by headless horsemen, phantom coaches and misers tending hoards of gold.

Barrie Rose is a welder who lives in Warwickshire. He believes he saw a ghost many years ago when he was courting the girl who later became his wife. She lived in an old cottage, dating back to the fifteenth century, in Barston, a village about eight miles from Coventry.

One Saturday night after going to a nearby cinema, Barrie Rose accepted an invitation from his future parents-in-law to stay the night at the cottage.

'After I got back I had some supper and went to bed. You could tell the place was old – the bed was held up on one side by two house bricks to keep it level.

'About three in the morning I woke up and as I looked across the room I saw a figure like an old man going through the bedroom wall into the next room. Well, it took me back awhile, I can tell you!

'Next morning I asked my mother-in-law-to-be if she had ever seen the figure. She told me she and her husband had seen it lots of times, but warned me not to tell the children, not to upset them. Well, they left the village, and I had forgotten all about it till last year when my sister-in-law wrote from Cornwall to see if I would go down for a holiday, as I had not seen her for thirty-four years; so I did.

'One night I was talking about the old times and mentioned the ghost at Barston, when she told me the rest of the story. It was said that the old man had buried a lot of gold coins under the back kitchen floor, and after he died he used to return from time to time to see if they were still there. The cottage was sold a few years ago and the new people had it all done over to make it more up to date.

'When they took the old red brick floor up, there were all the gold coins under the floor!'

Mr Rose was delighted to have this corroboration of his sighting of the old man all those years ago, and in 1988 he told me that the cottage at Barston is still there.

William David Smith (known as Bill), who has contributed a number of stories to this book, writes from his home in Suffolk, where he now lives in retirement. He was a lorry driver for fifty-two years.

One Saturday night in 1915, when he was a lad living in the south-west, he accompanied his uncle (a bareknuckle fighter) on a journey by local bus into Bristol. Returning very late that night the man and the boy were obliged to walk the last leg of the journey, from Combe Down to Norton St Philip.

'As we went up the hill from Midford towards Hinton Charterhouse I became tired, and my uncle picked me up and carried me on his shoulders. It was around 11.30 p.m. with a brilliant full moon. We saw something moving near an old stone stile on the right-hand side, in the dry stone wall, from which the ground dropped away sharply into the valley.

'I asked what it was, and my uncle said, "It looks like a sheep has got caught up. I'll release it." He set me down on the road and we went to the stile. There was nothing there. We looked over into the valley but all we saw were sheep paths, where the animals fed on the hillside, although there were no sheep anywhere in the field.

'My uncle got over the stile and as he did so there came a horrible unearthly scream: "Ow aragh!" Then silence. It seemed to come from the wall but when he reached it he found nothing other than stones and a few strands of ivy.

'He came back, lit his pipe and said, "We'll rest awhile." He sat me on the stile stone, and leaned against the wall smoking. As we talked, there came again this horrible scream, and about twenty to thirty feet below us something which looked like a man rose out of the ground.

'Uncle jumped over the wall and slithered down the hillside, but there was nothing there. Whatever it was had disappeared. He looked around and stamped about on the ground, then came back up, and said, "Where did it go? Did you see what it was?" I said, "It just went! I thought it was a man. He went back in the ground." But my uncle said there was no place he could go. The ground was solid.

'He took me by the hand and as we continued up the hill he was examining the wall. He stopped, and pointing to a large square stone let into the building of the wall, said, "Just look at that!" "What?" I asked. He said, "That stone! See that red 'M' on it? That is known as the Murder Stone. Years ago a man was murdered here, and that stone was placed to mark the spot."'

Mr Smith believes that he and his uncle saw the ghost of the murdered man on the hillside that night. He continues, 'Some few months after this, a workman saw what he thought was a rock protruding from the hillside. He dug round it to uncover an old stone coffin with no lid on it and no skeleton in it. The farmer had the coffin set up as a drinking trough for cattle near where it was found and it is probably there now if you go to look. It was when I was last there in 1927. And the "M" on the Murder Stone had been painted blood red.'

By 1928 Bill Smith had left childhood behind him and was working at Buckland Newton, a small village on the Dorset border. Having nothing better to do in the long winter evenings, he and his mate often walked three miles into the nearest village pub to play shove-halfpenny, darts or table skittles with the locals. After they were told of a short cut down Donkey Lane to the pub, they began using it. Mr Smith takes up the tale of the donkey:

'One evening, one of the locals asked which way we walked in to the pub and we told him.

'"You take my tip, don't you go that way tonight," he said. "This be the night the donkey gallop. If you do, you might not see mornin'. Folk here bin known to die o' frit when they sets eyes on he."

'I was interested and asked why. He said, "You take my 'vice, he baint no ornery donkey he, not that un aint, he got feet like a hoss, all white he be, an he run like a stag. He don't wait for no midnight he don't. He be 'bout all hours, and folks don't live long after they sets eyes on un." I said, "We won't see him if we go by the road, then?" He said, "Naw! Taint nivver bin knowed he go anywhere only up Donkey Lane. You won't git no man from village to go up there tonight."

'We spent the evening hearing about the donkey and decided we would trust to luck, and come home that way, thinking they had some trick to play on us.

'We got some distance up the lane and heard a sound as of a heavy horse galloping. The ground vibrated and we climbed the bank into the bushes, thinking someone had frightened a horse and driven him up the lane behind us. It was not altogether dark, there being a quarter moon and stars.

'Nothing came past, but the drumming of hooves seemed to be over our heads. We climbed the bank to look into the fields. There was nothing moving and the sound died way. It was uncanny and I felt a chilly wind, but there was no wind blowing. My mate said, "What do you reckon?" I said, "I don't know. But there's something strange. Come on, let's get out of it." We slid down the bank and continued our journey.

'On leaving the fields we saw the village constable waiting to meet up with the police sergeant. We told him what we had heard. He said, "Yes, I've heard strange sounds sometimes, and I've heard the tale about the donkey, but I've never seen it. There have been several reports over the years of men having seen a strange looking donkey-sized animal with hooves like a shire horse. But it has been argued that those who claim to have seen it have been drinking strong beer. I advise you to tell the old boys that you saw it, and it gave you a ride home, until it saw me and the sergeant!" I said I couldn't do that . . . We were both sober and we both knew there was something uncanny happening, though what it was we didn't know, and we never did find out. No one seemed able to explain it.'

Bill Smith had moved to Lancashire by 1929, and he worked there for a year on an estate which had been bequeathed to the Crown. The house, then no longer lived in, was open to visitors for eight months of the year, and looked after by a caretaker and his wife.

On arrival Mr Smith parked the van in which he lived on the

tree-shaded bank of a large lake. He was a keen swimmer and angler and was permitted to use the lake after the gates closed at 8 p.m.

'It had been a terrifically hot, humid day in June. Thunderstorms were frequent, and one could sweat standing still. I had spent some time in the lake, and before turning in I thought I would have a last good swim. It was around 10.30 p.m., deep dusk but no way dark.

'Looking around before diving in I saw four or five figures on the bridge over the moat and, thinking perhaps the caretaker had visitors, I decided to wait a while as I was nude. I heard a distant clock strike eleven and dived in, since it would now be too dark for anyone to see me underwater. I had my swim, climbed out and was rubbing myself down when I heard voices raised in argument, or anger, though I could not recognize the words or dialect.

'Thinking the figures I had seen earlier were unwelcome visitors who had been surprised by the caretaker or his wife, I decided he might need assistance. I ran to the van, pulled on a pair of shorts, picked up my torch and shovel and dodged from tree to tree in the hopes I wouldn't be seen.

'I could no longer hear voices but it appeared a scrimmage was taking place on the far side of the bridge. In the shadow of the balustrade I crept forward and heard two loud splashes as though something heavy had been dropped into the moat. I rushed forward with my shovel raised. There was nothing there. I looked into the water expecting to see ripples. There were none. Then I heard the front door of the house slam. I felt totally uneasy, as the door was always shut at 6 o'clock, and securely locked and bolted.

'The hairs pricked the back of my neck, the air was icy cold. I knew I had witnessed something which had no being. I shone my torch into the water. It was clear and still. Two or three fish nosed into the beam. I walked round the west side listening, but everything was silent. I came back and tried the front door. It was securely fastened. I went to bed, knowing that I had seen and heard something.'

The following morning Mr Smith saw the caretaker and described what he had seen. He knew nothing of any visitors or any disturbance. He had not seen or heard anyone around the house the previous night.

'It was not me,' he told Mr Smith. 'I don't have visitors.'

'I think you do,' replied Mr Smith. 'Supernatural ones!'

'We've never yet had any trouble,' said the caretaker. 'And I don't remember reading anything in the records. Had you been drinking too much, perhaps? It was awfully hot last night!'

Mr Smith assured him he drank soft drinks only, and there the matter rested.

'I couldn't convince him and I had no witness,' Mr Smith concludes. 'But I knew I had seen something and heard something. What was it? I had no way of finding out. I watched, night after night, but saw nothing further.'

Highway Encounters

A striking development in the recorded history of ghosts is the increasing evidence of incidents that occur on modern highways and involve drivers of all kinds of vehicles travelling at speed. These perplexing and sometimes frightening stories feature conventional ghosts as well as spectres that bear scant resemblance to the human form.

William James Hunter of Surrey has now retired from the RAF. In the summer of 1956 he was RAF Liaison Officer at GCHQ Cheltenham, Gloucestershire, living with his wife and two small sons in a rented cottage in the little village of Greet, near Winchcombe. He writes:

'Once a week I and two or three of my staff would meet after duty at Rossly Manor, a country club on the hill to the south of the A40 a mile or so beyond Charlton Kings, to play squash. After the game we would shower and meet at the bar for a quick drink before going our separate ways home.'

One fine clear night in August or September of that year, Jim Hunter finished his game of squash, and left the club at about 9.30 p.m.

'It was a pleasant evening and I believe there was a moon . . . so I decided to take the country route home rather than the main road around Cheltenham which would have been slightly quicker. My route took me a short way back along the A40 and thence into a lane, to the right to Winchcombe. A short way down this lane there was a large country house, owned by the Dowty Engineering people, I believe. Its only significance on this occasion, however, was that it was the only house for miles around, although some distance further on there was the occasional farm.

'The lane was winding and undulating and certainly, in the area with which we are concerned at the moment, it was heavily wooded on both sides. The particular stretch ran along a kind of ledge, from which it sloped down to the right and steeply up to the left, and was relatively straight for a while before dropping to the right at a fairly steep bend.

'About half-way along this stretch I noticed something out of the corner of my eye – a kind of light, some fifty to sixty degrees on the right from the direction in which I was travelling. It was not really a light, more of a glow in the darkness of the wood. (I should add that as aircrew my vision was good, certainly not "tunnel", and I was then in my mid-thirties.)

'Although I was unable to watch the light constantly, I was aware that it moved, and was proceeding up the hillside towards the lane. I had a feeling we were on a collision course. If it were a person I reassured myself it would see my headlights and stop before crossing the lane ahead of me. This glow grew larger and had taken on a human form. Furthermore it was strangely dressed – for I'm sure it was dressed. It wore a cloak of kinds, a dull crystal blue in colour. The figure was bare-headed, although I cannot recall a face. What startled me, however, was the fact that despite all the trees the figure moved deliberately and in a straight, undeviating way.

'Still unhesitating, it moved into the road directly in my path. I braked heavily but was quite unable to stop in time. This creature moved through the bonnet of my car. Automatically I prepared to open the door in order to get out to see if I had collided with something, although I neither heard nor felt anything at the time.

'What I did see was this creature, person, thing, continuing to move – it could hardly be described as a walk – across the road. And it continued up the hillside, up through the trees, still glowing and growing smaller with the distance. Again, it did not deviate or attempt to avoid the trees in its path and, strangely, it was never hidden by a tree. It certainly never looked back and I'm sure it never looked at the car.

'After an interval, which seemed like an age but could have been only a matter of seconds, it disappeared. But it had moved *through* the front of my car.

'Subconsciously and automatically I put the car into gear and drove around the lane towards Winchcombe and home. I found I was perspiring a little and had a feeling of numbness or unease.

But I don't recall being startled at the time. (There was no one else around.)

'I could think of nothing on my way home apart from telling my wife what had happened. I had a strong feeling, though, that she was not going to believe this one!

'And in twenty to thirty minutes, I suppose, I arrived home. It was only then that it occurred to me to look for any mark or damage on my car. But I could see nothing. I let myself into the cottage and walked into the sitting-room to greet my wife who said at once: "Goodness me! What happened to you? Have you seen a ghost?"

'To which I could honestly reply: "That's just it! I have!"'

Several days later, Wing-Commander Hunter was relating his tale to friends when one said: 'Well, of course, you know there's a long barrow above the hill on that corner?'

He still remembers vividly the sight he saw, and thinks the long barrow site might offer some kind of explanation. But he does not claim to believe in ghosts.

'On the other hand,' he writes, 'I am disinclined to dismiss their existence out of hand.'

Alan Berry of Birmingham, a storeman, describes an unsettling incident which happened to him in 1972, when he was twenty-three. He was driving to Birmingham from Tamworth after a night out. He stresses that at the time he was a normal young man who enjoyed a drink, but on this particular occasion he had not drunk any alcohol whatsoever.

'Tamworth is a small town in Staffordshire eighteen miles from Birmingham. At around 11.30 p.m. in March 1972 I decided to drive home from Tamworth in my ancient Ford Anglia. The old Ford was pretty reliable if you could get it started. This night was a good one; in went the key, over went the engine and I was on the way home. I thanked Henry T. profusely as this particular evening was very wet and windy.

'The old Ford and I soon left the comfortable houses and shopping centre of the town behind and headed into the rural landscape of Fazeley. That's where I saw him!

'Out of the passenger's window I saw a very tall soldier walking industriously towards Birmingham. My first reaction was to stop and give him a lift. However, something did not seem right about this individual. It was his dress. He was clad in very strange garb indeed. He wore a scarf or balaclava on his head, khaki in colour. I never saw his face. A greatcoat with large collar draped his thin frame and I could even see his gigantic army boots and those buckled garters that clasp the trousers tight at the ankles. I put my reservations behind me and decided to give him a lift; he was a soldier after all.

'That's when it happened. The only way I can describe our parting is this. Imagine the soldier was an image projected from a film camera on to a pool of water and suddenly, as I drove within ten or twelve feet of him, someone rippled the pool of water with his hand. I actually saw the soldier shimmer and fragment into the bushes and trees behind him.

'I have always maintained that on that dark windy evening long ago I witnessed something or someone not of this world, but I never got around to contacting the Institute of Psychic Research or someone of that nature to see if the soldier had been "seen" before.'

Mr Berry believes that if he had done so, and if the spectre of the soldier had been a familiar sight on that section of the road, he might have been spared the jibes he has been forced to endure whenever he has related his story to friends and colleagues.

John Crisp is retired, and his wife Patricia is now an invalid. They live in Hertfordshire. Twenty years ago they were living in Essendon, a few miles away from where they are at present, in a pleasant house with a spacious living room which had a wide open fireplace – at one side of which logs for the fire were stored in a large copper vessel. When Mrs Crisp heard of a similar container being offered for sale in a shop in St Albans, she decided to buy it to put on the opposite side of the fireplace. Hopping into her small car she drove off to inspect the copper pot. Mr Crisp writes on his wife's behalf:

'We lived in a long narrow lane with high hedges on either side, so my wife was driving very slowly and keeping her wits about her. It was about midday and the frost of a beautiful January morning was sparkling in the brilliant sunshine.

'Suddenly a horse and rider appeared from nowhere to her right and began ambling right across her way. She slammed on her brakes, stopping almost immediately, and watched in amazement as a young girl with long golden hair dressed in a bottle-green habit and wearing a little tricorn hat to match slowly crossed the road, only to vanish through the left-hand hedge.

'My wife sat for a number of minutes quite dumbfounded by what she had seen. As she said afterwards, it was a beautiful sight, the young girl with her head bowed as though deep in thought, and the metal parts of the bridle, reins, etc. shining like gold in the sunshine.

'Eventually she reluctantly started the car, went to St Albans and even managed to obtain the copper!

'She was shy of telling me or anyone else for a time in case we teased her; but when she did tell me my feelings were of envy rather than mockery.'

Neither Mr nor Mrs Crisp nor any of their local friends ever saw the beautiful young rider again, although they watched for her when passing that particular spot on the road.

Bill Smith (see p.207) had a similar adventure, not in a quiet lane, but on a busy highway. In 1936 he was employed as a night driver on the Dover to London route. One brilliant moonlit night he was driving a loaded lorry on the A2, headlights dipped, on schedule and therefore in no need to hurry.

'I had crossed Bexley Heath and was cruising down the hill towards the Dartford/Bexley crossroads in the valley at approximately 11.50 p.m. I saw something moving: a kind of reflected light on the Dartford road through the few trees, so flicked headlights to full beam and braked slightly. (Although I was on a major road, one has to be prepared for fools at night.)

'I was about forty yards from the crossing when a black horse and rider galloped across, causing me to brake heavily. The rider appeared to be reflecting the headlight beam. I cursed him for a fool, riding unlighted at that time of night . . . Then engaging low gear to pull away under load, I looked along the Bexley Road expecting to see his tail-end, but as the road was clear I assumed he had gone across the heath, and forgot the incident till 1942.'

In 1942 Mr Smith was again driving down the A2, for the first time in six years, when he noticed that in the intervening period an inn, the Black Prince, had been built on the Kent side of the same crossroads. He pulled in for a ploughman's lunch and in conversation with the landlord learnt that the inn had been named to commemorate the Black Prince who had made it a practice to bring his lady friends to a tavern on that site.

'"He is still supposed to visit us on a certain night of the year," said the landlord. "Dressed in his suit of black armour they say he rides his black horse from Dartford to Bexley, though I've never met him. Quite a few people who come in claim to have done so, and night travellers say he has caused accidents at the crossing."'

Mr Smith was fascinated. He related his own experience six years earlier to the landlord, who replied: '"People who claimed to have seen him said he always disappeared on the Bexley side."'

Mr Smith's recollection exactly tallied with other sightings communicated to the landlord, who assured him that he was not inclined to ridicule him because too many travellers had told him precisely the same story in the years he had been running the inn.

Bill Smith suffered another shock one night in December 1936 when he was at the wheel with his co-driver beside him in the cabin of a truck on the Worcester run, designated as a two-driver journey. Driving at night through thick fog, they reached Uxbridge very late, and pressed on to High Wycombe, where the heavy load and the gradient of White Hill leading down into the town forced Mr Smith to shift into a lower gear and slow the lorry down.

'Suddenly my driver mate shouted, "Look out! You'll hit him!" and into the beam of the headlights stepped a figure in a long black cloak. I braked hard, but was unable to stop before he disappeared beneath the radiator cowling.

'My mate opened his door and jumped out as the lorry came to a halt. I switched off the engine, engaged reverse and set the hand brake for safety. As I got out, my mate was coming along the road side looking underneath the truck saying "Where the hell is he! He must be hung up underneath, poor bugger. He must have been blind to walk into us like that!"

'I couldn't answer. I had the smell of death in my nostrils, and I was freezing cold. I leaned against the lorry not daring to even think. I knew in my mind we should find nothing. My mate put his hand on my shoulder and said, "It wasn't your fault Bill. No one could have avoided him. He just walked straight into us!"

'I reached into the lorry for my torch. He took it from me and crawled underneath the vehicle, shone it around, and shouted, "There's nothing under here!" He came out and started back up the road where there were several skid marks . . . He went beyond them, then came back on the offside of the road, saying, "There's nothing there! Where can he have gone?"

'We looked at the roadside which was banked as a cutting so he could not have been thrown off the road altogether – I knew, but I could not tell my mate, that we had seen something which wasn't there . . .'

The two men climbed back into the cabin of the truck and set off, Bill Smith agreeing with his companion's suggestion that they should find a policeman and report the incident, although privately he was convinced the figure had been a spectre. Seeing a policeman in a shop doorway in High Wycombe, his mate insisted that they stop the truck and speak to him, which they did.

Mr Smith described the incident in detail. The policeman put his hand to his forehead in a weary gesture and replied: '"What game are you blokes playing tonight? You're the third driver who has knocked somebody over who can't be found! We had a patrol car up there searching for an hour but they found nothing, and now you have the same tale! You're asking for trouble, wasting police time to chase shadows!"'

Telling them he would report their claim, he sent them on their way. Once again the two men climbed back into the truck and set off on their journey, travelling towards Oxford, in an agitated state. But the fates had not finished with them yet.

'As we ran out of West Wycombe towards Oxford we saw a lorry stopped and a driver with a wheel off. We pulled in behind to give him the benefit of our lights and got out. As we approached he straightened up and said, "Can you hear singing, or am I going daft?"

'We listened. We could hear a church service somewhere, but no organ music.'

The music appeared to be coming from the earth bank across the road and all the men could hear the sound which appeared to be a congregation or choir singing hymns although the words were 'strange and unintelligible'. The other driver was relieved when Mr Smith and his mate agreed that they, too, could hear the music, but could find no explanation for it. The other man begged them not to pull his leg.

'"I'm bloody scared," he admitted. "I knocked a bloke down other side of Wycombe. When I looked for him he wasn't there. I told the coppers and went up there with them for an hour but we couldn't find anything, only skid marks on the road; and then the coppers said I was drunk and they would pull me in for time-wasting. I don't drink and I don't smoke. But I know I saw a bloke walk into my front. He came from nowhere and he disappeared the same. I had a good look, he was dressed like a monk in long cloak with a hood over his head."'

Mr Smith told the other driver that they had every reason to believe him, and described their own experience, ending with the policeman's remark that no less than three drivers had reported the same type of accident that night. Whereupon the driver changing his wheel told him that, as soon as the police had released him, he had left the scene but almost immediately had suffered a puncture causing him to pull in to the lay-by, where he had just started taking off the wheel and heard the singing.

'"I was listening when a lorry pulled up behind me. The driver was scared stiff. He reckoned he had knocked a bloke down and when I told him about this singing, he wouldn't stop no longer!"'

To Mr Smith's knowledge, that driver, upset by his earlier 'accident', was the second man that night to report to the police that he had run down a figure in a long black cloak on White Hill.

Bill Smith and his mate, shaken by this latest revelation, helped the driver change his wheel and followed him to Witney where they parted company.

'We never stopped talking and wondering about what we had seen and heard for the rest of the journey,' writes Mr Smith. 'We were laughed at and ridiculed when we told people about it. But we knew we had witnessed an apparition and heard singing, although we had no way of finding out what it was.'

HAUNTINGS

Elizabeth Delmore is a poet who lives in Cumbria. As a child she often played at Nunnington Hall in North Yorkshire, an Elizabethan mansion now owned by the National Trust.

She enjoyed playing at the house but once she had to stay there overnight. 'I was frightened out of my wits,' she admits. Although she had seen nothing she had been terrified by the atmosphere inside the house. 'I know others who were, too,' she adds. Some years later in the vicinity of the same house she had another alarming experience. It was so upsetting that she made an entry in her diary, recording the event.

On 7 January 1936 Elizabeth Delmore and her friend Audrey (both in their early twenties), accompanied by Elizabeth's young cousin, fourteen-year-old John, were driving to a dinner party. Elizabeth was at the wheel, Audrey beside her, and John in the back seat.

It was a dark night but there was no rain or mist. They were travelling in familiar country along a well-known road, at this point taking them up a hill and through an avenue of very old trees. They reached Nunnington Hall and a second or two later passed it, continuing up the hill.

Then, as Mrs Delmore recalls: 'We saw two people walking up on the left-hand side of the road. As we pulled out to the right to pass them I looked at them, thinking I might know them . . . I heard a gasp from Audrey, looked back at the road and (the hair rises on my neck as I write) there was a figure right in front of my right wheel. In no way could I have failed to hit it. I waited for the impact. There was none. We passed straight through the figure.

'I said nothing, thinking I must have imagined it. But John, practical and unimaginative, said from behind me in a strangled voice, "What on earth was that?"

'We had all seen it. We all described the figure in the same way: we saw no features but a head covered with what might have been either a helmet of Norman type or a coif and indeterminate draperies. But none of us had *not* thought it was a live person. We had all waited for the impact. It had seemed inevitable. Relief that I had not killed someone and shock that there had been no impact were about even, and we all arrived at our dinner party a bit shaken.

'Some people scoffed at the story, but not when John confirmed what he had seen. None of us had had a drink before setting out. It was well known that the house we had passed was haunted, and it was thought that the avenue was haunted by nuns, though I had never heard of this before. I often drove that way and after that occasion always tried, when it was dark, to pull out to the right at the same spot, but I never saw anything there again.'

Now, unknown to Mrs Delmore, I contacted a former resident of Nunnington Hall whose name she had mentioned. She and Mrs Delmore had played together at the house as children, but had lost touch many years ago.

Unaware of Elizabeth Delmore's story, Mrs Susan Clive wrote as follows: 'I'm afraid I can't be very helpful to you as we never actually saw any ghosts at Nunnington Hall though we often heard and felt things, as did the dogs occasionally. One of my sons once saw someone and visitors staying did too, but nothing very exciting.' And then she adds the following comment: 'There must be something in the avenue, as a figure is sometimes run over by a car. This happened to another of my sons who saw and felt nothing, but the driver of a car following was rather shattered.'

Robert John Blenkinsopp of Yorkshire was the driver of that car. A highly respected company director, he has permitted his name to be published as a witness to the event.

That followed the same pattern as that of Mrs Delmore and her party, and it indicates the presence of a ghostly figure in the avenue outside Nunnington Hall over a period of forty or fifty years.

While studying at the Somerset College of Agriculture, Susannah Applegate of Somerset and her friend Ruth [named changed] were involved in an incident that made a deep impact on them. Ruth had travelled down the A39 on her moped to visit Susannah at the college and as the machine had had problems over the last few miles of the journey, Susannah agreed to follow her back to Chewton Mendip in her car when it was time for Ruth to return home. They arranged to meet for a meal at a certain point on the road.

'Giving Ruth ample time to start the moped and get going, I left college some twenty minutes after her. About half-way to our rendezvous, for which I thought I'd be late, I knew of a long flat stretch of road where I could make up for lost time. Approaching this stretch there was nothing else in sight and with Meatloaf blaring over my cassette player I went like a bat out of hell.

'Suddenly from nowhere two cars appeared on their side of the road coming towards me, both with their headlights full on. Dazzled, I slowed down and as they were about to pass me, a man wearing a long brown coat ran out from a gateway on my right, straight into the path of the other two cars. I braked, thinking he was going to cross my path to the minor road leading down to Cossington on my left. When my car came to a halt, I looked in the mirror, seeing nothing! I turned my head to look behind, hoping not to see a man prostrate on the road, and again saw nothing. There was no sign of the cars that seconds before had passed me, and no trace of a person.

'I looked at my watch. It was 9.30 p.m. the last light from what had been a beautiful spring day had now all gone. I felt a strange sense of being very much alone and lost on what was to me a very familiar road.'

Susannah continued her journey, shaking off the weird sensation caused by the incident, and by the time she met Ruth at Street, she had forgotten about it, and made no mention of it to her friend.

However, several weeks later Ruth again visited Susannah at the college and in conversation with friends related an odd experience she had had on the previous occasion, when Susannah had followed her home. She had been dazzled by the headlights of two cars, she told the group, and then was shattered to see the figure of a man walk out in front of the cars. Curiously, she added, she had felt no shock wave in the air from the passing cars, as would be expected when riding a moped.

'This chilled my spine,' Susannah recalls, 'realizing that Ruth had seen exactly what I had seen, only minutes earlier. We were both convinced that we had experienced something supernatural that night of 28 April 1981.

'The following year I decided to return to the same stretch of road at the same time on the anniversary of that night.'

Ruth refused to accompany her, but Poppy [*named changed*], a level-headed friend with an open mind, agreed to do so. They headed along the A39 aiming for the straight, flat area between

Bawdrip and Ashcott, running across the top of the Polden Hills.

'We travelled to the same spot in the car I had been driving the previous year, playing the same music and travelling in the same direction. We first passed the turning to Cossington with the Toll House on the corner at about 9.25 p.m. Nothing extraordinary happened, so we turned around in a gateway some 250 yards from the junction and approached it again, coming from the opposite direction.

'Twice we turned around and went back, only to see nothing. By now it was 9.40 p.m. and we decided to go home. We had to turn again in the gateway to face the right direction to return.

'As I drew out of the gateway there was not another car on the road. Up until this time there had been other traffic about each time we passed the Toll House/Cossington turning.

'However, as I pulled out and changed into second gear, a car with its lights full on came racing up behind me. I accelerated as fast as my car would go, thinking that the other car would crash into the back of us. Poppy turned around in her seat to look behind, and I was looking in the mirror, wondering why the car didn't overtake us as it could have done so easily on the clear road. As we passed the Toll House, now on our right, the pursuing vehicle just vanished! It didn't turn to Cossington, nor did the driver extinguish his lights.

'Both Poppy and I saw this and maybe we would have seen the figure of a man in long brown coat if we'd been looking ahead. I will never know as, although intrigued, to tempt fate once was enough for me. To tempt it again might prove disastrous. I feel that the second time I saw it, my Morris Traveller was taking the place of the first car, and if anyone had been coming the other way, they would have seen what Ruth and I had seen the first time.'

Susannah later made inquiries at a public house near the scene, and learnt that some years ago there had been a fatal accident in that area. But no one could provide any further details.

Pondering the extraordinary experience of having seen the ghostly vehicles twice, once with Poppy as witness, and once with the supporting evidence of Ruth's encounter, Susannah concluded that what they had seen was the image of an accident from the past in which the car in front had been dazzled by the car behind. The driver had failed to see the man in a long brown coat, possibly a poacher hurrying across the road from the gateway, and had hit him, braking sharply as he did so, when the car behind had crashed into the rear of his car, causing fatalities.

'I believe that what Ruth, Poppy and I saw were those unrested souls re-enacting that ghastly accident in the hope that if another life is claimed, it will set them free. I certainly felt that my life was in danger the second time I saw it.'

Ghosts of the Oceans

One of the most celebrated of all ghost stories internationally is the legend of the Flying Dutchman. According to Daniel Farson in the *Sunday Telegraph* (27 December 1987) there are still occasional sightings.

Frankie and Jeff Clarkson live in the same Devon village as Farson. They told him that when they were in their sixties they decided to add adventure to their lives by sailing around the world in their small yacht. So with great courage, they set sail for the high seas. According to Daniel Farson:

'Six days out of Cape Town, Mrs Clarkson was on watch and spotted a square-rigger in the distance – "a lovely sight with white sails against the dark evening sky . . . except that she was sailing against the wind. As I called to Jeff to come on deck, the ship turned with a single movement and came a mile nearer." Then she saw the solitary figure of a man and felt that something disastrous would happen if her husband saw it too. Simultaneously, the ship veered again and vanished over the horizon.

'When Jeff Clarkson joined her there was nothing to be seen, though he has never doubted her story, and nor do I. It was when they reached St Helena, and she described her apparition, that Mrs Clarkson learnt of the Flying Dutchman condemned to sail for ever as "the evil spirit of the sea".'

Daniel Farson poses the question: 'Could there have been an ill-fated ship sunk in this area, leaving an impression on the atmosphere to be seen by countless sailors ever since, thereby creating the legend?'

James A. Trowsdale of North Humberside works in an unemployment benefit office where part of his responsibility is payment of benefit to share fishermen unable to go to sea because of weather conditions, repairs to ship, and similar short-term but frustrating problems.

In his private life Mr Trowsdale is a lay minister attached to a local church whose vicar, the Reverend Tom Willis, is interested in the healing ministry of the Church of England. In addition to carrying out normal parish duties, Mr Willis was specifically appointed to work with problems arising from haunted places and psychic disturbances. (The public generally seem not to know that churches of many denominations take reports of psychic phenomena seriously enough to follow this practice.)

For the past twenty-five years Mr Willis has restored peace to people and places disturbed by supernatural phenomena, and he has often been accompanied by Mr Trowsdale in recent times.

'It therefore came as a surprise,' writes James Trowsdale, 'that my job and my connection with the Revd. Willis overlapped one day with a chance comment by the skipper of a fishing vessel, *Pickering*, which was undergoing substantial long-term repairs.'

The skipper, Mr Laws, told the counter clerk in the unemployment benefit office that he was fed up with the seemingly never-ending programme of repairs, saying that he had considered calling in an exorcist. He was taken aback by her comment that if he were serious he should talk to a member of the staff who knew about such things. He in fact, agreed to do so, and approached James Trowsdale.

'Initially I was a little sceptical as fishermen were often prone to having a bit of fun with the dole office staff,' writes Mr Trowsdale, 'and I knew Mr Laws was not a person to be scared very easily . . . When we met he related the following account.

'The boat was built some thirteen years ago by a father and two sons. While out fishing a couple of years later the sons were caught in the nets and tragically pulled overboard and killed. Filled with guilt and remorse the father later hanged himself from the crane on the deck. Later, during the press investigation, the *Daily Mirror* apparently discovered the father alive and well! It is certain, however, that at least one man died on board the vessel. It is interesting to note that possibly the men were Roman Catholics, as they were Irish, and the suicide may not have received a requiem Mass. (This is speculation on my part.)

'Shortly after that, the boat's name was changed and it was purchased by a local fishing company. Since then numerous events have happened which have given the boat a "bad" reputation among the superstitious fishermen.

'Three years after the boat arrived here, the then skipper, Targett [*name changed*], was walking along the harbour wall with a crewman. The skipper walked on ahead only to find that the crewman had disappeared: his body was found six months later and it appeared that he had fallen into the harbour. Last year another crewman's wife was badly injured in an accident with a ship's flare. It was hardly surprising the boat was considered bad, even if these events were sheer coincidence.'

This, then, was the background of the *Pickering* up to the point where the command was taken over from Targett by the new skipper, Mr Laws, who then told James Trowsdale about his own experiences in connection with the ill-fated vessel.

'Apparently the galley, cabin and brig all had certain "cold spots" in places where the crew normally worked or rested. In the cabin this became so bad that, despite a powerful heater and electric blankets, the crew were still aware of the chill. What brought things to a head for Mr Laws was one night when he was taking his rest alone in the cabin. Twice in ten minutes he felt the sensation of someone stepping on to his bunk to climb into the one above. When he put the light on to investigate, there was no one there.

'In addition to this, the boat was constantly requiring repairs. New engines would break down for no apparent reason, and on one occasion the steering broke down while the boat was at sea, leaving it going round in circles. When the engineers investigated the problems they could never find anything wrong.

'Mr Laws told me he was coming off the boat and handing over to another skipper.

'After a fortnight the new skipper contacted the Revd. Willis and asked him to bless the boat. He had experienced similar technical problems, and before he was to sail the following morning he wanted the vicar's help.

'On climbing aboard the Revd. Willis and I were both struck by the overpowering heat in the cabin. The new skipper told us that in his long experience he had never come across a boat which had so many mechanical problems – and on one occasion, a foul smell coming from the front of the boat. Another crewman said he had seen the figure of a man with a flat cap standing on deck.'

(Later, on returning to harbour, the clergymen spoke to a radar engineer who had been called frequently to check electrical repairs on *Pickering*. He described how the radar had shown a negative reading as if the wiring was 'back to front'. When reversed, the radar worked perfectly, only to change back to its negative reading as soon as the boat was at sea. The engineer admitted he was dumbfounded by this, declaring it impossible. He could offer no explanation for the behaviour of the radar equipment.)

'The boat put out into the bay and the Revd. Willis prayed for the souls of any departed persons to be at peace, and blessed the whole vessel with holy water. Neither the Revd. Willis nor I noticed anything unusual.

'After the blessing the boat put to sea and remains successfully fishing today, ten months afterwards. The skipper contacted the Revd. Willis to thank him and described how the boat now felt happier and peaceful.'

It was certainly a happy ending – to an episode featuring odd bedfellows: the unemployment benefit office working hand in hand with an exorcist from the Church of England. However, the Department of Employment emphasized when questioned about the matter, that the intervention by a member of their staff was entirely personal and not professional!

Another ghost ship is the Waratah *– though the haunting connected with it is of a different nature. Mrs Mildred North of Dorset sent me details of this gripping, and still unsolved, mystery of the sea which was drawn to her attention as a result of friends of her parents-in-law (let's call them the Griffiths) buying a house in St Albans in England.*

Later inquiries revealed that the house had been built around 1908 by an eminent man of the sea, Captain J. E. Ilbery, Commodore of the Blue Anchor Line, who had planned to retire at the end of a distinguished career when he returned from his final voyage to Australia on board his ship, the *Waratah*.

Captain Ilbery and his two sisters had lived together in St Albans for some years, and the elderly ladies had been preparing to move with him into the new house which was completed on time and awaited the return of the Waratah and its skipper. He had named the house after his ship.

For some reason, the Griffiths learnt when researching into the history of the house, Captain Ilbery had failed to occupy it, but they were unable to find out why. Apparently his sisters had stayed on in their old home and put Waratah on the market. It was subsequently sold, changing hands frequently over the years because none of its new owners appeared to want to stay in it for long, and rumour had it that Waratah was haunted. This information did not deter the Griffiths from acquiring the house, however, although it was not long before they became aware that Waratah was indeed subject to some inexplicable forces.

'At times a very cold, icy wind would blow, for no apparent reason. It was sufficient to wake a person, with a cold wind blowing on the individual's face. During a meal it would be felt as a cold draught on the neck. The icy breeze was strong enough to rustle papers and to blow over a vase of flowers, even when curtains were drawn. Needless to say, staff didn't stay very long!

'Eventually, a firm of builders was engaged to go over the house to try to discover where these cold winds were coming from. Nothing was found to explain the trouble, the house being soundly built. My parents-in-law and my husband often stayed there as friends of the family, but didn't experience anything unusual, except that the house appeared chilly, even in summer.

'But on one occasion, my father-in-law, a very "down-to-earth" civil servant, did experience something. He related that going upstairs one evening, with all the doors shut on the landing and in the hall, he experienced a sudden cold wind blowing around his head. It was strong enough to ruffle his hair, and cause him to pause to see whether a door was open. Apparently, all was as usual. He often related this incident.

'The family eventually moved away and we learned that the house, with various occupants coming and going, was eventually demolished with other houses, presumably for development.'

But Mrs North was to learn more about Waratah from an unexpected source. Several years ago a friend from Australia sent her a newspaper cutting describing one of the great unsolved mysteries of the sea – the loss of the ship *Waratah*, in 1909. Her friend was interested in the fate of the ship because a relative had been on board – it was purely by coincidence that Mrs North had found the article doubly interesting, on account of her knowledge of the house named Waratah in St Albans.

On 8 February 1956 the *Sun News Pictorial*, an Australian newspaper published in Melbourne, carried the following story:

WARATAH MYSTERY
by Jack Wilkinson

On the afternoon of July 1, 1909, the Blue Anchor steamer, *Waratah*, sailed from Port Melbourne bound for London. But she and her 211 passengers and crew never reached their destination – nor has any trace of them been found since.

Waratah, a twin-screw vessel of 6800 tons, was on the return leg of her second voyage. Less than a year before she had been launched into the Clyde. Captain J. E. Ilbery, Commodore of the Blue Anchor Line and a crack skipper, was in command of the ship.

The *Waratah* left Adelaide on July 7 and after an uneventful crossing arrived in Durban, South Africa, on the 25th. The following day she headed for Cape Town. At 6 a.m. on July 27 she passed the *Clan McIntyre* and exchanged greetings. That was the last time the *Waratah* was seen.

On July 28, the *Clan McIntyre* ran into a hurricane and heavy seas. It is now supposed that the *Waratah* foundered in this violent storm. When the liner was posted overdue an exhaustive search began. Three warships set out, and the Australian Government sent the steamer *Severn*, which combed the seas for a month.

The disappearance of the ship caused great concern in this country [Australia], for there were many Australians on board. On September 11 another ship, the *Sabine*, left Cape Town and made a search lasting 88 days and covering 14,000 miles. Many people refused to believe that the *Waratah* had foundered and many theories were put forward as to her fate or whereabouts.

However, in February 1911, the Board of Trade Inquiry decided that the ship had been caught in a violent gale, the first great storm she had encountered, and had capsized. Evidence at the inquiry suggested that the vessel was in a seaworthy state. But the latter finding has been disputed.

A passenger on the maiden voyage of the ship stated that she rolled fearfully, and on one occasion his bath water was completely drained away as she hung on a steeply-angled roll. He also said that one of the officers had said he would leave the vessel when it reached New Zealand.

One of the strangest sidelights of the mystery was the testimony of a Mr Claude Sawyer, who boarded the ship at Adelaide on her last voyage. He noticed the excessive rolling, and also that there was a permanent list to starboard.

A few days out from Durban he had a vivid dream of death. Acting on this premonition and his suspicion that the ship was faultily constructed, he disembarked at Durban and cabled his wife: 'Thought *Waratah* top heavy. Landed Durban.'

The amazing thing is that no trace of the ship or of the people on board has ever been found. About the same time of the incident one ship sighted what may have been floating bodies. Another ship reported what seemed to be a fire and explosion at sea off East London [a seaport on the southern coast of South Africa].

In 1930 what looked to be the hull of a ship on the sea-bed was sighted from the air in the same area. A search was organized, but yielded no further clues. In 1933 there was a similar report, but again with the same result. Occasionally a piece of flotsam suspected to be from the *Waratah* has been washed up but nothing substantial has been discovered.

Many stories and theories were put forward. One man suggested that the *Waratah* might have been sucked into a blowhole on the South African coast near East London. Tidal waves have been observed in that area and some think that might have been the cause.

But why a new and sizeable ship like the *Waratah* should have sunk when many lesser vessels weathered the storm is hard to imagine. It seems disaster must have struck suddenly without time for the lowering of the lifeboats. Even so, one would have thought that some piece of wreckage or some bodies would have been washed up or found at sea.

Whatever the cause, it spelt the end of the Blue Anchor Line, which was absorbed by P/O, and to this day the disappearance of the *Waratah* is one of the unsolved mysteries of the sea.

But the mystery of the house in St Albans *is* perhaps solved by that report from Australia. The elderly sisters of Captain Ilbery waited in vain for their beloved brother to return from his last command. And when the ship was reported missing and eventually given up as lost with all souls on board, the Misses Ilbery relinquished any thought of moving house and, electing to stay in their old home, placed Waratah on the market.

Did the old sea captain then return in spirit from his watery grave to enjoy the house as he intended? Was he responsible for calling up the salty sea wind to keep him company, and to ruffle the hair of Mr North senior as he climbed the stairs?

Part Four

POLTERGEISTS

According to Brian Inglis, an authority on the paranormal, ghosts may sometimes appear to be malevolent, but they do not as a rule inflict any injury, the notorious exceptions being, as he points out,

> poltergeists – noisy, fractious, often ill-tempered ghosts – which have been reported in every age, from every part of the world. They are rarely seen; commonly they are heard, and sometimes they leave obnoxious odours. They are distinguished from other ghosts chiefly because of the remarkable, often bizarre, physical phenomena associated with them. Objects, ranging from crockery to heavy tables, are heard to move, and often later are found to have moved, in empty rooms. Sometimes ornaments disappear, to be found later in another room. Accounts of poltergeist activity inevitably excite incredulity, but in many cases all attempts to track down a living practical joker have proved futile.

Like other ghosts, poltergeists appear in all kinds of buildings, from stately homes to police stations.

Catherine Berry lives in West Yorkshire. Six years ago, when she was a teenager, she was going through a traumatic period in her life. Her parents were divorced, and after living with her mother for a time, she decided to move in with her father who had recently rented a two-hundred-year-old house following the death of the previous occupant. Catherine describes its peculiar atmosphere:

'It was as if the house was stuck in some kind of timewarp. It looked as if it hadn't been touched for about a hundred years.'

Bare stone flags formed the floor and the old cooker, cast in solid iron, complete with full range of ovens, was still in working order.

'If my father had known then what he now knows, he could have sold the range for quite a bit of money. They are collectors' pieces now. Anyway, I helped my father to throw the lot into the back garden and the council carted it away. My father redecorated downstairs and had a cooker fitted in what was to become the kitchen, complete with a stone sink!

'I duly moved in with my father and everything seemed fine for a few days. Then small things started to happen. At first it was just noises that I noticed, bumps and bangs and the like; but the strange thing was that I could sit downstairs or in the bedroom until two or three in the morning reading and I wouldn't hear a thing, but as soon as I retired to bed and the light was turned out the noises would start.

'I thought at first it was just because it was a strange house to me and it was the house's own noises that I hadn't got used to . . . But they were different every night. It was as if as soon as you had moved out of the downstairs room to go to bed, someone or something else moved in and continued to get on with some kind of unseen duties it had not been able to perform during the day.

'Furniture sounded as if it was being dragged across the floor or picked up and dropped from some height, as all the house shook, doors being opened and closed. One night I even heard what seemed to be someone doing the dishes only to find the morning after, to my disappointment, they were still to be done.

'Up to this point my father was oblivious to these goings on, which I had not yet mentioned to him. Then after a few sleepless nights I did so. He said he had heard a few noises but thought they were being caused by me. He presumed I was moving things about in my bedroom after he'd gone to bed.'

Concluding that neither of them could have caused the noises, father and daughter decided to investigate. The house was at the end of a block, with solid stone party walls two to three feet deep. They agreed with their neighbour, an elderly woman living alone who claimed to be in bed each night by 10 p.m., that she could not be the source of the noises experienced.

However, they did discover something slightly disturbing about their own house from her: 'The previous occupant, a man who had lived there for many years, had died in his chair next to the fire and it had been over a week before anyone had found him.'

As time went by the noises in the old house not only continued, but intensified.

'One night my father had been awakened by them from his sleep and I discovered him creeping down the stairs clutching an iron bar. Just what he was hoping to discover I don't know, but there was nothing to be seen.'

After Catherine had been living in the house for a period of four months, her father moved out to live with a friend. Catherine chose to stay alone in the house. This decision marked a further increase in the number of inexplicable happenings.

'Things started to disappear and then reappear. There was not any chance of me just mislaying items in the house, as furniture to put items on or in was at a minimum, just one small wall unit in the living room and one built-in wall cupboard and one table.'

By now Catherine had named the spirit or ghost 'Albert', after the old man who had died in the house. He was, she discovered, 'Very careful as to the things that he took – not things you could do without but money, important papers, hairbrushes and combs and a potato peeler. Most of these items would disappear for two or three days, then they would reappear in the most obvious places, for example on top of the television set. But I was beginning to wise up to Albert and he was getting more predictable.

'One evening I came home and put my house key on the table next to the door. The next morning it had disappeared. I looked around the room and its contents. Apart from the furniture I have already mentioned . . . [which was too obvious to serve as a hiding place] there was a bag of music in the corner of the room which had been left there by a music teacher, a friend of my father's . . . Sure enough at the bottom of the plastic carrier bag, underneath all the sheets of music, was the key. As far as the rest of the items which disappeared and reappeared are concerned, I never discovered where they went. In fact one pair of the two pairs of curtains I possessed completely disappeared, never to return.

'I feel it necessary to go into such detail about these happenings so you can see how strange they were in the circumstances.'

Throughout this period lights were turned on and off, and Catherine heard furniture being moved about during the night and the following morning she would find it had shifted from its position of the night before. On one occasion she woke to discover that a large solid wooden box containing hand tools had moved itself from the corner of the room to within inches of the side of her bed. The tools included a wooden plane, an iron bar and other heavy metal implements.

'While there were also numerous other small incidents which occurred, strangely enough after the initial period when I was frightened, these incidents didn't bother me in the slightest – in fact when I was used to them I found them mischievous if not even quite amusing, although my friends at the time refused point blank to come into the house!

'Now twenty-two years of age, I have concluded that the things that happened to me then seemed to be connected with my very disturbed state of mind at that time.

'Until I had arrived at the house all was apparently quiet . . . When I was under more mental stress than other times, the incidents were more noticeable. For example, the racket during the night before my father left was unbelievable; I don't think either of us got a wink of sleep. And when I had finished my job the same unrest occurred.

'However, if my conclusion is to be believed, then would it not put the ghost in the category of a poltergeist? In which case, if we are to believe the experts, this was all energy which had been directed from within me.'

Catherine Berry believes that categorizing the experience is not much help: she had had months of disturbed rest and inconvenience that had been caused by some unknown force.

Her story ends in a puzzling manner: 'About a month before I left the house . . . everything stopped. Yes, it all just went quiet. This is when I knew there had definitely been something sharing the house with me.'

Mrs Jacqueline Davies married a widower and moved into the house in London in which he had lived with his former wife Cynthia [name changed]. *She has been there three and a half years now, and believes the house is haunted by her predecessor. I suspect she would have sympathy for Catherine Berry as she has had comparable events to contend with, and finds herself blamed for causing them.*

'I first began to notice that objects were in places where I hadn't put them about three months after I had moved into my husband's house in London. One evening I was filling in an application form for a holiday for my fifteen-year-old son. I knew that I had placed on a ledge . . . a voucher for a £10 reduction off the holiday he wanted, and it just was not there . . . the next morning I found it in the extension on the top of the washing machine. I had not been using the washing machine and if I had taken it in myself I should have left it in the kitchen. I thought that it was very strange but thought no more about it.

'Then one evening when I was sitting in the lounge with my husband and we were on our own, I said to him, "When I go out shopping next I must buy myself a couple of brushes to use when I do the washing up as we haven't got any." I had looked for some in the house and I couldn't find any; but about twenty minutes later when I went into the kitchen (my husband had not left the lounge room), there was a new brush resting on top of the washing-up bowl – and that was when I believed that the house was haunted. I also knew whoever it was was friendly and had helped me.'

After that Mrs Davies had similar experiences several times a day. She was not particularly bothered by the presence of the helpful spirit, but did find it irritating at times, especially when some objects were removed and failed to turn up again until a week or more later, and then in a place she would not have expected to find them.

'One evening about half an hour or so after I had washed up, I came into the kitchen and found a mess. A large amount of washing-up liquid had been spilled on the kitchen table and, as far as I can remember, the bottle was on the floor. I wasn't too pleased about that. I also found a tube of ointment on my bedroom floor which had been pressed out in one long line – very naughty!

'One afternoon I opened my wardrobe door which has a full-length mirror in it, and there was an old photograph of my husband's late wife . . . All my husband said was that he thought that he had thrown out all the old photographs, and he quickly removed it, so now I was quite sure that it was Cynthia who was moving the things around, as I felt that it was her way of showing me that she was there.'

Mrs Davies describes her husband as a tidy man who became annoyed from time to time by objects being removed from their usual place. Both he and Mrs Davies's son blamed her for moving items in the house which *she* claimed were being moved by Cynthia.

'Last week the key to the porch . . . was missing, and we all say that we haven't taken it. So my husband had to have another one cut. I noticed only this week that a small trophy won by my husband many years ago had moved twice in one day. My husband said that he had seen my son move it, so I asked my son and he said that he hadn't . . . Only last week my husband found something in his car which he says he didn't put there . . . He is the only person using the car.'

Mrs Davies finds it distressing that her family will not believe her when she claims that some unseen force is responsible for the activity in the house.

'For the first year that I was married, my stepson lived with us. He is very religious, and in the dining-room there were dozens of religious books. The interesting thing about it is that while he and the books were in the house nothing moved about in that room. Also while he was living here things moved about more on Fridays than on any other day of the week. Since my stepson's departure there is much less movement of objects around the house, though there has been more during the past two weeks than there has been for some months.

'I came downstairs to find on the floor in the hall an old brooch that one of my children had bought me. I haven't worn it for years. My husband and I came home one day and we found the french window open in the dining-room, even though it is always kept locked. My son was in the house at the time but he said that he hadn't been into the room.'

On another occasion Mrs Davies had commented during the evening how much she enjoyed reading books by the Brontë sisters. When she went up to bed that night she found one of their novels by her bed. It was a book she had not read, and she was not previously aware that there was a copy in the house.

'At one time my photographs were being moved a lot. The one of me in the bedroom was moved the most. One evening I found it in three different positions.'

Eventually, tired of being accused by the family of moving the objects herself, Mrs Davies sought help in having the house exorcized; but her husband refused to allow it, and the activity continues.

In her final letter to me, dated 11 November 1988, Jacqueline Davies writes: 'Last week some of my artificial flowers were removed from the lounge and placed in a little vase on the mantel piece in the next room; and my twenty-year-old son said that at about 11.45 at night, when he was the only one still up, as he went downstairs a shower of water hit his face.'

Harold Webster (see p.198) remembers clearly an ancient farmhouse in Oxfordshire which he visited some years ago. Owned by his wife's cousin, it was an attractive building surrounded by stables and orchards.

During restoration work the landing wall was painted, but every time it was finished a mysterious black line appeared on the fresh new paint. Nonplussed by this, the owner decided to investigate further by poking a hole in the ceiling. Climbing up to look through the aperture, he saw to his amazement an ancient bed, some candles, and festoons of cobwebs covering the recessed window which, as he proved later, was not visible from outside the building.

He became aware of thumps and noises constantly occuring during the night and, intrigued by the discovery of the secret room, he resolved to find out more about the history of the house.

According to local legend, the building had at one time belonged to the Earl of Clarendon who quarrelled with Charles II. Realizing that he would be pursued relentlessly by the king's men, the earl constructed a secret chamber in the farmhouse in which to wait and watch for troops crossing the marshes of the surrounding countryside: his plan was to escape as soon as they appeared. Clarendon did in fact oppose Charles II, and spent some time in the Tower of London as a result, but the identity of the man (or men) who might have used the secret room is open to conjecture.

Mr Webster and his wife stayed only one night in the house. They were so strongly impressed by the 'eerie, spooky feeling' that they mentioned it to their hosts, and obtained details of the discovery of the secret room before they left.

POLTERGEISTS

When David Stevens (see p.100) was living in a three-hundred-year-old cottage in the village of Gurney Slade just north of Shepton Mallet on the A39 between 1983 and 1985, he had some extraordinary experiences.

'I was living alone and, a few days after moving in at the end of October, I was upstairs fixing some fittings in the bathroom when I heard a voice downstairs calling my name. The doors were locked and there was nobody at either the front or the back. I wondered if the sound came from the television although no character of the name Stevens featured in the programme. It was a little eerie, but I put it down to coincidence.

'Two days later I returned home in the evening from the school where I teach to find that two small pictures that I had hung on the wall of the second bedroom had lifted to hang at right angles to the vertical. I tapped them and they dropped to the normal position. The next day they were again hanging at right angles. At that stage I began to wonder if there could be anything of a supernatural presence in the cottage. It is one of the oldest buildings in the village and part at least was originally a barn or stable. Perhaps I should at this stage point out that I am not one who ridicules the idea of ghosts. I have always been keen that they should exist but at the same time have been wary of letting the imagination take control.

'The next happening was very odd. Late one night I was sitting on the bed in the second bedroom and glanced idly at the coat-hanger I had carelessly dropped at the top of the stairs on the landing. Suddenly, without warning, the hanger lifted itself up on end and proceeded to jump down the stairs one at a time. I had not been drinking and the hanger was at the foot of the stairs next morning. There had been no draught or vibration to shake the hanger loose and indeed it had been dropped several inches back from the top stair.

'At Easter my parents were staying in the house while I was away. During the night my mother, who was sleeping in the second bedroom, had a strange dream in which someone beckoned to her. Sleep-walking, she got out of bed, stubbed her toe sharply on the balustrade and awoke just in time to stop herself from falling down the stairs. What disturbed her, however, was the intense feeling of evil that was all around, and this was something she couldn't explain. It could, of course, be the result of a fertile imagination; but this episode was brought back sharply into focus a few weeks later when I awoke in the middle of the night and felt this atmosphere of evil myself. It seemed to be restricted to the second bedroom which I also used . . . This happened for the next two nights and then the evil atmosphere vanished as suddenly as it had come, and was never felt again.

'The following Christmas a supernatural film called *Carrie* was being shown on television. It was interesting to find that whenever the main character revealed her psychic powers the lights on our Christmas tree went out and there was slight interference on the television screen. This could well have been a complete coincidence and I should have dismissed the matter from my mind had it not been for the other events.

'At this stage no manifestations had been observed. During the spring of 1985 I had a week's study leave. One morning I was reading in the sitting-room and happened to look across the hallway into the dining-room which was sited directly underneath the second bedroom. The sun's rays were streaming through the window and picking up the dust as it rose from the carpet. Suddenly the dust seemed to take on the shape of a man in a cloth cap staring out of the window. This was just an outline, with no actual bodily substance and reminded me of a stable lad. It lasted for only a few minutes and then it was gone. I had not been thinking of ghosts at the time, my mind being fully occupied with my research. I never saw the man again but I like to think that if there was a presence in the house, I actually saw it on that occasion when, perhaps, the dust was attracted to some presence in the atmosphere and clung to it with electrical energy.

'Several months later I found it necessary to move house. No strange happenings had taken place in the meantime, but about a fortnight before moving I was writing a letter in the dining-room when there was a crash in the kitchen. On investigation I found that a spatula had jumped out of its rack and shot across the floor. That certainly could not have happened unassisted, and any doubts I might have had about some form of presence were now completely dispelled. This proved to be the last strange occurrence.

'It is worth observing that all events took place on one side of the house, the part that once might have been a stable, and in the second bedroom that could have been a hayloft.'

David Stevens adds a final comment: 'The person who purchased the cottage was a young lady. Two months later the property was back on the market and it took two years to sell. One can't help wondering if she saw or heard something, but I don't suppose I shall ever find out.'

Anthony Vardy (see p.122) lives in Derbyshire, a county that had been familiar to the Vardys over a long period. The following story was related to him by members of the family who lived in the house described.

'My paternal grandfather was police superintendent in Belper in the late 1800s and early 1900s, and he lived in the police station with his family – my father, my two aunts and my uncle.

'One day a prisoner was brought some food by a young constable. The prisoner sharpened his spoon on the cell wall, and when the constable returned, the prisoner stabbed him and killed him. Not too long afterwards my grandfather had the cell converted into a storeroom for crockery and cutlery, and that was when "things" happened.

'The attic was a living-room and was partly carpeted. Quite often the family was forced to search the attic for the "person" responsible for walking on the wooden floor and then across the carpet and finally on the wooden floor on the other side – but there was never anyone there! What was even stranger was the sound of a motorbike starting up upstairs, and going across the floor.

'Often the family were woken by the sound of smashing crockery and crashing cutlery coming from the converted cell. Grandfather would go downstairs with loaded revolver to find – nothing!

'In fact the motorbike and the walking sounds went on until the old station was sold off as a private house. I don't know whether anything happens there now.'

Mrs Joyce Long lives in Surrey. She wrote to me about the bizarre experiences of her husband Eddie, who was a shop-fitter before his retirement.

POLTERGEISTS

Five or six years ago, Eddie spent five months converting a cinema into a shopping facility after the premises had been used by several large commercial companies. He followed his usual practice, when working far from home, of taking with him a camp bed and bedding, and sleeping on the job during the week.

On the first night, sleeping at the rear of the old cinema building, he was kept awake by the banging of doors. In the morning he thought he had discovered the problem: a pair of heavy doors left unfastened. He assumed they had been blowing back and forth, although there were no apparent apertures for a breeze to enter the building. He jammed the doors together with cardboard, making it impossible to move them.

'That night he settled down for a peaceful night's sleep,' writes Mrs Long, 'but once again the doors were banging. In the morning he went to investigate, and found that the cardboard had been thrown into the middle of the room, and the doors were banging free again.'

Although he had been made uneasy by the door business, Mr Long was nevertheless set on staying in the building and continued to sleep on the premises. One night he heard running water, and when he went upstairs to investigate, he found the hand-basins wet – they were never in fact used – without the taps being turned on. He returned to his bed and settled down to sleep, only to hear the sound of running water once again. Deciding that discretion was the better part of valour, he remained where he was.

He worked on site for five months, sleeping in the shop every night during the week. However, he did move his bed to the front of the shop for easy access to the exit because of the continuing supernatural activity. He refused to give in to the presence in spite of being – according to his wife – awake 'quaking every night until about 5 a.m. when things quietened down and he could get some sleep'.

'It was about this time that a local lady came into the shop and asked if he had heard about the ghost. Twenty years ago, apparently, the cinema projectionist had hanged himself in the projection room and had haunted the place ever since. The suicide was reported in the local papers. The cinema closed down soon afterwards, and none of the shops that opened on the premises after the conversion stayed for long.'

One night Mr Long was startled by the sound of a buzzer which he could not locate, although the source of the sound was definitely inside the building. Next morning he searched high and low for the origin of the sound, with no success. When he told this story to his brother-in-law, he learnt that it was the practice in cinemas to use buzzers instead of telephone bells in projection rooms.

'The most frightening thing that happened was waking up one morning to find rolls of wallpaper taken from the fitments and laid end to end along one of the gangways,' he told his wife. Throughout his time, Eddie Long had seen nothing in the shape of a ghost, but the noises and peculiar happenings continued to disturb him. Even so, he still persevered, determined not to let the supernatural presence in the shop evict him until he was ready to leave. A colleague of his was less tenacious.

'One night when Eddie had come home unexpectedly, someone who had gone to help him with the work and intended to stay the night with him was so frightened by the noises he ran out of the shop, leaving everything open, and refused to return, even in daylight.'

Mr Long was probably unusually sensitive to paranormal activity. He has told his wife of a number of strange and inexplicable happenings at various shops in which he was working, some involving himself, others his workmates. But the cinema ghost was by far the most frightening and active presence he ever encountered.

Bill Smith describes his many baffling experiences as 'incredible . . . absorbing and fantastic', but admits that he is no nearer to solving the mysteries presented by them now, at the age of eighty, than he was as a young man. However, he makes an interesting observation: 'I have been startled and astounded many times by apparitions, hearings, phenomena unexplainable. But I have never been harmed, though touched by icy sensations many, many times.'

In 1928 Mr Smith was working on the land. One day, eating bread and cheese with two farmhands during a break at a property in

Sherborne, he entertained them with a description of his encounter with the ghost of a donkey (see p.208).

'The younger man was very vociferous, the older quiet and morose. He had been shell-shocked in France during the First World War and was deaf to anything but shouting.

'"Old Jim got ghosts up where he live," said the younger man. "His missus be an old witch. They sez as how she harbour them." He tapped the old boy on the shoulder and shouted, "You got ghosts up your place, hain't you Jim?" The old boy said, "Har, but I ain't niver seen 'em. I think 'tis missus mucking about. Her sez he be thar, orlrit."

'I said, "If we came up there do you think we could see it?" The old man replied, "He doan't come every day. It be ony sometimes he come, and shift things about. He be a b . . . y nuisance times. Kep shiftin' things. You niver knows where you'm goin ter find it. He ony come at night when dark be on, an' opens doors, and she say he mak noises, but I doan't hear un. I be deaf. I laughed tother week, smoke wouldn't go up chimney. So missus set fire to it next day. An' do you know that devil, he smoked us out that same night. Not a mite of smoke could we git to go up chimney. I told her she warmed his ass up, and he were a havin' his venge on her."

'I asked him if it bothered him and he said, "Naw! I ain't a worrit. He nivver don't do no harm, 'tis only mischef. Missus get upset sometimes, but her be a gittin' used to un. You'm welcome ter come if'n you wants, but I cain't tell if he will show hisself cos you'm there. You can stop all night but you'll hev to sleep in chair. I only got one bed."

'He told us where he lived and I said we would go and see him one night. The following week he said, "You ought to a bin up my place last night, that old sod he jammed the door so us couldn't get out. An missus said he were a-laughing like hell, then when we give up trying, door opened on 'is own. Sort of tricks he plays."'

That night Mr Smith and his mate went up to Jim's cottage but nothing happened and they decided to return home. On the way his mate fell flat on his face on the path.

'I laughed but he lay there shouting, "Let go! Let go! You'll break my ankle!" I wasn't close enough to hold his ankle, but he swore someone had held it tight.

'We went again next night. Nothing happened until we tried to open the door to come away. It would not budge. I said to Jim, "You've locked it!"'

Jim's wife told him that that was impossible – they had no key to the door and never had had one.

'I tried again, then examined the lock, thinking someone had locked it from outside. It was not locked. There was no bar across. Then as I went to the window the door flew open, striking my mate in the back and sending him across the room. But there was no one outside.

'We went again the following evening and as we got near we saw the door was wide open and smoke was pouring out. Thinking the place was on fire we ran forward, only to find Jim and his wife coughing and spluttering in the garden.

'"That old sod," said Jim. "He got us smoked out again."

'I shone my torch up to the top of the chimney. No smoke was coming from it. We listened for sounds but heard nothing. We looked around using our torches, but could see nothing. Then as I shone my torch to the top of the chimney again, smoke was billowing from it. We went in the cottage. The smoke was clearing and the fire blazing merrily in the grate.

'A few moments passed and a loud screeching occurred outside. My mate rushed out and [again] fell flat on his face shouting, "Let go! Let go!" I shone my torch on him. There was nothing to stop him getting up, but he said, "Get him off my back! I'll kill the b—!" As I was replying "There's no one on your back", we heard again this loud screeching coming from the lane. My mate scrambled up and we ran down the path. Then we heard the missus scream, "He's here!" We looked back. The house was in darkness; the lamp had gone out.

'We went back, shining our torches. There was nothing there. As we went in Jim said, "Light be gone out!" We shone a torch on to the table where the lamp had been. It was gone, and in its place stood a candlestick with about an inch of candle in it. Jim lit it. We searched for the lamp. It was nowhere in the room. Yet no one had entered or left the room except us, and we were outside when the lamp went out.

'We closed the door, and as we stood talking a cupboard door opened and something heavy fell to the floor. I bent down and retrieved a packet of candles and placed them on the table. The missus said, "Are they yours?" I said, "No. They just fell out of the cupboard." She said, "They aren't mine. I only buy half a dozen." Jim got up from his chair and said, "You better be agoin'. This be a gettin' a bit too much for my likin'. I bain't a sittin' up no longer. If'n you wants to stop you can. There's wood and coal for fire, and you can have a chair apiece. I be goin' outside a minute."

'He went to the door and tugged at it. It would not open. He said, "He got it jammed again!" I rushed to look out of the window, but all I could see was a strange greenish-yellow glow which seemed to be moving. I said, "There's a fire outside!" My mate lifted the latch and the door opened easily, and on the doorstep was the lighted lamp, the globe blackened by a smoking wick. I felt as though an icy hand had touched the back of my neck and turned quickly – there was nothing behind me.

'It was weird. We had no explanation, and Jim said, "Don't you come here no more. He don't like you!"'

Mr Smith can offer no explanation of these events, which have been a conundrum to him for years. The spirit or presence had done no real harm, but 'Why,' he asks, 'should a ghost be so mischievous?'

The Bath Evening Chronicle *for Monday 11 April 1988 published the following story:*

'Chopping boards, loaves of bread and tins of tomatoes fly across the kitchen at a Marshfield pub – if the owners ignore their friendly poltergeist.

'Roy and Jeannette Lane, of the Lord Nelson pub and Carriage Restaurant in Marshfield High Street, say the poltergeist has made himself known every two to three months.

'"If you are in the kitchen you think someone has come in through the cellar, but when you turn around there's no one there," said Mrs Lane. "If you decide not to turn around then something will be thrown.

'"It's as if he's saying 'Look at me'. It used to startle us but we've got used to him now. The dogs aren't allowed in the kitchen but if they're passing through on their way for a walk then they jump around trying to catch something by the cellar door.

'"But since my husband installed a darkroom above the kitchen about three months ago we haven't heard a peep out of him."'

Disrupted Holidays

A tempting resolution to the problem encountered by owners of houses inhabited by troublesome poltergeists, who have difficulty in disposing of their property, is to let it to unsuspecting holidaymakers.

In June 1962 George Phillips-Smith (see p.193) rented a holiday home on the outskirts of Brixham, Devon, for a fortnight. He and his family were pleased on arrival to find themselves accommodated in a modern detached house overlooking the harbour. Their pleasure was soon clouded.

'Our first night there was memorable for the activities of a horde of mice chasing around behind the skirting boards, preventing sleep, and taking no notice of the rain of boots and shoes aimed at the noisy spots. At first light the mice cleared off, only to be replaced by the twittering of a lot of birds, seemingly nesting in the grid-type ventilator in the bedroom wall, the outer grille of which was obviously broken.'

In the morning Mr Phillips-Smith investigated possible sources for the noises. But he found no mouseholes anywhere. The outer grille of the ventilator was in excellent condition, and there was no sign at all of feathers or bird droppings – nothing, in fact, to indicate the presence of either mice or birds in the house. Unsettled but relieved by this discovery the family began their holiday in good spirits.

'The next night we were awakened by heavy hammering on the wall which divided us from the room where my elderly father-in-law was sleeping. My wife fled around, assuming the old chap was in trouble and needing help. To her surprise, he was fast asleep, awakening only when she switched on the light. It was he who suggested the place was haunted.

'We never saw a thing during the whole holiday; but on two nights I was aroused by hammering on the side panel of the bath, and one day when we were all in the lounge there were heavy footsteps overhead.'

The noises of mice and birds which were so disruptive throughout the first night, were not heard again by the Phillips-Smiths. However, there was another odd matter to record. Neither husband nor wife liked being in the kitchen alone. 'There seemed to be some sort of atmosphere about that room, but we never got any explanation for it.'

After receiving a fortnight's rent in advance when they came, the owner had left the family to its own devices, and they did not see him again. And during the time they were there, the Phillips-Smiths saw no one, not a single neighbour with whom they could discuss their experiences.

They have still to find a theory to explain what it was that caused the disturbances.

In 1955 Bill Smith and his wife decided to go to Cornwall for a holiday. Inviting another married couple to join them on the basis of shared expenses, Mr and Mrs Smith managed to rent a double-fronted cottage near Penzance for a fortnight during the owners' absence abroad.

As he was familiar with the road and experienced in driving long distances, Mr Smith took the wheel and drove through the night while the rest of the party snoozed in the car. They arrived early next morning to find the key under a flat stone by the door, as arranged. The house proved to be ideal for their purpose, offering both couples a bedroom on the top floor and a sitting room on the ground floor with shared bathroom and kitchen facilities downstairs.

Having had breakfast when they arrived, Mr Smith decided he needed to get some sleep after his marathon drive of nearly four hundred miles, while the rest of the party took the car into Penzance. Mr Smith recalls what happened when he went upstairs to bed.

'I got between the sheets but though tired I couldn't seem to lose myself in sleep. There was a nasty cold draught, although the temperature was in the seventies. I got out of bed and closed the window which I had opened earlier to dispel the musty smell in the room.'

He returned to bed, pulled the blankets up over his head and was nodding off when the bedroom door suddenly slammed shut and he heard someone moving about the room. Annoyed at being woken, Mr Smith pulled the blanket more firmly around his head and, assuming his wife had entered the room, he spoke to her with some irritation.

'Please don't slam the door! I'm trying to get to sleep! I think I'm overtired, and it seems so draughty in this old house!'

There was no reply. The bedroom door slammed, and that was followed immediately by the slamming of the door to the next room. Mr Smith heard footsteps going down the stairs, and the front door then slammed shut. Thinking his wife had left the house, he settled down again.

'I thought, that's it, now I can sleep.'

Once again, just as he was drifting off to sleep, he was startled by the slamming of two doors – which appeared to be those downstairs. Exhausted by now, he fell sound asleep. But a little later he awoke, cold and uncovered. The bedclothes had been pulled back, and so he assumed his wife had returned to the room and was teasing him. Losing his patience he hauled the bedclothes up and covered his head again, hearing as he did so the opening of the bedroom door. He waited to hear it close, but there was no sound.

'Thinking my wife was in the room, I said, "For God's sake let me sleep! I've been awake all night to get you here!" The bedroom door slammed, followed by the other, then I heard heavy footsteps on the stairs and someone laughed loudly.

'I had had enough. I was irritable, and rushing out on to the landing I shouted down the stairs, "It's not funny! You slept on the way down but I couldn't!" The back door slammed. I went back to put on my trousers as I was wearing only underpants. But the trousers were not there!'

Disconcerted, but thinking his wife had taken his trousers away as a joke, he decided to run downstairs as he was to collect their suitcases and bring them up to the bedroom.

'I went down. The house was empty, back door and front door locked. I grabbed the cases and took them upstairs and then went to the other bedroom door and tapped. No answer. I opened the door and peeped in. The room was empty.

'I had a feeling I was not alone in the house. I took the cases into my bedroom. My trousers were where I left them, loose change and keys in the pockets. Had I been sleep-walking or dreaming? . . . I got into bed then looked at the time: it was only an hour since I had turned in.'

'My wife woke me at 4 p.m. with a cup of tea, saying, "Come on, wake up or you won't sleep tonight." She saw the cases and said, "Have you been downstairs?" I was trapped, but said the pixies must have brought them up, or perhaps Harry did. I dared not say what was in my mind.

'I got up, had a meal, and we went out for the evening together. When we came in, the table was laid – crockery and cutlery laid out for a meal. No one had done it before we left. We went to bed. Doors kept slamming, and there were footsteps on the stairs. The bedcovers were turned back. The room became icy cold. My wife was scared, although she tried to laugh it off. I told her Cornish pixies often played pranks on strangers.

'We didn't know that Harry and his wife were in a similar plight until 4 a.m. when we heard heavy footsteps on the stairs. I went out on to the landing. The front door opened and slammed. I went down and examined it. It was locked and bolted. It was almost daylight, and our holiday twenty-two hours old. I met Harry on the landing as I went back up. He said, "What are you playing at? We haven't had a wink of sleep!"

'We went downstairs and made some tea. I told him I couldn't tell him what it was but to explain the noise to his wife by saying I couldn't sleep and had been up all night. We took the tea upstairs, and heard no more. The truth came out later.

'We lasted the fortnight, but it was touch and go. Things moved without being touched by any of us. We got used to doors slamming. Nobody got hurt, and we went out all day. But it was the last Cornish holiday for us!'

Violence

Physical injuries inflicted on people by supernatural forces are rare, but not unknown.

David Stevens was once a victim of such an attack.

'As a small child,' he writes, 'I was playing in the garden while my family had a picnic tea. Apparently I suddenly started screaming loudly as though I had been stung. My mother could find no evidence of this, and when I stopped yelling the matter was forgotten. However, when being bathed that night, mother found deep claw marks all over my chest and back; they had obviously been the cause of my distress.'

No explanation for the marks on the little boy's back was ever discovered.

Christina Foyle had a similar experience, which was mentioned in an article by Daniel Farson in the Sunday Telegraph *on 27 December 1987.*

According to Farson she once spent a night in a reputedly haunted room and woke 'to find two tooth marks on her shoulder; wounds which her doctor told her had been infected by a germ unknown for years.'

Daniel Farson himself had a restless night when he was invited in 1987 by the owners, Camilla and Gerald Harford, to stay overnight in a certain attic room at Little Sodbury Manor, north of Bristol.

When I visited this splendid house overlooking the Severn Estuary recently, I learnt about the history of William Tyndale's room, believed by generations of inhabitants to be haunted.

It is an attractive room; spacious and comfortably furnished with antiques, it is half-timbered with oak beams and plaster, and houses an open fireplace which would have warmed the active fingers of the heretic William Tyndale. Four hundred years ago he is thought to have sat in this room working at his translation of the bible into English, during the period he was retained by the owner of the manor, Sir John Walsh, as chaplain and tutor to the Walsh children.

Tyndale's heretical comments upset the Catholic community in Gloucestershire, and reluctantly Sir John asked him to leave the district. Tyndale left for London, then travelled to the continent. His new bible was published and copies smuggled into England created a furore among the clergy. Tyndale was lured into a trap, captured and eventually charged with heresy. On 6 October 1536, in spite of Thomas Cromwell's efforts to save him, he was taken out to the courtyard of Vilvorde Castle, Brussels, 'there tied to the stake, and then strangled first by a hangman, and afterwards with fire consumed'.

Since that time Tyndale's room at Little Sodbury has contained some form of 'presence': a number of people who have stayed in it have reported to their hosts that they were woken during the night believing they were being strangled.

Daniel Farson, having seen one ghost some time before his visit to Little Sodbury and being keenly aware of the room's reputation, was nervous of the night to come. After dining with the Harfords, he left them reluctantly to climb the stairs to Tyndale's room. He, too, woke at one point convinced he was being smothered, only to find that the heavy bedspread had risen to cover his face.

'There is no doubt my sleep was disturbed,' he reports, and having got up once during the night to make the hazardous journey to the bathroom down slippery wooden stairs, he was feeling even more shattered than usual when he woke in the morning. He hurried again to the bathroom in order to rinse out his mouth 'which seemed half full of liquid. I was shocked to see a stream of crimson blood pour into the basin instead of water, and assumed this was simply a matter of bleeding gums, though my dentist could not explain it, nor has it happened since.'

Some people believe the evil presence in the attic room at Little Sodbury Manor may not be the spirit of William Tyndale, but that of his murderer, the man who strangled him. Daniel Farson discussed his experience in Tyndale's room with Peter Underwood, a leading writer on the topic of ghosts and president of the Ghost Club. He was intrigued by Underwood's conclusion: 'It seems that the evil presence may well be that of the person responsible for strangling Tyndale before he was burnt as a heretic. This particular influence could be a case of derangement in respect of time and place; the manor where Tyndale concentrated and worked so hard could well provide the atmosphere necessary for an impression of the cruel nature of his strangler to become locked there in some way we do not understand.

'Your experience of a mouthful of blood (something Tyndale would have experienced in his last moments) is interesting,' continued Underwood. 'If there was no natural or physical explanation (as seems likely) then it would appear to be a case of the superphysical affecting the physical.'

Note

Readers who have experienced incidents similar to those described in this collection are invited to contact the author at the following address:

Vivienne Rae-Ellis, PO Box 5159, Bath BA1 2ET, UK.

Select Bibliography

The first attempt to mount a scientific investigation of ghosts and hauntings was begun by a committee of the newly founded Society for Psychical Research in 1882. Its findings can be read scattered through the first ten volumes of the Society's *Proceedings*; in Edmund Gurney's *Phantasms of the Living*, 1886; and in Frederic Myers's *Human Personality*, 1903. There was a disposition then to avoid the term 'ghost' because it had become identified in the public mind with wraiths of the dead. In indexes, the subject was more likely to come under the heading 'phantasms' (though that did not catch on for long), 'apparitions', which has remained in common use, or 'hallucinations'. A follow-up investigation conducted by Eleanor Sidgwick appeared in Vol. 33 (1923) of the *Proceedings*.

Other serious studies which have appeared this century are, in chronological order:

Camille Flammarion, *The Unknown*, London, 1900; *Death and its Mystery*, London, 1922
Ernesto Bozzano, *Phenomena of Haunting*, London, 1920
Sir Ernest Bennett, *Apparitions and Haunted Houses*, London, 1939
G. N. M. Tyrrell, *Apparitions*, London, 1943
Celia Green and Charles McCreery, *Apparitions*, London, 1975
Andrew MacKenzie, *Hauntings and Apparitions*, London, 1982; *The Seen and the Unseen*, London, 1987
Ben Noakes, *I Saw a Ghost*, London, 1986

Two other works deal specifically with poltergeist phenomena:

Alan Gauld and A. D. Cornell, *Poltergeists*, London, 1979
Guy Lyon Playfair, *This House is Haunted*, London, 1980

Index

Adelphi, Salford, 177–82
airfields, 52, 198–9
Alderson, Karen, 121–2
Aldous, John D., 132–4
Allison, John, 18–20
animals:
    ghosts of, 34, 83–97, 127–8, 208–9
    reactions of, 8–9, 12, 13, 42, 98–101, 121, 204
apparitions:
    of the dead, 5, 27, 37, 38, 45–53, 54, 55, 56, 59, 60, 61, 66, 67, 69, 71, 79, 149, 173, 194
    of the living, 75–7
Appledore (Poplar Hall), 12
Applegate, Susannah, 221–4
Armadale, Western Australia, 114
Askew Arms, 193–4

'Banks, Tom', 132
Barford, Pamela, 78–9, 161–2
Barnes, Eva ('the Poetess'), 87, 122–3
Barnsley, 37–8
Barrow Court, 118–19
Barston, 206–7
Bath (Bathampton Lane), 21
Bath (The Circus), 58–9, 63
Bath (Daniel Street), 63–4
Bath (Theatre Royal), 172
Batheaston, 125
Bathurst, Charlotte, 60–1, 66, 194–5
Beamish Hall, 162–3
Belfast (Divismore Park), 108–11
Belper, 244
Benghazi, 90–1
Berry, Alan, 214–15
Berry, Catherine, 235–8
'Best, Claudia', 61
Biggy, John, 200

Billingham, Co. Cleveland, 55
Birmingham (Lionel Street), 183–4
'Bishop, Deirdre', 35–6
Black Prince, 217
Blenkinsopp, Robert John, 221
blood, 141–4, 256
Bodmin Moor, 197
Borley Rectory, 33, 164–6
Boxall, Hilary, 85
Bradshaw Hall, 155–9
Bradshaw, Thomas, 155–6
'Brenda', 176, 189
Brighty, Helen, 115–16
Brisco, Mr, 166
British Spiritualists' Association, 6
Brixham, 251–2
Brown, Theo, 139
Browne, Adrianne, 55
'Brunell, Miss', 125–6
Buckland Newton (Donkey Lane), 208–9
buildings, phantom, 18, 22
Burks, Eddie, 199
Burton Agnes, 47
Busby Stoop, The, 193
Byrne, James N., 127–8, 193–4

Cadwell, Nancy, 93–7
Cameron, Hilary J., 167–8
Carlton Miniott, 193
cars, 8, 68, 222–4
Cartwright, Miss S., 185–7
cavaliers, 8, 65
Chadwick, Brenda, 201
chairs, 14, 46, 183–4, 193
Chapman, Ann, 49
Chappell, Gwerfyl, 41
Charles I, King, 155–6
Charles II, King, 241

INDEX

children:
  ghosts of, 7–8, 45, 57–8, 70–1, 79, 82, 109–12, 188, 190–1, 195
  seeing ghosts, 18–19, 37, 41, 71–4, 78–82, 188
chills, cold spots, 14, 27, 31, 32, 117, 122–3, 170–1, 200, 204, 229, 252–4
Chopin, Frédéric, 151
Church, Joan, 26–7, 42–3, 45, 54–5
churches, 143–4, 164–8
Clarendon, Earl of, 241
Clarkson, Frankie and Jeff, 225
Clive, Susan, 221
clothes, 3, 20, 21, 35, 41, 45, 46, 47, 54, 57, 60, 62, 64, 65, 82, 134, 149, 161, 200–3, 215–16
coaches, 15–16, 18
Colyton Cottage, 129–30
Cooper, Sydney Ernest, 113–14
Corsten, 93–7
Corwen, North Wales, 41
Cotton, Gillian, 176
Coverdale, Miss, 18–20
Crisp, John, 215–16
Croft Castle, 47–8
Crofton Hall, 166
Crook, Lake District, 112
Crown Hotel, 23–6
Cruse, Leslie, 204–5

Dacre House, 49
Dartmoor, 124, 138–9
Davies, David Lloyd, 75
Davies, Jacqueline, 238–41
de la Mare, Calina, 47–8
de la Mare, Giles, 47, 76–7
de la Mare, Walter, 76–7
Deer Abbey, 132
Delmore, Elizabeth, 220–1
'Diana', 152–5
dogs, *see* animals
'Dorothy', 159–61
Drunken Admiral, The, 195–7
Dumpton Hill, Devon, 20

Ealing (Montpelier Avenue), 17–18

Elliott, Beryl M., 71–3
Elsworth, Graham, 37–8
exorcism, 19–20, 43, 110, 155, 189, 227–8

Fairhurst, Patricia, 86–7
Farson, Daniel, 225, 255–7
Fedrick, Rosemary, 98–9
Fletcher, Douglas, 80
Fletcher, Jill, 4–7
Flying Dutchman, 225
Ford, Ernest, 200–2
Foyle, Christina, 255
Franklin, Henry, 75

Gainsborough, Thomas, 63
Gambrill, Rita, 112–13
'George, William', 68–9
ghosts:
  felt, 60, 68, 124–8, 160, 183, 196
  guardian, 9, 63–74
  heard, *see* sounds
  identification, 54–62, 149, 153
  of animals, *see* animals
  smelled, 117–23, *see also* smells
  solidity of, 24, 35, 50, 174
  violent, 255–7
Goatham, Brenda E., 79–80
Godfrey, Craig Alexander, 195–7
Godfrey, Leone, 197
Glossop, Canon, 43
Grace Dieu Ruins, 205
Grant, Alice, 39
Greenwich (Park Vista), 12–14
Grey Ladies, 132, 160, 166–7, 172
Gurney Slade, 242–4

Hadfield, Fred, 203–4
'hairy hands', 138–9
Hale, South Manchester, 107–8
Hardcastle, Colonel H. M., 155–8
Hare and Hounds Hotel, 194–5
Harford, Camilla and Gerald, 255–6
'Harris, Dr', 17–18
Hauton, George, 143–4
Headon, Gordon, 23–6

262

INDEX

Heaton, Irene, 155–9
Helby, Dr Ernest, 138
Helmn, Paul, 117–18
High Wycombe (White Hill), 217–19
highway encounters, 141–3, 212–24
Hine, Jacqui, 125
Hobart, Tasmania, 195–7
Hodges, John Richard, 44, 63
Hodgson, W. F., 198–9
Hodkinson, R. H., 177–82
Hopwood, Margaret, 107, 126–7
horsemen/women, 99, 216
hospitals, 173–6
Houghton-Brown, Geoffrey, 58–9
Howarth, Irene, 119–20
Hughes, Charles, 114–15
Hunger Hill, Westhoughton, 201
Hunter, William James, 212–14
Hutchinson, Rosemary E., 89

Ilbery, Captain J. E., 228–32
Ilfracombe, 133
Inglis, Brian, xv–xvii, 235
Inn Farm House, 197
Irwell River, 180
Islington (Liverpool Road), 52

Jacobsen, Mary, 136–8
Jaekel, Lionel Geoffrey, 139–40, 182–3
Jamaica Inn, 197
Jeffreys, Judge, 130
Jenkinson, Brenda, 198–9
Jones, E. Christine, 173–4

Kendal (Market Place), 182–3
King Arthur's Castle, 119–20
King's Lynn (Paradise Grange), 42
Kirkman, Fred, 200–1

Lambert, Peggy, 70–1
Lancaster, Doris Olwen, 53
Lane, Roy and Jeanette, 249–50
Laws, Mr, 226–7
Layer Marney Tower, ix–x
Lee Bay, 133

Lee (Bromley Road), 38–40
Lee (Dacre House), 49
Leicester, Sgt, 51–2
Lightfoot, Arthur, 65
Linton-on-Ouse, 198–9
Little Sodbury Manor, 255–7
Long, 'Barry', 244–6
Long Hanborough, 99
Long, Joyce, 244–6
Lord Nelson, Marshfield, 249–50
Lynall, Erica, 20–1

McCarthy, Rosemary, 21–2
McKeown, Don, 162–3
MacLauchlan, Juliet, 9–12
McMahon, Mrs F., 201
McNeill, Hester, 112
McParlin, Michael, 106
Maguire, Margaret A., 107–8
Maidenhead, 26–7
Man, Isle of, 86–7
Manchester (Hale), 107–8
Manchester (Longsight), 59–60
Manchester Warehouse, 177–82
Marshfield, 249–50
Maunday, Ann, 49
Messing Church, 164
mist, 99, 121–2
Monaghan, Mivhael, 108–11
monks, 41–4, 156
Moody, Angela, 174–5
Moss, Norah, 61–2
Murder Stone, 208

Neagle, Dame Anna, 172
Neale, Mary Cathrine ('Molly'), 190–2
'Neale, Mrs D.', 46–7
Neville-Statham, Victor, 33–4, 164–6
Newey, Patricia, 63–4
Newman, Shelah, 30–2, 50, 87–9
North Hill House, Winchester, 36
North, Mildred, 228
Nunnington Hall, 220–1

Offen, Margaret, 66–7

INDEX

Old Deer, Aberdeenshire, 131–2
Organ, Moreen, 111–12
Orkneys, 139–40
Ouija boards, 7
Outhwaite, Lucy, 82, 124
Outhwaite, Mary, 32–3, 82, 124, 130–1

Palace Cinema, Westhoughton, 201
Palmer, David H., 127–8
Paradise Grange, 42
Pavlova, Anna, 172
pets, *see* animals
Phillips-Smith, George, 193, 251–2
photographs, 132–5
Pickering, 226–8
Pickering, George, 49
Pittkin, Dorothy Mary ('Peggy'), 56–8
poltergeists, 235–50
possession, 136–40
premonitions, 17
presences, 113, 129–35
Pretoria Pit, 202
Price, Ernie, 48
pubs, 193–7

Rastan, Charlotte, 138–9
Rattray, Louise, 62
Raybould, Eric B., 141–3
Read, Jack, 91–3
Read, Joan, 12–14, 38–40, 48–9, 202–3
Reay, Mrs J., 166–7
Red Lion Hotel, Westhoughton, 201
Redcar, 190–2
Reynolds, Simon, 28–30, 148–50
Riding, Jean, 120–1
Robinson, Robert, 76
Romeland Cottage, 43
Rose, Barrie, 206–7
Ross, Jim, 34–5
Rowe, Margaret, 78
Russell, Mr, 183–4
Rutherford, Harold V., 41
Ryde, Isle of Wight, 91–3

St Albans (Romeland Cottage), 43
St Batholomew's Hospital, London, 176
St Cuthbert's Vicarage, Billingham, 55
St John's College, Oxford, 168–71
St Mary in the Marsh (Old Rectory), Kent, 9–12
Salford (Adelphi), 177–82
'Sally', 187–9
Sawyer, Claude, 231
Sayer, Louise Mary, 62, 150–2
Schloss Moritzburg, 148–50
Schtraks, Pascale, 69–70
sensitives, 4–14
Sherborne, 246–9
Sherman, Sarah, 49
ship, phantom, 225
Skeat, Francis W., 43
smells, ghostly:
  gas, 151–2
  ozone, 192
  scents, 120, 167, 172
  tobacco 8, 12, 117, 119
  unpleasant, 9–12
Smith, William David (Bill), 207–11, 216–19, 246–9, 252–4
Sone, Olive S., 7–8
sounds:
  banging, 115, 241, 251–2
  breathing, 116, 186
  carriage wheels, 19
  crying, 109–10, 111–12, 160
  footsteps, 4, 34, 36, 42, 45, 63, 66, 68, 82, 112–14, 149, 179–80, 185–6, 188–9, 253–4
  horses' hooves, 99, 209
  knocking, 115, 157
  music, 11, 151, 161, 164
  of human presence, 4, 11, 180, 207
  singing, 107–8, 167–8, 195, 218–19
  talking, 43, 106, 109, 173
  voices, 106, 109–10, 187, 188, 210, 242
  see also poltergeists
Southwark (Bankside), 202–3

INDEX

spiritualism, 6–7
Stamers-Smith, Eileen, 168
Stamers-Smith, H. A., 168–71
stately homes, 148–63
Stevens, David, 100–1, 242, 255
Stevens, H. W. R. ('Roy'), 90–1
'Stevens, May', 67–8
Stott, Edward A., 51–2
Stringfellow, Janet E., 59–60
'Susan', 15–17

Taylor, Winifred, 52
Theatre Royal, Bath, 172
Thringstone, 204–5
timewarps, 15–22
Tinkerbottom's Farm, 157
Tintagel, 119–20
Toms, Dr, 43
towns, 200–5
train, phantom, 81
Traquair House, 167–8
Trowsdale, James A., 225–8
Turton Tower, 158–9
Tyndale, William, 255–7

Underwood, Peter, 257

vapours, 121–2
Vardy, Anthony, 122, 244

Versailles, 62
violence, 23–40, 158, 255–7, *see also* poltergeists
voices, *see* sounds

Wade, Mena, 83–5
Walker, Ida, 55–6
Walker, Thomas Henry, 98
Walsh, Sir John, 256
Waratah, 228–32
Watson, Mary M. ('Mollie'), 80–1
Wear, River, 106
Webster, Harold, 198, 241
Westhoughton, 200–2
Westonbirt, 194
Whannie Moors, 136
Whicker, Juliet Mary, 79
Willis, Reverend Tom, 226–8
Winchcombe, 212–14
Winchester (North Hill House), 36
Winlaton (Selby's Stile), 34–5
'Winthrop, Sarah', 50–1, 64–5, 100
Wire Mill, 32
Wood, Ann, 132
Woodyatt, Mrs S. M., 20, 129–30, 134–5
wraiths, 32, 201, 203
Wright's Tenement, 118
Wroxeter, 44